# Harder than Hardscrabble

NUMBER SIX
*Clifton and Shirley Caldwell Texas Heritage Series*

# Harder than

*Oral Recollections of the Farming Life*

# Hardscrabble

*from the Edge of the Texas Hill Country*

EDITED BY THAD SITTON

UNIVERSITY OF TEXAS PRESS, AUSTIN

Publication of this book was funded by the United States Army, Fort Hood, under delivery order 7 of contract DAKF48-99-D-0009.

Publication of this work was made possible in part by support from Clifton and Shirley Caldwell and a challenge grant from the National Endowment for the Humanities.

COMPILATION AND EDITING COPYRIGHT © 2003 BY THE UNIVERSITY OF TEXAS PRESS

Printed in the United States of America

First edition, 2003

∞ The paper used in this book meets the minimum requirements of ANSI/NISO Z 39.48-1992 (R1997) (Permanence of Paper).

LIBRARY OF CONGRESS CATALOGING-IN-PUBLICATION DATA

Harder than hardscrabble : oral recollections of the farming life from the edge of the Texas Hill Country / edited by Thad Sitton.
    p.    cm. — (Clifton and Shirley Caldwell Texas heritage series ; no. 6)
Includes bibliographical references and index.
   ISBN 0-292-70199-3 (alk. paper) — ISBN 0-292-70238-8 (pbk. : alk. paper)
   1. Fort Hood Region (Tex.)—History. 2. Fort Hood Region (Tex.)—Social life and customs. 3. Fort Hood Region (Tex.)—Biography. 4. Country life—Texas—Fort Hood Region—History. 5. Ranch life—Texas—Fort Hood Region—History. 6. Farmers—Texas—Fort Hood Region—Biography. 7. Ranchers—Texas—Fort Hood Region—Biography. 8. Texas Hill Country (Tex.)—Social life and customs. 9. Oral history.
I. Sitton, Thad, 1941– II. Series

F394.F6365 H37   2004
976.4'287061—dc22                          2003 16597

To former residents of

*Antelope, Bland, Boaz,*
*Brookhaven, Brown's Creek,*
*Clear Creek, Cold Springs,*
*Crossville, Eliga, Ewing,*
*Friendship, Harmony, Hubbard,*
*New Hope, Okay, Palo Alto, Pidcoke,*
*Reese's Creek, Refuge, Ruth, Schley,*
*Seattle, Sparta, Spring Hill, Stampede,*
*Old Sugar Loaf, New Sugar Loaf,*
*Tama, Turnover, and Willow Springs*

# Contents

PREFACE AND ACKNOWLEDGMENTS  ix

CHAPTER ONE. *Introduction: Lost Worlds*  1

CHAPTER TWO. *Homeplaces*  17
  Lay of the Land  17
  Chores  29
  Gardens, Home-Use Field Crops, and Fodder Crops  35
  Domestic Livestock  44
  Fishing, Hunting, Trapping, and Gathering  51
  Medical Self-Help and Town Doctors  60

CHAPTER THREE. *Money Crops*  71
  Cotton and Other Crops  71
  Cash-Crop Livestock  90
  Minor Money Crops  98
  Part-Time Cash Labor for Others  107
  Peddlers and Country Stores  115
  Visits to Town  120

CHAPTER FOUR. *Settlements*  193
  Country Schools  193
  School Entertainments  208
  Family Visits  213
  The Sporting Life  222
  House Parties and Dances  226
  Neighbors Helping Neighbors  235
  Churches and Religious Life  241

CHAPTER FIVE. *Modernizations and the Takeover*  251
  Communication Breakthroughs  251

Roads and Automobiles   257
Government Programs and the Takeover   263

EPILOGUE: *Sixty Years Afterward*   280
APPENDIX: *The Fort Hood Oral History Project*   283

SELECTED BIBLIOGRAPHY   289
INDEX   291

*Photo essay follows page 126*

# Preface and Acknowledgments

MORE THAN FORTY small rural communities once existed on the 339 square miles of land that now make up Fort Hood. Many of these communities began in the 1850s and lasted only a few years, but others lived on for almost a century. All the surviving communities ceased to exist early in World War II, when the government acquired the lands for the army training base of Camp Hood. Other communities disappeared as the government purchased more lands to expand Fort Hood during the 1950s.

Over the past two decades, researchers at Fort Hood have been documenting all of the known historic and archaeological sites within its borders—over 2,200 locations that range from ancient Native American campsites to early-twentieth-century farms. Field investigations and archival research were the primary strategies for documenting sites from the historic period, but oral history interviews began to be used to augment earlier approaches during the 1980s and 1990s. Building upon that experience, between 1995 and 1999 researchers conceived the Fort Hood Oral History Project as a means of documenting people's informal memories of rural life before World War II—valuable data, never written down, and important to preserve for historians and generations yet to come.

From 1998 to 2002, teams of historians and photographers busied themselves meeting people, conducting audio and videotaped interviews, and copying old photographs. These labors resulted in a valuable archive of historical information about the fast-disappearing rural world.

Special thanks go to U.S. Army Fort Hood and to Dr. Cheryl Huckerby, Director of the Fort Hood Cultural Resources Management Program, for their support of this worthwhile project.

Funding from U.S. Army Fort Hood made this book possible, but nothing would have been accomplished without the participation, cooperation, and support of the many former residents of the Fort Hood settlements. To them, their families, and their forebears, this book is respectfully dedicated. Thanks also to the Texas Collection of Baylor University, which graciously agreed to serve as a permanent repository for the project's oral history tapes, transcripts, and historical photographs. I also owe a large debt to my fellow historians, Marie E. Blake, Amy E. Dase, Martha Doty Freeman, and William S. Pugsley. Thanks, finally (and emphatically), to Doug Boyd of Prewitt and Associates, who organized the Fort Hood Oral History Project and at the end hired the fox hunter to hunt the fox.

—THAD SITTON, AUSTIN, TEXAS

# Harder than Hardscrabble

# CHAPTER ONE

# Introduction

## *Lost Worlds*

This book uses oral history to tell the human story of 339 square miles of countryside on the hardscrabble western edge of the cotton South, a farming and ranching landscape that became the giant military base of Fort Hood in central Texas. This area occupies southern Coryell and western Bell counties, on the northeastern perimeter of the Hill Country, but in many ways it could be anywhere on the southern periphery where soils become marginal, rocks lie close to the surface, and rain thins out. Like a lot of other southern places, this does not look much like "cotton country," but it once was.

Eli Whitney's invention of the cotton gin in 1793 had triggered an explosive expansion of cotton culture to the west. From a high of only 6,276 bales in 1792, national cotton production soared to 16,736 bales in 1794, only one year after Whitney's gin, to 115,073 bales in 1802, to 337,720 bales in 1820, on the eve of the settlement of Texas. Southerners had gone "cotton crazy," and soon the cotton boomers moved west, launching a wave of cotton expansion that rolled inexorably westward through time and space to 1930 and the blue, arid hills of Coryell County, at the edge of the Texas Hill Country.[1]

With Coryell and Bell county farmers contributing their part, the last big expansion of Southern cotton came in Texas. All across Texas during the 1920s, people cleared cutover pine forests, sandy-land hillsides, and floor-prone bottomlands and broke the ground for cotton. Texans plowed a record 16,813,000 acres for cotton in 1929. During that year, the value of Texas agriculture was over $11 billion—three times the value of oil, and cotton still remained the king. Texas far outdistanced all other southern states in cotton, producing over one-third of all the cotton picked in the United States throughout the decade of the 1920s. By 1924, 56.7 percent of all Texas cropland—16,658,356 acres—lay in cotton. Mississippi came next with 44.9 percent of its cropland in cotton (but only 3,011,444 acres).[2]

Texas produced over 25 percent of the world's cotton each year, ginned it in nearly four thousand gins, and led all other states in percentage of gross income derived from cotton. One economist estimated that one-third of the total population of the state was directly involved in cotton farming in 1929 and that many thousands more were involved in ginning, warehousing, merchandising, compressing, and transporting cotton or in cottonseed processing.[3]

Cotton farming, however, was a gambler's trade. The value of lint cotton at ginning time ranged from 5 to 45 cents in the two decades after 1910, and every season the inexorable and unpredictable play of weather determined how much each farm family had to sell.[4] As one retired farmer told me, dry-land cotton agriculture had always been a "crapshoot," with each year a new roll of the dice.

Cotton farming also was the great unifier, and the stories told in this book about plowing and hoeing and picking and wagoning to the gin could just as well have come from sand-hill East Texas or upstate Mississippi as from the edge of the Hill Country. In Coryell and Bell counties, as at other marginal places across the zone of cotton culture, local farmers hedged their bets on the great gamblers' crop with sideline money enterprises, raising cattle, goats, sheep, corn, and small grains, and sometimes the sidelines become mainlines. They further hedged their bets by producing most of the food consumed on the family farm—garden vegetables, field peas interspersed in the corn, hogs in the woods, chickens, turkeys, milk cows, and all the rest.

This rural world was very different from the present, and during oral history interviews former natives of the place struggled to convey its essential strangeness. Across a single human lifetime, the cultural change had been immense. Grandparents who had grown up hauling drinking water from the spring creek to their homeplaces, a barrel at a time, with a one-mule farmer's "sled," found it hard to explain this practice to their incredulous grandchildren, who were growing up surfing the Internet.

We know the mule-powered, coal-oil-illuminated countryside was different, but I am not sure how well we appreciate the nature of that difference and what it felt like to live out there. Many of us, even some historians of the farmer's lost world, have the grandchildren's problem of understanding. Interviewees seemed well aware of the difficulty. At some point during most of our oral history interviews, the elderly persons hesitated, then tried to find words to convey just these things. They told of an isolation so severe that every passing stranger became a object of great interest and where "fifteen miles down the road was like another land."⁵ They described the darkness of the nights and the brightness of the stars in a time before electricity. They commented upon the immense silence of the countryside at a time before humming machines—when farmers shouted back and forth to each other from distant fields, the next Model T on the dirt road could be heard coming from miles away, and the only industrial sounds were the distant steam whistles of cotton gins and passing trains.

Some memories of the historic sounds of the countryside had already disappeared into Coryell and Bell county graveyards by the beginning of the twenty-first century, doubtless along with many other unrecorded details of rural life. "The grassroots historian must do his work before the night cometh, in which no man can work," C. L. Sonnichsen once observed, in properly biblical tones.⁶ In 1992, 102-year-old Walter Cole of Jasper County told me of the sounds of the mule- or horse-powered bale presses of his childhood. As the animals went around and around the bale press, compressing the boxed cotton under the wooden screw, the squeal of wood grinding on wood rose to a crescendo that carried for miles across the autumn landscape.⁷ None of the people interviewed in Coryell and Bell counties between 1998 and 2001 was old enough to recall the squealing of the bale presses in cotton season, though this doubtless had been an authentic sound of the place. For how many other common details of rural life had the oral historians arrived too late?

At most locations, this exotic rural world transformed into something else during the two decades following World War II. Roads improved, schools and stores and gins and churches consolidated into bigger and better versions of themselves in nearby market towns and county seats. Small-scale, dry-land cotton farms could not compete with the new large-scale, fully mechanized agriculture and became obsolete. Existing farms became larger, and "cattle and coastal" (bermuda hay) replaced much row-crop farming. Many people still living in rural areas now commuted to jobs in town.

However, none of these trends fully worked themselves out in this stretch of the Coryell County and Bell County countryside. There, a still-vital rural society died within a few weeks in 1942 with the forced sale of land for the U.S. Army tank-training facility of Camp Hood.

Army bases had to go somewhere, and by the nature of things in a democracy authorities usually established them "nowhere," in areas of empty countryside, where the taking of private lands was least disruptive to people's lives. That was perhaps the case here, but triangulated between the three market towns of Gatesville to the north, Belton on the southeast, and Cop-

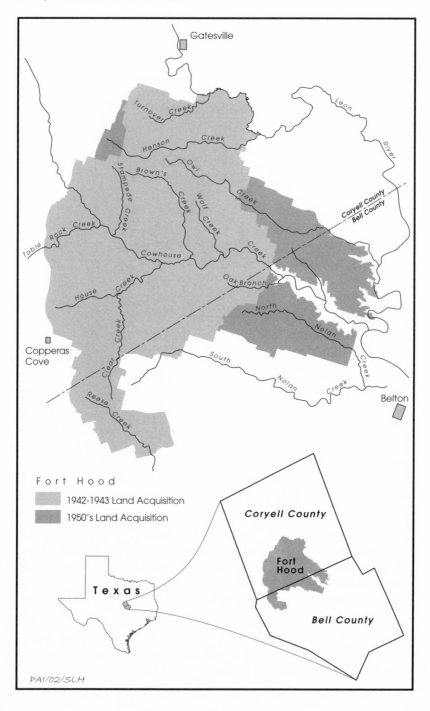

Fort Hood

1942-1943 Land Acquisition

1950's Land Acquisition

PAI/02/SLH

peras Cove to the southwest lay more than twenty island communities—
"settlements" in the southern lexicon—dispersed, informal rural communities whose time had run out.

This doomed nowhere was a complex place, akin to thousands of similar landscapes across the eastern half of Texas and the South. Pidcoke, Sparta,
Antelope, and one or two other settlements had discernible community
centers, where church, school, and store were close together. Most had a
more dispersed infrastructure, with the elements of community scattered
across the landscape along with the farmsteads of the families that gave
them their allegiance. Most settlements had a church, or churches, and a
school. Some had a store or post office, or had previously had them. Somewhere in almost every settlement was a farmer who also operated a syrup
mill or a grist mill to provide the community with the survival staples of
molasses and cornmeal.

Some of these settlements might look like "remote countryside with
scattered farms" to a stranger passing through, but when questioned, farm
families almost always professed a community membership. They believed
they lived somewhere—that they were part of some settlement, some community, no matter how faint or far away.

Historians often have failed to recognize the importance of the settlement as a basic social unit of the southern countryside, Frank Owsley argued in his classic study of the Old South.[8] Typically unincorporated and
unplatted, settlements were poorly represented on official maps, and historians have turned out to study them only after obliteration by reservoirs or
military bases triggered mandatory salvage research.

Overlapping fields of membership linked a farm family to its home settlement—ties to church and school. Of the two, schools were more important. There might be multiple churches in a community, and the
congregations might or might not cooperate, attending each other's services on alternating Sundays, but the schools cut across congregational lines
and served as core social institutions. They functioned as community centers, filling important social needs beyond education of the young. Major
social affairs and entertainments centered on the school, as did political
"speakings" and other community-wide events. If any issue rose to general
community concern, people gathered to discuss it at the school. In many
ways, the school and the community, the settlement, were one, and as some
rural people said, "When the school dies, the community dies"—ominous
words, even before 1940, considering how many smaller rural schools were
consolidating into larger ones.[9] Local officials or distant scholars rarely had

reason to map the array of informal settlements across a rural county, but the common school district maps of the 1920s and 1930s came very close. As anthropologist Oscar Lewis noted in his study of the Texas blacklands farther east, rural school districts and settlements tended to coincide.[10]

Perhaps most important, each of the twenty-odd settlements that ultimately became part of Fort Hood had functioned as mutual-aid communities, domains of neighborliness, face-to-face societies in which neighbor stood ready to help neighbor in time of trouble. If your house burned, or you needed help building a new barn, or someone got sick and could not get weeds from the cotton or put meals on the table, neighbors sprang into action to help out. They did this in a spirit of Christian brotherhood and sisterhood but also in full knowledge that the next time their families might be the ones needing help. Kin group and community functioned as the only social net anyone had, and to be thought of as a bad kinsman or neighbor was not something you could afford.

The first settlements of Coryell County emerged in the wilderness, soon after the establishment of Fort Gates in 1849 on the Leon River at the present site of the county seat of Gatesville.[11] By 1852, when most troops pulled out of Fort Gates to relocate to new forts farther west, four first-generation settlements had established themselves to the south. These were Ruth, Spring Hill, Antelope, and Old Sugar Loaf, all of them on army roads. Additional settlements came later, ten in the Fort Hood area by 1868 and about thirty—the maximum number at any one time—by 1913.

Before the Civil War, frontier stockmen sparsely inhabited the area, with farming mainly for subsistence. Farmers had no easy way to get cotton to market until the coming of the railroads in 1882; cattle, and to a degree sheep, could be driven to the railhead. Families distributed themselves across a semiarid landscape of flat-topped, brush-covered hills, intermittent grassy prairies, and heavily wooded bottoms of the Leon River, Cowhouse Creek, Brown's Creek, and their feeder streams. Indian raids by Comanche and Apache harassed settlers into Civil War times, and periodic drouths marked Coryell County as a marginal farming area. Corn was critical for a subsistence agriculture, providing "fuel" for work stock, feed for domestic animals, and food for human diet, but the local corn crops failed from lack of rain in 1856 and 1857, causing considerable hardship.

Every southern agriculturist breathed a huge sigh of relief each year that his main subsistence crop of corn grew big enough in the field to form ears. Then and only then did he know that no one in his family would actually go hungry that season. However, during a long succession of years, perhaps one each decade, from the drouth of 1856 to the drouth of 1925, local fields produced little corn.

This was a backwoods frontier society until after the Civil War, as historian Martha Doty Freeman noted in her overview of agriculture at the settlements that would become Fort Hood.

> Recollections of life until the Civil War emphasized the self-sufficiency of the agricultural unit, normally comprised of two parents and their children, the males of whom stayed at home to help with production until they reached their majority. Typical housing consisted of log structures that had stone or board chimneys, dirt floors, and hide doors. Furnishings were simple, and those described by members of the Blackburn family near Palo Alto were not very different from those described by a former slave who had lived on a small "plantation" near Gatesville. A table in the Blackburn home was made of 3-foot-wide post oak boards, and a cradle was a hollowed-out split oak log. The family owned a spinning wheel, and after Mrs. Blackburn worked in the corn fields all day, she sat up at night carding, spinning, and weaving. Beds often were made of split ash logs through which holes were bored and rope threaded to substitute for slats. Cow hides, or occasionally buffalo hides, were put on top of the rope. In similar fashion, former slave S. B. Adams described the "log huts" in which the slaves lived, as well as furnishings such as spinning wheels and looms. Bedsteads were "corded criss-cross with cow-hide strings"; food was prepared in the fireplace; and, like their White neighbors, the slaves wore homespun dyed with colors extracted from vegetable matter.
>
> Diet frequently was beef, and sometimes fish, but variety was achieved by killing opossums, squirrels, and rabbits, and by raiding roosts, where boys blinded birds and then "knocked them senseless with sumac sticks." Gourds were used widely, providing receptacles for milk, salt, lard, cracklings, hominy, and gunpowder. Even the family dog was not immune from the generally opportunistic behavior that characterized early frontier life. One settler recalled that "Bird Clements made shoes from dog hides, and my beloved dog Trip was slain for this purpose."[12]

This "generally opportunistic behavior that characterized early frontier life" had not disappeared from the area by the 1930s, when winter robins still were blinded by torches at night and thrashed from roost trees with long poles, then used for robin pot pies, and when at least one old man went around wearing shoes made from a worn-out basketball salvaged from the nearby rural school. The tough skin of the dead basketball worked even better than dog hide.[13]

Populations of both Coryell and Bell counties swelled in the two decades after the Civil War and rose steadily to a peak between 1910 and 1920, at which time Coryell County's population topped 20,000. Bell County had over twice that. Stock raising and subsistence farming continued to be the norm until the 1882 arrival of railroads to Gatesville and Killeen triggered an agricultural boom. From the 1880s into the Depression 1930s, cotton became the main money crop for the area. Waves of new settlers (mostly row-crop farmers from the deep South), the advent of barbed-wire fencing, and the terrible winters of the 1880s ended the frontier stock-raising era.

Stock raising itself did not end, of course, not in this landscape so marginal for row-crop agriculture. Most farmers kept some cattle behind fences. Locals raised many sheep from the late 1880s into the 1890s, though these proved even more vulnerable to harsh winter weather than did the cattle. An enthusiasm for "hair goats" struck Coryell and Bell counties in the 1910s and lasted into the 1930s. Angora goats (detractors called them "hooved locusts") thrived where no other stock could live and not even the most optimistic cotton farmers would try to grow cotton.

Cotton remained king until the government's anti-cotton programs of the 1930s, though cotton in this landscape was "a hard row to hoe," even in the best of times. Drouths occurred periodically, one just after the turn of the century and another in 1925. Beyond the local dice-roll of weather, international prices of the gamblers' crop followed a mysterious (to the farmer) boom-and-bust cycle from the Panic of 1893 to the Great Depression. Most farmers preferred to recall the rare good years of ample rain, bumper crops, and 40-cent-a-pound cotton.

During the cotton era, certain generalities held true. Being out on the limb with one-crop agriculture proved chancier for renters than for landowners, who had bigger gardens and more pork in their smokehouses. Agricultural "diversification"—the raising of other money crops and various livestock—was practiced by many farm families, just in case. Farmers here raised more small grains, broomcorn, goats, and sheep than did others on the blacklands farther east. Pressures on the limited arable land increased until, by 1910 in Coryell County, slightly more farmers rented land than owned it. Tenants "on the thirds and fourths" brought their own work stock and agricultural machinery to their rented farms and paid landlords with one-third of the corn and one-fourth of the cotton. Sharecroppers "on the halves" brought only their labor and that of their families and paid landowners with half of everything produced. Few big agribusiness sharecropper farms flourished in the settlements that became Fort Hood, however; here cotton farming was mostly small-scale. In a common landowner-renter situation, a farmer rented to two or three of his grown sons, to other relatives, or to neighbors.

The economic wild ride of cotton agriculture was even wilder for renter families, no matter who their landowners might be. In years of local crop failure, it was these families that temporarily relocated to pick for others in the cotton fields of West Texas, the Red River Valley, or any other place where farmers had "made a crop." Renter dissatisfactions (and the anger of small landowners with the railroads) show up in active Farmers' Alliance organizations during the 1880s and local majorities for Populist presidential candidates during the 1890s.[14]

The Depression thirties followed the boom-and-bust twenties, and cotton prices dropped to record lows and remained there, and life became (as William Powell told me) truly "harder than hardscrabble." Some claimed to see the Great Depression as only business as usual; things had been tough in the past. The subsistence side of the farms supported families as before, no matter the price of the cotton. People scrounged and recycled and went without, somewhat heartened by observing that none of their neighbors, even those with large landholdings, seemed much better off. The area remained a backwater, although modernizations and consolidations went on as at other places across the South. Schools merged into larger rural schools, improved roads led to closure of country stores, community gins lost out to larger and faster gins in the market towns, farmers hauled crops to more distant markets by truck or tractor.

The 1940 Census for Coryell County revealed a marginal southern farming society in transition: 74 percent of farms had an automobile (down from 80 percent in 1930); 52 percent of farms hauled water from over 50 feet away from the house; 80 percent had outdoor privies (others had none at all); 87 percent had no indoor bath or shower; 51 percent did not have an icebox; 68 percent had no telephone; but 57 percent had radios, some of the quartz-crystal-and-headphone variety that required no battery power. Except for a few Delco battery and wind-powered systems, none of the farm families in the Coryell County settlements had electricity.[15]

Even the government's New Deal programs had no unusual impact in Coryell and Bell counties. The Federal Emergency Relief Act led to the killing of livestock. The Soil Conversation Service worked with the Civilian Conservation Corps to build fences, sod pastures, and terrace fields. A relatively small percentage of families went on federal relief. WPA projects employed only 7 percent of the total workforce of Coryell County in 1939.

By 1941, however, a much more drastic government intervention in local affairs loomed just over the horizon, and like a blue norther of early spring it swept swiftly down upon an unsuspecting countryside. In November of that year, appalled by what Hitler's Panzer divisions were accomplishing in Europe and in full realization that its notion of static tank defense systems now was obsolete, the U.S. government activated the army's Tank Destroyer Tactical and Firing Center. The army desperately needed a large base to train its new tank and anti-tank divisions to try to stop the Panzers, and it had nothing big enough. It began a hasty search to find a location for a base.

War arrived the next month on December 7, 1941, with the Japanese attack on Pearl Harbor. A week or so later, rumors increased about a possible large army base somewhere in the Temple-Waco area. The rumors seemed hard to believe for local farmers, but soon people saw strange, close-mouthed army survey teams abroad in the land. Some people laughed when they first heard of a possible army base, but the laughter quickly died. The army considered several large sites west of Waco and chose one just west of Valley Mills. After furious political lobbying from boosters in Bell and Coryell counties, the army then reversed itself and chose a site mostly in Coryell County. "Camp Hood" was on the way, patriotically named for Texas Civil War general John Bell Hood.[16]

In this time of national emergency, matters moved swiftly. On January 14, 1942, the army announced the establishment of its military base in Coryell and Bell counties. Lands quickly were taken by the government, acting under its Fifth Amendment powers of eminent domain, vastly strengthened by the Second War Powers Act of 1942. Some farm families had two months' notice or more to move out, some received as little as fifteen days' warning. Army estimators generally awarded low values for the land and did not compensate for improvements—farm buildings, barns, fences, pecan orchards, and the like. Government land payments trailed government eviction notices by months—in some cases by years. With so many land seekers forced on the market all at once, supply and demand (and greed) drove local land prices sky high, and farm families found it virtually impossible to take the money the government paid them for their farms and buy comparable farms just off the reservation.

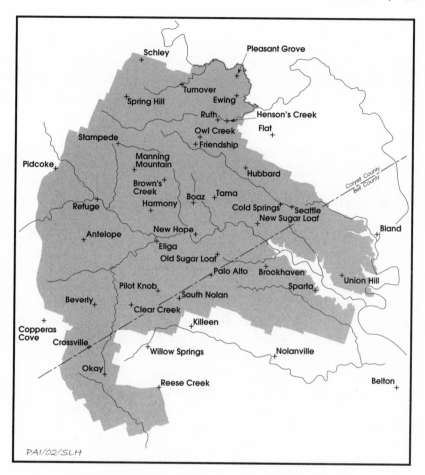

Schley
Pleasant Grove
Turnover
Spring Hill
Ewing
Ruth
Henson's Creek
Owl Creek
Flat
Friendship
Stampede
Pidcoke
Manning Mountain
Hubbard
Brown's Creek
Refuge
Harmony
Boaz
Tama
Cold Springs
Seattle
New Sugar Loaf
Bland
Antelope
New Hope
Eliga
Old Sugar Loaf
Palo Alto
Brookhaven
Pilot Knob
South Nolan
Sparta
Union Hill
Beverly
Clear Creek
Copperas Cove
Killeen
Crossville
Willow Springs
Nolanville
Okay
Reese Creek
Belton
Coryell County
Bell County

PAI/02/SLH

Many of the farming families and settlements affected by the forced relocation had only just begun slowly recovering from the Great Depression, and the circumstances of their treatment during acquisition by the government caused them great hardship. In her study of the Fort Hood "taking," researcher Sylvia Edwards relied heavily on interviews with people who had been relocated, and she stated the situation bluntly.

Families who moved off their lands did so regretfully, but with a sense of patriotic commitment to the war effort. They held their tongues out of loyalty. The hope of future success on distant battlefields did little, however, to assuage the bitter draught of selling homesteads. Coupled with the personal blow of abandoning their homes was the criticism to which landowners were exposed from their neighbors if the landowners even questioned the sums being offered for their property by the government. Frequently, they were accused of being treacherous and reminded that they could be losing sons as well as homes. Many did both.[17]

All families suffered economically and psychologically from the speed of the forced land sales; they had little time to adjust to circumstances. Reactions to the taking varied greatly from family to family but basically divided along renter-landowner lines. Restless rent farmers, who customarily moved to a new place every year or so, might shed few tears about the coming of the army base. They might even be at the front of the hiring line for the barracks construction crews. Landowners losing great-grandfather's hallowed ground had a much more painful perspective. A farm wife told her daughter-in-law that she was happy about the land seizure, since "That's the only way in the world I'd ever have got away from down there," but three agonized farmers committed suicide, one with his pocket knife as army trucks drove up to load his household goods. In any case, by mid-September of 1942 Camp Hood opened for business.

By the end of the twentieth century, the island settlements of Fort Hood existed only as archeological sites and in the memories of the hundreds of former residents, many of whom gathered yearly at reunions in the peripheral communities of Killeen, Belton, Copperas Cove, and Gatesville. Their numbers dwindled, however, and beginning in 2000 U.S. Army Fort Hood funded a major oral history project directed by Prewitt and Associates of Austin, Texas, to record those memories before it was too late.

The full text of every interview has been printed in *Just Like Yesterday: Recollections of Life on the Fort Hood Lands* (2003), edited by Amy E. Dase, and all tapes, original transcripts, and other materials have been placed in the Texas Collection of Baylor University. Other publications published by the Fort Hood project are "Agriculture and Rural Development on Fort Hood Lands, 1849–1942: National Register Assessments of 710 Historic Archeological Properties" (2001), by Martha Doty Freeman, Amy E. Dase, and Marie E. Blake, and *Imprint on the Land: Life Before Camp Hood, 1820–1942* (2001), by William S. Pugsley. *Harder than Hardscrabble*, the last work of history from the project, is the "popular" fruit of the oral history research.[18]

This publication is different from the scholarly studies of the Fort Hood settlements mentioned above. If I had a guiding intent, it was to step out of readers' way so they could make direct contact with the primary sources, with the voices recorded on the interview tapes. The voices are powerful, even at times disturbing, and a little chaotic and redundant. Sometimes they are hard to interpret by the historian, but trying to make sense from contending voices is nothing more than the experience of "doing history." This should prove an interesting exercise for the reader. "Everyman his own historian," Carl Becker argued long ago, and so, I might add, is every woman.[19]

My other "agenda," or intellectual baggage, was the belief that life in the countryside was stranger than we usually think, that the economic historians who have mainly held the field in scholarly interpretations of rural life have often been one-dimensional in their depictions of it, and that few scholars have listened very well to what the "natives" have to tell us. This book is one historian's attempt to really listen and an opportunity for readers to listen along with me.

Certainly, the natives are ambivalent; their message is complicated. You will read in the following chapters of the power of old-time family ties and community traditions of "neighborliness" that go far beyond current urban or rural practice. But to accompany the good memories are those of physical hardships also far beyond modern experience, seemingly unending work, mind-numbing isolation, and the threat of early death from what today would be considered minor medical conditions. Furthermore, when the close, face-to-face ties of kinship and neighborhood went wrong, they went very wrong. Long-simmering family antagonisms, "bad blood," and violent "feud" incidents are hinted at but are underrepresented in the accounts; some things were still too painful to put on strangers' tape recorders.

By design, our interviews were permissive, wandering, and allowed interviewees to place their own emphases and to bring up topics they deemed important to talk about. Many of the recurrent topics came directly from the natives' remembrance of place, and some are surprising. "Waste not, want not" ruled as the iron dictum of the countryside, but you will read of the frugalities of a true materialism, where daily dishwater became a component of hog slop, and weekly bluing water from Saturday washday served also to bathe the family's children, one after another (then, as often as not, to swab the floors). "Worn out" files—good pieces of steel, nonetheless—were recycled into many different tools. Cotton sacks, dragged to death on the rocky land, became "jumper jackets," hand towels, and a score of other useful things. Historians consistently have evaluated family farm life from a cash-crop perspective, but former country dwellers were more likely to discuss memorable complexities of the subsistence side of the farm—gardens, milk cows, barnyard fowl, field crops grown for family use, hunting, fishing, and foraging. Everyone took great pride in "living off the place," with little more than flour, salt, sugar, tobacco, and coffee required from the store.

Even more unexpected emphases emerge in the oral recollections: dogs (to work stock and patrol for snakes), water sources, soil types, and more. In the Fort Hood settlements the "more" includes rattlesnakes, over and over again. I have been privileged to collect similar oral histories at several other places in rural Texas, but I have never recorded so much material about poisonous snakes, which abounded in the area. People joked about the snakes, but they were a serious matter; sometimes it was like cultivating field crops in a minefield. One woman narrowly survived a painful rattlesnake bite inflicted in the cotton patch, as did her three brothers; their father had not been so lucky.

There is much humor in the telling about these things, even about the hardships and the tragedies. I have not especially selected for this, it permeates the oral testimony. It is a wry, even at times a dark, humor, a far cry from nostalgia, born of people's sense of amazement at the enormous cultural gap between the world they grew up in and that in which they spend their final years.

Other former natives of the rural world tell similar stories to those of people from the Fort Hood settlements, but perhaps as a result of the takeover there seems a certain fervor of remembrance, a keeping of the faith more intense than at other places. This is visible at the yearly community and family reunions, though the ranks thin out. The Hill family still returns each year to take their ritual drinks, one by one, from the lost homeplace spring.

**NOTES**

1. Thad Sitton and Dan K. Utley, *From Can See to Can't: Texas Cotton Farmers on the Southern Prairies* (Austin: University of Texas Press, 1997), p. 10.

2. Elma S. Moulton, *Cotton Production and Distribution in the Gulf Southwest*, part 3 of *The Commercial Survey of the Gulf Southwest*, Domestic Commerce Series, no. 49 (Washington, D.C.: Government Printing Office, 1931), p. 3.

3. Ibid.

4. Ibid., p. 4.

5. Eddie Wegner, quoted in Sitton and Utley, *From Can See to Can't*, p. 40.

6. C. L. Sonnichsen, *The Grave of John Wesley Hardin: Three Essays of Grassroots History* (College Station: Texas A&M University Press, 1979), p. 26.

7. Walter Cole, interview with Thad Sitton, July 9, 1992.

8. Frank Owsley, *Plain Folk of the Old South* (Baton Rouge: Louisiana State University Press, 1949), p. 25.

9. For a detailed social history of Texas rural schools and their important role in community life, see Thad Sitton and Milam C. Rowold, *Ringing the Children In: Texas Country Schools* (College Station: Texas A&M University Press, 1987).

10. Oscar Lewis, *On the Edge of the Black Waxy: A Cultural Survey of Bell County, Texas*, Washington University Studies, New Series, Social and Philosophical Sciences, no. 7 (St. Louis: Washington University, 1948), p. 76. County-wide maps of the myriad common school districts for many Texas counties are included in the 1813-page *Report of the Results of the Texas Statewide School Adequacy Survey* (Austin: Texas State Board of Education, 1937).

11. This historical section of the introduction derives from the research of my colleagues at Prewitt and Associates: Martha Doty Freeman, Amy E. Dase, and Marie E. Blake, "Agriculture and Rural Development on Fort Hood Lands, 1849–1942: National Register Assessments of 710 Historic Archeological Properties," U.S. Army Fort Hood, Archeological Management Series, Research Report No. 42, 2001. The authors cannot entirely be held responsible for my summary paragraphs interpreting their lengthy and detailed social and economic history of the Fort Hood lands.

12. Ibid., p. 22.

13. Several accounts in the chapters that follow report "bird blinding" of robins. Interviewee Andy Wolf told of the "basketball shoes."

14. Freeman, Dase, and Blake, "Agriculture and Rural Development on Fort Hood Lands," p. 101.

15. Ibid., p. 114.

16. William S. Pugsley, *Imprint on the Land: Life before Camp Hood, 1820–1942* (Austin: Prewitt and Associates, 2001), pp. 147–150.

17. Sylvia Edwards, "Land Acquisition in Coryell County, Texas, for the Formation of Camp Hood, 1942–1945: A Civilian Perspective" (master's thesis, Baylor University, 1988), p. 15.

18. Martha, Amy, Marie, and Bill later became my co-researchers on the oral history project, so this book is best regarded as a joint product of all our labors. All quote selections and editings were my own, however.

19. Carl Becker, *Everyman His Own Historian* (New York: Crofts, 1935).

# CHAPTER TWO

# Homeplaces

## Lay of the Land

*Rather often a sense of amazement registered in people's voices as they cast their minds back sixty years and more to describe the physical circumstances of the farms they grew up on. Situations were spare indeed, although landowners usually had more outbuildings and amenities than did the renters. People built their houses more to survive the heat of Texas summers than the cold of winters, when the north wind coursed up the "dogruns" and huddling in the "fireplace room" often had to suffice. If good-tasting, clear, clean water was available close to the house, the family counted itself lucky.*

### NORRIS SIDNEY GRAVES

I was born at Pidcoke [in 1924], in the vicinity of Pidcoke, about six miles from Pidcoke, where they had to pump sunshine to find me. Oh, it was a pitiful, poor old place. I've seen it since. Cows would come up on the porch and things like that, you know. But that's the best Mother and Dad could do, and that's where I was born.

### JOE D. INSALL

My granddaddy was a Confederate soldier for four years, and he went to Mexico when Lee surrendered because he couldn't put up with Yankees. Anyway, Daddy and them settled on Clear Creek. My brother and sister were born there, and I was born at Antelope in 1930. It was right in the bad part of the Depression. Dad owned eight acres, and he built our house out of an old house he tore down.

We had some pretty good land. It was partly sandy and partly black, grew sweet potatoes and watermelons real good, and we grew nearly everything we eat. We were about the poorest people in the neighborhood because we didn't have but eight acres. Dad worked on WPA sometimes, and my grandmother lived with us. She got a Confederate veteran's pension, or old-age pension, I don't know which. It was fifteen dollars a month.

When someone got sick, they were just in bad trouble. I think I was nine years old before I went to a doctor. When the doctor delivered me, my dad gave him this gold railroad watch to pay for it because he didn't have no money. And when my sister was born three years later, he gave him a Jersey milk cow. That's the way we did things. This old Rawleigh peddler would come around ever so often selling this toilet soap and stuff. It was a lot better than the homemade lye soap. My mother would trade him a chicken for a bar of it. He had a chicken coop on the back of his car.

I don't know how we survived. Caught a lot of rabbits. There was a [patch] of grass and broomweeds just up on the hill from where we lived. A lot of rabbits lived there. This old dog would chase the rabbits in that rock pile. I can still seem him now up there wagging his tail and barking on top of them rocks. I was a little bitty feller, about seven or eight years old, and I'd run over there and move the rocks and catch that rabbit. Knock his head over a rock and head home with him. I was even too little to skin him. But we ate a lot of rabbits.

### WILMA EARL COLVIN EDWARDS

My parents had come back and rented my grandfather's rent house at the Boaz community on Brown's Creek. That's where my first days were spent. It was remote and rocky, and cedars were thick behind the house, and rattlesnakes were the biggest in the world all around that place, but none of us got bit. I have so many memories, you just wouldn't believe it.

It was just a small, as they called it, "box house." It wasn't a bungalow. It had a living room and a bedroom and a kitchen and a big screened porch that we slept on in the summertime, because it was hot. The people that had lived in it were just renting, so they didn't paper it or anything—just a house. They did leave their wood cookstove for Mother, because she had nothing. But Mother could be put on a rock and make it look like a mansion, she was just that kind. She papered it, they got curtains and made it homey. They bought a rug. But it was hot hot and cold cold cold, I remember that. We had no indoor toilet, and the mud was so deep that a child might get lost in it. Daddy built a wooden step and walk out towards the well so we wouldn't have to walk in the mud to get in the house.

Daddy and Mother did everything, they were real industrious people, they didn't mind work. Mother canned. Oh, my Lord, how Mother canned food! There was an old religious song, "Work for the Night Is Coming," and when mother was doing all this work, trying to get our life back together, she hummed and sang that all the time, "Work for the Night Is Coming." I found out later what she meant.

### GLADYS MERLE KEENER CHASTAIN

Dad lost his place, and we moved to Silver City and sharecropped on Mother's brother's farm. Dad worked the farm, and when he sold the hay, the cotton, and everything, he'd give Uncle Lee Hopson his quota. Dad worked for the man across the road, who seemed to be financially better off than we were. He had Dad build a rock fence and paid Dad a dollar a day. I can remember seeing my father come home with his hands bleeding from handling these big rocks.

So, Dad farmed and Mother gardened, because if she didn't garden, we didn't eat that year. She canned everything she could get her hands on. Mama was a great cook, and we always had food to eat, but we wore hand-me-down clothes from my cousin Neta out of Killeen. I always liked to see my uncle come, because she'd sent her leftover clothing for me to wear. For me, it's like Christmas, 'cause Uncle Lee was gonna bring me Neta's clothes.

We didn't have running water, and we didn't have an outhouse. It was like the song says, "out behind the barn," and glad you didn't have neighbors living too close. We had to haul water in barrels from down on the branch, and probably the cows were upstream. We did have a rain barrel at the end of the house and caught rainwater. It would get tadpoles in it, but we would strain that, and that's what we would bathe in and wash our hair in—the rainwater that the tadpoles had been strained out of. Mama would fill a big washtub full of water and heat the water on the wood cookstove. Us girls would get the bath first, and then Dad got his bath, and poor Mom got the last bath. In the same water, mind you! Lots of people wouldn't tell this story, but it's the truth, it's history.

My two youngest sisters slept in one bed, and then there was the pot-bellied stove, and then you went into the other room where me and my sister Faye slept. But the wind came through the windows so and through the cracks in the wall that you could even see the snow. If it was snowing, it would seep through. Mother would have so much cover on us that once you went to bed, you didn't turn over because it was so weighted down with cover. Also, she would put the flatirons that we ironed with on the cookstove and heat them up and wrap them in old leggings or something and put them in the bed with us to heat our feet. But when you talked, you could see your steam blowing, it was so cold in that room.

We didn't have clothes closets back then, you had a wire stretched across the corner, and that's where you hung your clothes, what few clothes you had. We didn't have a clothesline outside. When we washed we hung our clothes on a barbed-wire fence, and when they dried the wind would blow them off. So, you'd just go along on the ground picking up your clean clothes.

### ANDY GORDON WOLF

My mother was Effie May Hill and my dad was John Daniel Hill, nicknamed "Tuck" Wolf. His daddy was named "Uncle Jack." That wasn't his name, either. His name was John. But my dad and his brothers all lived there [at Wolf Valley] at one time, and their names were Buck, Tuck, Jack, and Jim. That's nicknames.

All of them gone, ain't none of them left. I guess that my dad was the only one of them that ever tried to own anything, all the rest of them just rented. Uncle Jim, he worked for us and helped make a crop for a long time. We hired people to work on fence and things like that, my daddy did, all the time. He was a trader, and I guess he had a little money—must have had it. But all the boys in the country just about, they's growing up, worked for us at one time or another for fifty cents a day and keep, fifteen dollars a month. That's not an eight-hour day, either. When you woke up in the morning, you got out and fed the cattle and everything before daylight, and when it got daylight, you was ready to go to the field or the post yard.

The neighbors, they wasn't rich people and poor people, they's all poor. Even the rich ones was poor. Didn't have no electricity at all. We used kerosene lamps and a kerosene lantern if you had one. Sometimes you'd have to go out at night and have to light one of them lanterns to see how to get around or get on an old rattlesnake.

I think we got along pretty good. My dad, he was trucking back in the thirties, and he'd go sometimes and be gone two, three days. My mother would go with him. So me and my brothers got along pretty well by ourself. When you got hungry you'd go out and get a hen egg and fry you an egg or something. You never were hungry. Might not be what you wanted to eat, but you always had something. And we squirrel hunted and rabbit hunted. A good cotton-tailed rabbit is hard to beat, and squirrels, you could always kill squirrels.

Back in the thirties, didn't nobody have [piped-in] water. We'd go down and pull water from a spring well that was eighteen or twenty foot deep and throw water on one another. Use that old lye soap. I don't know if you ever got clean or not, but you sure got enough of it pretty quick. That water was like ice.

### JOHN DANIEL WOLF (ANDY'S OLDER BROTHER)

We lived in three different houses there on my grandpa's place. One of them was the old house, the first one built on the ranch when my great-uncle settled that country. That house had a ten-foot porch all the way across the front and an eight-foot hall down the middle. Then, over here was a big room and a fireplace with a kitchen on the back of it. And over here was a big room with a fireplace and a storage shed on the back of it. You filled this room with two or three beds and this one with two or three beds, and then in the summertime you moved all those beds out on that big porch. We lived in that house quite some time, then we moved to a little three-room house down in the pasture. Had a lean-to roof porch across the front, and very crowded.

There was no air conditioner or anything, you moved your bed out on that porch so you could get air circulation. By about nine o'clock [at night], it's pretty cool. If you didn't have a porch and had a big live oak tree out in the front yard, you'd move your bed under that live oak tree.

Some of the time we're living in a house that was built back when all you did was put up one-by-twelves and stripped it. You had no insulation, no nothing. The wall was one-by-twelve thick, with a strip on the outside. The weather and water would get against that strip, and after five or six years that strip would crinkle. You could see through them, see through the wall! The roofs were horrible, lots of time buckets all over the place to catch the water running through. A time or two we did put new roofs on.

Cut wood for the fireplace for winter and for the cookstove. Sometimes it was four or five o'clock in the afternoon before you got the house warmed up. If you let the fire go off in the night before, it took a tremendous long time to get that silly thing warmed up again.

### LOUIS J. TOMASTIK

I'm the youngest of six, born in 1928. All of them were born east of Temple in the country. I was the only one born in Fort Hood. I say, "I wasn't born, I was hatched among the rattlesnakes and rocks." I tell you, there's some rattlesnakes around there. I've seen a-many of them.

We hauled many many loads of rock out, but pretty good land, pretty good cultivation there. Wasn't nothing like the blacklands around Temple, it was shallower land there, but it made half-decent crops. They'd plant usually cotton, corn, and some oats.

The house had two or three bedrooms, then the living area and the kitchen. It was pretty old, it was in the old times. In summer it was real neat. It had a breezeway from the south to the north, about eight or ten foot in shade, and a lot of times it was the coolest place in the house 'cause of the way the wind hit. We were living on a kind of little hill and bluff, and then a rock ledge there. The ledge was about two foot or so, and we used to watch the northers when the rains were coming in from northwest during the spring—blue norther. We'd set on those rocks and watch them after sundown. Farming, you've got to know a good lot about weather, or you try to out-guess it. Dad taught us a lot about weather, learned us to be weather-wise.

We killed about six hogs each winter and make two or three different kind of sausage. Had to make head sausage, too. In Czech we called it *jelito*. You fry it and bake it, it's for breakfast. That was delicious. Gosh, my stomach is . . . ! I feel the juices coming just thinking about it.

We were the only Czech family around [Antelope]. You wouldn't be taught any English until you were about four years old, and you'd learn your native language fluently. You'd know maybe five, six hundred words in English when you started school, enough to get you by, and then pretty soon you catch up fast.

### ROBERT E. GAULT

Our homeplace [on Cowhouse Creek] was a little bit airy. It was about a seven- or eight-room house built back around 1905, somewhere along there. What I loved about it was the porches. We had a porch on the east clear across the house, had one on the south halfway across, and then on the north by the kitchen and dining room we had another porch. So we had three big porches. And course, we had big windows, in those days you used windows for your air conditioning. That's all you had was just wind coming in. It was a real comfortable house. It was ten-foot ceilings, of course, had a big old fireplace. I used to tell them, I had to take a bath in a tub in front of that fireplace, and I'd burn on one side and freeze on the other. Baths in the winter were rough. In the summertime I didn't worry about it, [I'd] go to the creek. It was about half a mile, just a nice walk when I was a kid. I didn't mind. I didn't like those bull nettles down there, though, sometimes. You ever get in bull nettles?

### JUANITA GRIFFIN DUNCAN

The house I was raised in [at Brookhaven] was a great big old house. It had three bedrooms. It was a great big old T-shaped house, the roof was T-shaped. It had two big rooms at the front of the house with a hall between and a porch all the way across the front. You went down the hall, went into the kitchen area, went through the kitchen to the living room—the fireplace room, where we had the fireplace to heat the house. And then there was a bedroom off of that, and then the dining room off of the kitchen, and the back porch. That was the house that we lived in.

One bedroom had two beds, a dresser. We had no closets in that house, we hung our clothes on the wall with nails. In the other room was the dresser and a piano and a bed. In the kitchen was a big wood cookstove and a woodbox set as you went out the back door. There was a closet to put canned foods in the corner there, and there was a big table we called the cook table. Then of course in the dining room was a big long table with a bench that we older kids sat on, and as you grew older you got to sit in a certain place by my daddy. The rest of us sat around the table, but four of us would sit on the bench at one time.

The other room was a bedroom. My grandmother Griffin lived with us at one time, and she lived in that room. She had her belongings—she had a bed and dresser, trunk, and all that stuff.

Then, in the fireplace room there was a bed, and we had what was called a washstand. That's where we had our radio. And then in the corner we had a square table and a great big kerosene lamp that we studied by, because we had no electricity out there for a long time. In the hall we had what was called a milk cooler that had a water basin on the top and a pan on the bottom that the water overflowed through. Usually, it was an old ragged sheet that you tore up and pinned around that to keep it cool, and the wind came through and kept the water cool. That's how we kept our milk.

Then, on the back porch, we had water that came from the windmill out the back and had a washbasin that we washed in, and the towel hung on the back door. We had a woodbox out there that we put our wood in. On the front porch there was a little table that held two wooden water buckets that we put our drinking water in. We carried our drinking water from a spring up the branch from where we lived.

We had screens, we had a telephone. The fact of it is, we had the only telephone in that little community there. We had the only washing machine, a gasoline-[powered] Maytag. We had the first and only one for a long time. We were a large family, but we never went to bed hungry, we had clothes to wear. Of course, my mom sewed and made most of the girls' clothes.

We lived at the end of the road. Whenever you saw a car coming, it was coming to our house. That was the last place they could go.

### JUANITA MANNING FLEMING

On the Manning Mountain, it was a six-room house with a big hall down the middle of it and a double fireplace. We had to go to the springs in the hollow, about a quarter of a mile from the house, to do our washing and our laundry and stuff, and we had to pack our drinking water from down there. We had kind of a climb. It was down in a gully, the springs was, in the side of a hill. We caught it fresh as it come out of the springs. Fall down and spill our buckets and have to go back and refill them!

No outhouse. We had to go to the barn, wherever we could get out of sight, and had to squat. And we didn't have an outhouse down there at Eliga when we left the Manning Mountain. We had to go under the hill or use the henhouse. We had to squat unless we went to the henhouse. I believe Daddy put a little two-by-four across the corner, and we used that.

### TOMMIE L. SHULTS HAFERKAMP

We lived in an unpainted house [at Friendship]. There were three bedrooms. Well, actually our living room had a bed in it. There was a kitchen, but we ate and cooked in the same room; it was a long shed room on the south end of the house. And there was a front porch and a back porch. The front porch had a shelf where the drinking water, the water bucket, and the dipper were kept.

One room we called the "fireplace room," because that's where the fireplace was. That's where we lived, mostly, during the wintertime. Then there was—I suppose it was the hall, but it had a bed in it—a room we called "the little dark room," because it had no window in it.

There was no electricity. We didn't have electricity at all until after we moved out of there. We had kerosene lamps. It was a great day when my mom was able to buy an Aladdin lamp. It has a kind of a mantle, I don't know what it's made of, very delicate, but it produces a bright light like an electric light. You had to be very careful or it would collapse.

Bare wood walls, single walls, and the outside was unpainted. The [interior] walls of the house were papered, but with builder's paper. It's very heavy paper, it isn't like wallpaper today. You didn't have canvas under it, but it kept a lot of the wind from the cracks.

We had a wood cookstove that was the only way of heating and cooking. And for our milk we had a water cooler, a milk cooler. It had three shelves with a pan on the bottom, and you pinned a cloth [around it], a white cloth that you had to keep real clean or it smelled fishy, yucky. Mother had one sewed together from white feed sacks, because it had all the seams in it. To have fresh milk in the summertime, we'd catch the fresh water from the windmill, pour it in the top tray, and keep that cloth wet. And then it would drain down into the bottom tray, and that kept the milk and butter fresh, at least for one day. Then it went "blinky," we called it "blinky blue-john."

The water situation, we had a deep well with a windmill over it. We didn't have any creeks running through our place, so in the summertime it was bad. If the wind didn't blow, we were very careful with the water. In 1934, in the hot summer, the windmill was broken, I believe the sucker rods were broken. It was hot! The stock had water to drink, but we didn't have. Oh, it was awful, we had to haul water from a neighbor's house in barrels. Anyway, some people came to help Papa pull the pipe and fix it, because neighbors did that, they just helped each other when somebody needed a well fixed or something. But somehow the pipe fell in the well, and what I remember is that Papa came over to the shelf for the water bucket on the front porch and just sat down and cried. That's the first time I ever saw Papa cry.

### JOE D. INSALL

We didn't have any water supply [at Antelope], just a cistern where the water run off from the house. Daddy tried to dig a well or two, hand-dug, and somebody witched it, but he was pretty bent out of shape because they lied to him. No water.

The cistern set up above ground, [but] daddy hauled water from [Mr.] Tomastik. He had a fifty-five-gallon wooden barrel, probably an old vinegar barrel. He built him a slide out of some logs with a platform on it and set that barrel on it. He'd go fill it up, he'd drag it with some horses. He put a piece of wagon sheet with a barrel hoop on top so it wouldn't slosh out or get anything in it. [The Tomastiks] had a big spring well. It was probably ten foot in diameter, and it wasn't too far down to water. They had a pump on it.

### WILLIAM AKE POWELL

I was born near the Friendship Cemetery in 1921. We lived there when I was just a little boy, I don't know how long, but [then] my daddy bought an old farm that somebody had let go back during the Depression. Nobody had lived there for a very good while. And he and my Grandpa Powell built a house on it, a little bungalow. Four-room bungalow house, no ceilings, no screens on the windows, but it had a porch on it, porch on the front. I was probably six or seven years old when we moved over there. We farmed that place and helped my grandpa and grandma. They lived about half a mile through the woods from where we lived.

One thing I remember about it, [that place] had laid out all those years, and we killed forty-five rattlesnakes the first year we lived on it. We tried to kill all of them when I was growing up. We went up to my Grandpa Dorsey's one Sunday afternoon to eat lunch with all the kids and grandkids. My daddy had an old Model T Ford that didn't have no top on it, had a little hoopy bed on the back. We was coming through the woods, and a big old rattlesnake started cross the road. And he's going to run over it with that car, and that thing stood up! You could see his head above the fenders on the front of that thing, and it was hitting! We finally got it killed, and it's close to six foot long. We tied a wire on it and dragged it back to my grandfather's to show it to everybody.

My Grandpa Powell, he was the first one on Owl Creek. It was part of a grant that his people got after the [Civil] War. And he had a brother named "Bun"—Bunyon, I believe was his name—and he was given the next place next to my grandpa's. And then on the other side of him was my Uncle Jim, that was another one of my grandpa's brothers. And on the other side was another one, his name was Uncle George. And then on the other side of him, right next to him, was one named Emmet. And they was all Powells, brothers, right down that creek, right down Owl Creek.

And then my Grandpa Dorsey on my mother's side, he had almost everything. He did hay baling, he did threshing. He had the blacksmith's shop, he sharpened the plows and put shoes on the mules and the horses. And had bees, he'd sell honey, had a lot of bees. He had it all, and his place was the next place west of my Grandpa Powell's place, they joined. So my mother and daddy was raised up next to each other.

We just lived on that farm and raised cotton and corn. There's a lot of flint rocks. Man, you never seen as many rocks, you'd sure wear out the hoes trying to get the cockleburs and the grass out of it. It was a kind of a reddish brown dirt and had a lot of flint rocks in it. Every time it rained, every time you plowed it, you plowed up a bunch more. It'd wear all your equipment out, wear you out, too. We used to haul rocks and build fences and everything else out of them, pick a lot of them up. And that's post-oak country where we was at. After them post oaks all been cut down, you just cut them sprouts about two or three times a year. They'd come up and get about that high before you'd know it. We'd take a grubbing hoe and go cut all of them down.

There used to be an old gray wolf every once in a while would come through. They didn't stay too long, they'd be a-going from one place to another. And there used to be a panther used to come through every once in a while and shake everybody up. They'd hear it scream and raising sand and making all kind of racket. And a lot of times the dogs would go under the house when that panther would do that. They wasn't about to go see what it was. They knew what it was, I guess.

### ROBERT E. GAULT

I had four brothers and one sister, but we were scattered out so much in age. My dad was forty-nine and my mother was forty when I was born. So I was unexpected, I imagine. I was always my mother's pet. My oldest brother was fifteen years older than me, and the next one was fourteen years older than me, and the next one was twelve years older than me, and then my sister was six years older than me. The oldest brother was a bachelor, and he stayed home until the army took him. He was always there, but he was slow and deliberate. When I was twelve years old, I could out-pick him in cotton and hoe two rows to his one. He's just that way, he'd pull a boll of cotton and stand up and look around and get another one. And if he got two hundred pounds, he's all right, he didn't care.

My sister and my next-to-oldest brother was real good pickers. My sister was the only girl, I guess she had to be mean. She could ride a horse and shoot a gun with anybody, and anything like that. Played softball, she was pitcher. She was tough, I'll guarantee you, and she used to pick five hundred pounds of cotton a day. Every time I got in a fight with her, I got a whipping. I tripped her one morning, and she fell and hit the dresser across there and broke her nose, and Dad like to beat me up. I told him it's worth it that time.

### ERNEST ALLEN COLE

Our house [at Okay] faced west. It had a bedroom and a big living room–bedroom. Then it had a side room were my daddy had built a box and lined it with tin. In the fall, when they had sales, he'd buy either six or seven sacks of flour, and we'd keep it in there. And we kept sugar in there, the bulk stuff in there. We had a fireplace in the north room, that's where we'd [stay] in the cold wintertime. And you didn't spit in the fireplace in our house. That was taboo, because Mother liked to put sweet potatoes in there and bake them in the ashes. Those sweet potatoes were Jamaica yams, and sweet juice would come out of them in the ashes. You'd brush the ashes off the skin and eat them.

Most of the homes [at Okay] were about half farm, half ranch. They grazed cows, mules, horses, goats—an awful lot of Angora goats—where the hills start. And the homes, about half of them were painted and about half of them weren't. A lot of them were made out of rawhide lumber, which is lumber that is a little rough, and the homes were usually on the rocky hills, caliche hills. If you took all the rocks off, there wouldn't hardly be any hill there.

A lot of them, for their water system, had cisterns. Some of them had hand-dug wells, and a lot of the hand-dug wells were down close to the barn and horse lot, and they had quite a bit of typhoid fever back in the late 1800s. Some of them had bored wells, and you'd see a lot of people there with iron stains on their teeth, which was iron fluoride in the water causing that. My mother, when she died in '96, I believe she had lost one of her teeth, and my Aunt Byrd, I'm not sure if she'd ever lost a tooth. She died at about 102. My Uncle Jarvis, who died at about 98 or so, he lost a tooth one time, and the dentist wanted four hundred dollars to make one to fit in, so he made his own. He made him a mold and poured himself a pewter tooth he kept in his pocket when he ate. But this is the kind of people we're talking about, that lived there.

Mother had had ten [brothers and sisters] in her family—the first crop. There were fourteen to start with, and four of them died. One got kicked by a horse, the other three, I think, had typhoid fever. I know my Aunt Byrd used to tell me, when something didn't do right she'd say, "Well, you know, I had typhoid fever when I was seven, and so it did that." That was the one that lived to be 102.

My mother's father, Finis Henderson, he had the first batch of kids, fourteen kids, and ten of them lived. And the next batch was four kids, and they all lived. He was a rancher and a farmer. He had six or seven farms, and he owned those mountains that are up there, and he principally raised sheep and cattle on them. But he gave the community the land where the school, the church, the little store, and the blacksmith shop was. These hills or mountains, most of them were covered with cedar or juniper, mountain juniper.

He said he never went past the third grade, but he was quite a mathematician, and apparently he read the H. G. Wells history of the world, because to me he knew everything. Every morning, he got up at four o'clock and made coffee, and he drank a glass of buttermilk with cornbread in it, and that was his breakfast. I spent an awful lot of time out at Grandpa's house.

He'd take me up on the mountains, up on the hills out there, to look over the property, and see how the goats and cattle were doing. He called me "Boy" all the time. He had about fifty grandkids, so he couldn't remember the names.

As my mother told it to me, the [New Liberty Hill] community decided they wanted to build a school, make a community, and they wanted to have a post office. Well, they submitted several names to the post office authorities, and they'd already been taken. So they had to reassemble, they were getting some other names, they had a list up there, and someone in the group says, "Well, that sounds like it's okay with me." So somebody wrote down "Okay."

## Chores

*In farm families of the mule-powered cotton era, nearly everybody worked in the field, and everybody without exception had their daily round of tasks, their chores. These assignments began soon after children could walk and continued until they married and left to do chores on their own places. At most farmsteads, chores began before daylight and ended after dark. Chores by their very nature were not optional activities; firewood had to be brought in for the stove or you did not eat; lamps had to be filled with kerosene or you did not see; milk cows had to be milked or the cows cried out in discomfort. Within the farm family "chore discipline" had to be sternly enforced. By many daily necessities, chores strongly tied the family to its homeplace.*

### NORMAN RICKETTS HALL

As a child, I gathered up the eggs. We had boxes and you had hidden nests, 'cause all the chickens were running loose—no pens. And we had turkeys, we had geese. That was unusual, to have geese. We had fourteen geese. Every morning about ten o'clock they'd walk out in the field and take off and fly to a pond, which must've been two or three hundred yards, and land. And they'd walk back, we never understood that. But I gathered up the eggs, and mother had me sweep the porch sometimes, as a very young child. They never made me learn to milk, and I didn't volunteer. No matter what happens, you've got to milk. Holidays, they were just work days. Then, as I grew older, I worked in the fields.

### J. W. SHULTS

We weren't hard to control at school because our dads and moms worked off our energy. We'd come in from school, my little sisters would have to wash the dishes and start supper because my mother helped my dad with the animals and with the farming, too. Mother would help Papa with the cultivating of the land, and then in the fall she'd pick cotton and help him pull corn and that sort of thing. I'd help shuck the corn for the hogs and milk the cows and gather up the eggs and do those kind of things.

We had to keep the varmints out—shut the chickens up in a house at night and the goats and sheep in a pen at night to keep stray dogs and varmints from getting them. Even if it was raining or cold, we had to cut wood to where we'd have wood to heat the house or to cook with. It didn't matter how cold or rainy, we had something to do. The animals had to be fed.

### FRANKIE JUANITA TRANTHAM

I'd have to get up early of a morning. Now, my mama never stayed in the bed until after daylight. Before daylight she was up! Getting breakfast ready and this and that, and she'd always call me, she'd say, "You better get up! You got to go milk." And I'd go before breakfast and milk those six or seven cows. She always milked at night, but I had to do it every morning.

My mother skimmed the cream off of all of it, I'm sad to say. My mother would not let us drink [it]. She'd send it by my dad when he'd go to town, she'd send that off and sell it. She'd sell cream, and sometimes she sold some butter. And she sold eggs, we had a lot of chickens all over the place. They just went wherever they wanted to. Of course, there were no neighbors for them to bother, so they just went everywhere. They roosted in the trees at night, we didn't have no chicken house.

It was my job every afternoon in the wintertime to carry in enough wood to do in the fireplace that night and the next morning. We called it stovewood, 'cause it went in the stove. That was my job—and carrying water. We had a water spring that was built up with rock around it, about waist-high. I'd have to put my bucket down in the water and let it turn over and get full. Then I'd bring it out of the spring and take it to the house for use. It was good water, too. And cold!

### JOE D. INSALL

Feed sacks was the only way to go [for underwear]. They just had one big old button on the front, 'cause [my mother] didn't spent a lot of time on them. In the summertime when I'd get up, that's the first thing I pulled off, put on a pair of overalls and a shirt, and that was what I wore. Barefooted, and a big old cheap straw hat. Only thing I had to do back then was get in the wood and chips where Daddy'd chopped wood and put them in the wood box by the cookstove. 'Cause he'd get up and pour them chips in that cookstove and put some kerosene oil on them. Had this little can that set back there, light a match to it, and then pile some wood on, and you'd have a fire going. I guess he made the coffee. We had these snuff glasses, they had three rings on them, I'd put one ring of coffee and two rings of milk. It was pretty much like hot chocolate.

We hoed weeds in the garden, and we had four acres of corn, and Daddy didn't even plow it. We hoed it. And I knew I needed to be down on the creek a-fishing real bad. We'd hoe, but our heart wasn't in it. We played a lot. We didn't have nothing to play with, but we'd make something. We'd make rubber guns and shoot these rubber bands off of inner tubes. A bunch of us boys would get together, and we'd just run around and shoot at one another and chunk wet corncobs, just a lot of stuff like that. Built me a corral and [I'd] catch bugs and put them in there for animals, stayed pretty busy all the time.

### JUANITA GRIFFIN DUNCAN

I'd get the eggs and feed the chickens, and later I had to milk the cows. We had five cows to milk, and I milked three [because] my brother could always piddle around enough so I'd have to get the third one. We had to get it done so we could go to school, and we walked to school most of the time. It was about three to three and a half miles, according to whose field you cut across.

We drank a lot of milk, and we liked buttermilk and clabbered milk. Do you know what clabbered milk is? We always waited until it soured before we made the clabber milk, before we churned and made buttermilk. We had a big old three-gallon splatter churn, and that's what we churned our butter in. Usually, in the summertime, sometimes we didn't have any milk except enough to make the bread with, because the cows had gone dry. See, if she has a baby calf, when that calf gets big enough to wean, she quits giving milk, and then you have to wait for her to have another baby. We just had regular, mixed-up cows. We usually would have two-gallon pail buckets, and they'd be three gallons [of milk] in both of them. We drank it and made butter. We fed it to the dogs and if we had turkeys we let the milk sour and put it on the stove and cooked it and made what they call curds to feed the turkeys.

### ARCHIE SPIVY WRIGHT

Me and Ocie, my oldest sister, milked the cows all the time, every night
and every morning—early in the morning before we went to school, and in
the evening after we got in from school, along about night. We'd milk three
or four cows then. The cows were out for the day, and we kept the calves in
the pen. At night we'd let the cows in and milk the cows. Of course, we'd
tie them calves off. Had a rope we tied the calves off with to milk the cows,
then turn the calves loose and let them suck. Of course, they'd suck a little
at the start, and then we'd take them off and tie them until we got through
milking and then turn them loose. Most of the cows wouldn't let you milk
them without that calf sucking some, hardly.

### WILLIAM AKE POWELL

Me and my brother carried the water in a bucket for cows. And, man, they
drank a lot! My grandpa had a well [that] had one of them long buckets on
a rope, and it's about sixty foot. I guess that bucket held three or four gallons. He had a bunch of old Jersey cows. They sold cream and butter, that
was one of their deals, and every week they took a can of cream and a can of
butter to town. They also had a milk separator to get the cream off. You had
to turn that thing by hand, I've turned it lots of times, too. And he had all
them old cows, and we had to water them by hand when the creek would
go dry. We'd have to draw that water, and they'd drink it faster than you'd
pour it in that trough. By the time you got another bucket drawed, that
trough was dry. It's bone dry, they're standing there waiting on it.

We used to go to town in a wagon. We'd get up and leave early, and it'd
be dark when we get home, but we still had to do our chores. In the wintertime we used to feed them the prickle pears. We'd build a fire, take a pitchfork, burn the stickers off of them, and them old cows just loved that. That
was another chore we used to have. And my grandpa and grandma would
have a big garden, and me and my brother used to have to pick all them
beans and help shell them. They'd store the dry beans, and we'd pick them
when they'd get dry and shell them, and my grandpa would put them up.
We'd have them all winter.

Uncle Jeff, he had the mill to grind the corn, and he ground everybody's
cornmeal. One of my jobs, about every other Saturday, was to go down to
the barn and shuck and shell and nub this corn, get it where it's cleaned,
and do a flour sack full, all you could put in a flour sack. We had an old
black mare, and I'd saddle this mare up, get that corn up in front of me, and

I'd take it to the mill and get it ground. He'd keep part of it for the grinding, and I'd bring the rest home. That was about every two weeks, and it's always on a weekend.

### ERNEST ALLEN COLE

On the farm you had chores, and I know one of my chores was cutting wood for the kitchen stove. My dad was one of these [that] haul the wood out of the woods. We'd go cut trees, and they had to be what they called Spanish oak that made good kitchen stove wood. I had to chop that and haul it in for Mother. I had to feed the horses, usually. I had to feed the chickens. I had to slop the hogs. I don't know how those hogs could stand it, but she took the dishwater and fed it to the hogs. They had a hog trough, a V-shaped trough. You put it in there, and those hogs would just go wild over it, and it had soap and everything else in it. I don't know how they stood it.

My mother washed every Saturday morning, and I hated that. We had a cistern, and I had to get up, pump water, put it in a wash pot, build a fire under it, shave soap in it, pump two tubs of water, get this water boiling, and she brought out the clothes. I think she soaked them in one tub, then put them in a pot, and I had to sit there with a broomstick poking it. And after we did that, we had to pull them out and wring them out, rinse them twice, and then blue them. We had a hand-operated wringer, but it was easier to just squeeze them out. We had some of them on the clotheslines, but we had a lot of shinnery oak there on the hill, and we'd spread them out on that. They dried better that way.

Of course, you changed the sheets every week, and every kid took a bath ever week, too. We had a big old tub that you took your bath in. It was in the yard or in the house, I believe sometimes Mother put it outside and let the sun warm it up. Started out with the littlest [kid] and ended up with me, 'cause I was the oldest. You took a bath either Friday or Saturday morning after washing. A lot of times the kids washed in the tub where the bluing water was. That wasn't real dirty.

In the summertime I'd never take [a bath], I'd just go down to the tank and go swimming. I wore kind of a coverall, and I could take them off a-running and hold them in my hand and jump in the tank without ever slowing down.

### GLADYS MERLE KEENER CHASTAIN

My sister Faye liked outside work better. I liked inside work better—you know, doing ironing. Washing day, we were in the back yard. In the wintertime, I can't remember, I guess your clothes stacked up, because you sure didn't go out in icy weather to wash clothes. You had to wait for a sunshiny day. But you got out there, and Mother heated the water in a wash pot. Then we washed on a rub board. We'd rub and rub and rub them. We always had clean clothes and clean linens. You washed them and rinsed them, and us girls would be the ones that rinsed and wring them out and then hung them on the barbwire. Then the wind would blow them off, and you'd go along on the ground and pick them up.

And we always had a clean house. We had wood floors with big cracks in them, and she would scrub them with lye. They would be the cleanest floors and felt so good in the summertime—just felt so good and cool and clean. We always had a clean house. It didn't look like much, but it was clean.

### Joe D. Insall

We didn't have any water supply—not to wash with. Me and my mother would go down on Cottonwood Creek. There was a crossing there, and it was rock, and the water was shallow. We'd haul that wash pot on that little wagon, and a wash tub, and bunch of clothes, rubbing board, and all that stuff. If they were real dirty, you had to rub them on that rub board with that lye soap. She'd take that homemade soap and cut it up in little pieces so it'd dissolve in the wash pot. Didn't know what bleach was. My job was to keep the fire going around the wash pot and punch the clothes, like the agitator on a washing machine. She had a hard time keeping me on the job, because I was usually chasing a red horse minnow or perch.

### Melba Goodwin Bennett

My mother saved everything—the string from a flour sack, also feed sacks. Her flour sacks were used for her kitchen towels. She made her own towels for the kitchen from the flour sacks, also feed sacks. We didn't have feed sacks for a long time until I was older, but flour did come in sacks, and she always saved every one of those. She would rip the thread that put those together and save every bit of that twine, and then the boys used to get some to spin tops. She also used it to sew with. The boys made tops out of spools by driving a wooden peg in the holes.

She made all our clothes, she pieced quilts, she made our doll dresses. We always had dolls at home. My mother always, if nothing else, [would] make a sock doll. I remember my dad buying the first treadle sewing machine for my mother. It was quite an expensive thing. If [people] had a treadle sewing machine, they were rich people.

My dad would not let us girls wear overalls at the house, or pants. We had to wear some kind of a dress. When we moved to the Gardner farm, we did get to buy some pants to wear to the field because it protected us. When we came to the house, we went immediately to our bedroom and changed clothes. He thought it was a disgrace for a woman to wear pants like a man.

## Gardens, Home-Use Field Crops, and Fodder Crops

*Although the yearly dream of cash in hand focused on cotton, cattle, sheep, and goats, families survived by "living off the place" and often were more subsistence farmers than agribusinessmen. Historians of the farming life have somewhat neglected the large gardens, special "potato lands," home-use field crops, and menagerie of domestic animals fed by corn, but farm families did so at their peril. Families preserved home-produced foodstuffs with almost a religious fervor, and in these matters housewives took charge.*

### T. A. WILHITE

Planted a little bit of nearly everything [in the garden], just about whatever you want to eat. Some of that, you didn't want to eat them, you didn't want them, and you wouldn't plant them. But everything that's fittin' to eat and you liked, why, you'd plant a lot of it.

### JOHN DANIEL WOLF

We raised a little bit of everything, a little bit of everything. My mother even raised some English peas. English peas are very difficult to grow in our part of the country. We had ear corn, and she canned some corn. She canned green beans and put up a good many vegetables like that. I remember a number of times when we were going to have company, the broomcorn dealer from Sealy came by. [I'd think], What's my mother gonna fix? How she's gonna fix a meal for that man? And she'd make a dang meal that was fit for a king! Where'd she come up with all that good stuff?

We raised green beans, we raised Irish potatoes, we raised onions—a good supply of those, about a year's supply. Usually, in canning corn, we'd get together with a neighbor and just put up a whole hell of a lot of corn. And vegetables like that, green beans, the same way. My mother had methods of making pickles of different kinds, she put them in a crock, and they come out just wonderful, beautiful pickles with a beautiful taste. And she would make relish of different kinds and can it. We were able to get hold of fruit. I remember my dad and some of the neighbors getting together and going over here near Gatesville to where they raised a lot of peaches and things, and he'd come back with four or five bushels of peaches. They'd can peaches for a day or two.

### ROBERT E. GAULT

We didn't buy much at the store when I was growing up but sugar, things like that, maybe a box of prunes. We raised our potatoes and put them in the barn and kept them, and we had our beans and peas put up dry. And the things we couldn't dry, we canned. You just didn't buy much, we had our meat right there. That's what carried us through the Depression years. You see, people raised their own food. But Dad had to buy coffee, he had to have coffee, my dad was the biggest coffee hound I ever saw. He'd come in and take that old cold pot and turn it up and drink out of it.

Mother put her canned goods in the pantry in the house, and then we had a storm house [where] she put things like sauerkraut. She made sauerkraut, she'd take them old crocks and have a lid on there that's loose and sauerkraut down there. Got it ready, and then she'd can it. And we made hominy, too. They use an acid and you soak it for a long time, that'll take that end off that corn, and take the hide, the peeling, off of it. It took about seven days to make it. I loved hominy, I always did.

And black-eyed peas, that was an experience, too. You pick them by hand and by bucket and just take them over there and pile them up, put them on that tarp, and they'll be dry enough you can just shell them right out. Lay them on a tarp and beat them, throw the hulls away, and you got your peas there. We used to put up a barrel of brown peas a year. We loved them, and it's cheap. My dad had to have white lima beans, we had to grow them, too.

### NORMAN RICKETTS HALL

I guess it was the days of the Depression that we tried to be self-sustaining. I've heard Mother and Dad say, "Well, you know, we're not poor, we've got almost eight hundred acres of land, but we don't have any money." So the pressure cooker came out. I remember we canned chicken. And there were people that owned a pressure cooker that would come to your home and would help you can, and they got half of what you canned. Corn was big. I don't eat corn today because I ate my share back when. You picked the ears, and you shuck them, and then you cut the top off, and then the rest of it. Lord, that corn! We could've fed Fort Hood. And we canned beans, practically anything in the garden.

### H. P. BROOKSHIRE

Had everything: peas, beans, corn, cucumbers, tomatoes, radishes, lettuce, onions, potatoes—it was all in there. They'd plant a hundred pounds of seed potatoes every year, and if you got a rain, they'd make. When we lived over at Spring Hill, they had a potato patch down below the barn. I'd have to clean out the chicken house and scatter it over the potato patch, and they generally made lots of potatoes. Maybe that hundred pound might make a pickup load. They'd store those potatoes all over the house and in the barn and everywhere.

We kept all of our canned vegetables in that root cellar. Mother put up at least three hundred quarts of pinto beans every year. I still don't like pinto beans, I've shelled so many of them. Daddy would plant a row of corn and a row of pinto beans, they called them "dough beans." You get them when the shells start turning speckled. She canned them, then they'd let the rest of those beans dry out, and when they dried out, go in there and pull them up and just take a broom handle or something, an old wagon sheet, which is a tarp, and just thrash all them dried beans out [on the wagon sheet].

### WILMA EARL COLVIN EDWARDS

Mother canned food! They had no garden spot there [at Boaz] because that was pastureland and cedar, but in the field toward Granddad's house, they had these big field gardens, an acre of this and a half acre of that, like peas and corn and all sorts of vegetables. She told [Daddy] that she would can everything she possibly could, and they wouldn't have to buy groceries. He would not borrow money for anything, especially after the Depression.

And so she canned just hundreds of cans of beef and everything in the year of 1931 and '32, all kinds of vegetables, and preserved all kinds of fruits. They bought a canner and a sealer and a pressure cooker. Mother was not frail but a small woman, a thin-type person. She never weighed but ninety-eight pounds most of her life, and she couldn't lift these. She'd stand over that hot stove all day long, and pregnant with my brother part of that time. Daddy would help her lift these big cookers. They held I forgot how many quarts.

I'd snap beans. They had to watch me though, because they were not the stringless kind of beans. I'd do what I could do, and the neighbors would help each other. The menfolks would go pick all that stuff and gather the corn. Corn was quite a process to can. You had to cut it off the cob and all that. I remember washtubs full of beans sitting on our porch, and both grandmothers would come and help her to can, prepare the vegetables to can. We'd just snap [beans] from early to noon or later and get stuff ready. They canned sometimes until eleven o'clock at night.

You utilized every inch of everything. You didn't waste any food. You ate it, or you fed it to the pigs, or something.

### MARGARET BERT WILHITE BOUNDS

We'd make butter, and there was a spring house, and we'd put that down in that. It would be cool, keep the butter from melting. It would be a [little] house built over the spring run, and it never quit running. It would be cool in that house kind of built over it. It was high enough that I could walk in it. 'Course, I wasn't too tall then.

I don't know how old we were when we got an icebox. It was a big old wooden box, and the iceman would come around, and you had a card, and it had twenty-five, fifty, seventy-five, or a hundred, for whatever amount of block ice you wanted. You put that in the window. He'd come about twice a week.

Canning corn was a full day. My daddy would usually hitch up the mules and put them to the wagon and go to the cornfield. He would cut the stalks, it would have the roasting ear on it, and he'd just throw the whole thing in the wagon and bring it up under the shade trees, and he would pull the roasting ear off and throw the stalk to the mules. He would cut both ends off [the ear] with a big knife, and we would take and husk it, and then we would silk it 'cause Mama didn't want any silks in [the canned corn]. Then she would cut the kernels off in a big dishpan, scald the cans, put the corn in the cans and seal them, then she would put them in the cooker and cook them. It was a just about all-day affair.

My mother canned just about everything that she could get her hands on—out of the garden or out of the orchard, either one. She would can green beans and new potatoes, and sometimes she'd can carrots and potatoes and tomatoes and onions. It would be a form of soup already in the can, which she could add other things with it. We'd let part of the beans dry, then we would pick them and shell them and have the pinto beans, as people know it now, in the dried form. It would be [stored] in big containers in the smokehouse. Sometimes she'd wash feed sacks and store them in that. Onions she'd hang up to dry in part of the smokehouse, not where they smoked the meat but [in] another little building there onto it. You'd see onions hanging up, and potatoes. Lots of time she'd scatter them out on a screen wire with a wood frame around it, so they could get air and wouldn't rot as quick. Sometimes she canned cabbage as cooked cabbage, and sometimes part of it went in there where the potatoes were on the screen thing, so the air would circulate and it wouldn't rot.

And like fruits, she would can peaches, she'd make preserves and peach jelly and plums. A lot of time she'd cook the plums down and have the plum juice to make jelly whenever she needed it. Then we'd go pick wild grapes, and she'd make grape juice and grape jelly. And we'd pick pears and take them and wrap them in a newspaper, and put them in a pasteboard [box] and put them under the bed, 'cause it was dark and cool under there. We'd have pears, fresh pears, way on into the winter. When we was going to school, she'd put a pear in our lunch.

For school, she would fix a big biscuit and fix a sausage and mustard [to go in it]. When Daddy killed hogs, she'd make sausage and stuff a bunch of little cheesecloth sacks and hang them in the smokehouse. But then she would cook some and put them in a big old crock jar—I guess that thing was five gallons, it might have been more—and she'd cook them and just lay them one on top of the other, and when she got it about full, she'd pour melted hog lard over that. Then, when she got ready for breakfast or [was] fixing our lunch, she'd just go get however many patties and put them in the skillet and finish cooking them.

Then, when daddy would kill a beef, she would can a lot of that beef, and sometimes we would share with the neighbors. Sometimes my mother would invite the ladies over to give them some fresh beef. Then, when they killed a beef, they would share with us and the other neighbors.

### ERNEST ALLEN COLE

We had a big garden [at Okay]. Some reason, the sharecroppers didn't do this. That's the reason they're sharecroppers, I guess. How they got enough to live, I don't know. But we planted a big garden. Mother had a little garden right there by the house. I remember Daddy hauled black soil from down at the cow pen up, and it had about that much black dirt on top of that chalky stuff. The first thing we got out was leaf lettuce, Mother liked to put it in the skillet with grease, and radishes. That's what we raised in that little [garden], and sometimes turnip greens. But in our big garden down from the house, down below the hill where the soil was pretty good, we had beans, black-eyed peas, potatoes. Then down on the wet lands where it didn't dry up so much, that's where she would have her big crops—tomatoes, sweet corn—I remember one year she planted eggplant. That was the worst thing I ever tried to eat! Anyway, we raised sweet potatoes and a lot of Irish potatoes down there.

She would can. We had a storm cellar, and it had shelves in it, I'd say we'd have two or three hundred yards of canned food in that cellar. There'd be canned tomatoes, there'd be canned beans, there'd be canned peas, black-eyed peas. When they was green, can those. There'd be jars of jelly. We had a peach orchard, Alberta and Indian peaches. Indian peaches was a kind of white-pink peach. We gathered the peaches and cut them up and put them on the roof of the house in the sun and let them dry. You'd have to take them down at night and put them back to keep the dew off of them. And so we had dried peaches. We had a lot of Irish potatoes, seemed like we always raised red ones. And Daddy would put the sweet potatoes in the haystack where the cows couldn't get to it. He'd put the sweet potatoes in the haystack, and that'd keep them. You'd go down and dig some up when you wanted them.

### CLEMENTS W. "SPEEDY" DUNCAN

Basically, my mother never wanted to go to South Texas. When we lived up here, when we lived on what we could make to eat, my mother would can all summer. And when we moved to South Texas it took about three Model T's to haul the quart fruit jars of everything. She had everything you could can: peaches and beans and corn, and on and on. We got down to this old house, and there was nowhere to store these canned goods. It would hold a quart fruit jar on a flat two-by-four, so we lined the whole five rooms with fruit jars full of everything. In a few nights it come a cold spell, it wasn't supposed to be thataway down there, and it busted them jars at night, sounded like rifles going off. I don't remember what was the loudest sound, the fruit jars busting or my mother crying. We scooped it in the washtub and carried it out and dumped it. Quite a project mopping up the floors, and my mama crying all the time.

### WILLIAM AKE POWELL

My grandfather's name was William Henry Dorsey—"W. H."—people used to go by their initials. He went down on Owl Creek, and the land was a little bit rough, wasn't cleared quite enough for cotton and corn, but it's good dirt. He went down there and cleaned it up and made him a patch down there right on the creek, and he used to plant cushaws and pumpkins right in there. It was good black dirt along that creek, and I've seen him haul them old cushaws and pumpkins out of there by the wagonload. Man, he raised some big ones down there.

A cushaw is more of a pumpkin. It's bigger on one end, some of them are striped, some of them are yellow. They used to bake it. You'd put sugar or something on it, bake it, and I remember them cutting it in squares. They'd cook it on the shell, they'd cut it and put butter and sugar on it. And they'd keep. You could put them in the barn or somewhere. Put them where they wouldn't freeze, and they keep all winter. And I used to pull the tomatoes, green, in the wintertime, before the frost got on them, and put them in cottonseed. They'd get ripe in there, and they'd take them out right along.

### JOE D. INSALL

We never did grow pumpkins, but we had cushaws. It's kind of like a summer squash, the hard ones that you can keep until they freeze. We had a bunch of them big old cushaws, and we put them in the hay in the barn. My mother'd take one of them and cut it up in little squares and put some cinnamon on it. Don't like cinnamon, nutmeg, either one. She'd bake it, and you just ate it off the rind. I'll tell you, her pumpkin pie was about as next to nothing that you can get. Sweet potato pie is not bad. We always grew sweet potatoes, and Dad would take cornstalks and stand them up like a tepee on this sandy land we had. He'd dig a little hole and put the sweet potatoes in there and then cover the whole thing up with sand. Then, when you wanted to get some, you just dug in the side and pulled a few out.

### T. A. WILHITE

Corn was my main crop. We had what you call a John Deere Stag in them days. You could hook four mules to it, and it'd run around as deep as you want it to, and you throw up a bed of dirt, you put a good bed of dirt on it. It had iron singletrees, and they's three of them to work three mules to. They could pretty well handle it, but I wanted four. I could just whup them on out and get a lot done with four.

All our corn down there, sell it right where I sold the cotton. Old man Johnny Boren told me, me and one of his boys was the only ones that ever had put four loads of corn in the barn every day. We could get that corn gathered and throwed it in the barn. I'd scoop it out. On one side of the wagon I'd have the boards on pretty high like cotton boards. On this other side it's back down lower. I was on this side a little bit lower, and I was just picking two rows and throwing them over in there. And didn't take me but just a little to get a load, either! I'd have two mules hooked up to the wagon, and they was pulling that load of corn. You'd get up to their side and they'd start. And then after they got up there a little ways, you'd holler "whoa" at them, and they'd stop. Everything just worked off like a clock.

### ROBERT E. GAULT

We raised white native corn. It's a big ear of corn, [Dad] wouldn't have yellow corn. We raised that old big white corn, and, boy, you talk about good roasting ears. Dad said that little old yellow dent [corn] is too little, he just never would go with it. If you'd got yellow meal around that place, he'd run you off. Edwin Thompson, who lived on the prairie, he raised the same thing, and they swapped seed. The seed grown on the prairie went to the creek, and the creek seed went to the prairie, and they claimed they got better production like that. They picked the ears, and shelled that, and swapped out seed every year. It worked out good for us.

We always [pulled the corn and threw it in a wagon]. After you had one row down, then you worked the sides. Now, some people would skip over, they'd have a down row about every other time. A down row is heck to pick, 'cause that was all on the ground. When I was a kid, that's what I got, the down row all the time. But you know, I went all through school, and my dad never would let me stay out and work. When I was a senior in high school, we had corn in the field that needed to be out, look like it was going to rain, and I took off school that day. He finally let me do it. That's the only day I ever took out of school to work.

### MARGARET BERT WILHITE BOUNDS

That blackland, if you stick to it when it's dry, it sticks to you when it gets wet. They used to say that. The bull nettles growed sometimes in the corn. 'Course, we'd chop them out, but sometimes they growed back. Before I was big enough to pull corn, I drove the corn wagon. Those mules would step in a bull nettle, and, oh, they'd take off running! Daddy would tell me, "Hold on to the reins!" And Mama'd say, "Turn loose, turn loose!" 'cause she's afraid they'd drag me out. But I'd hold on, and he'd jump on the back and work his way up and finally get a-hold of them and slow them down.

When I was driving the corn wagon, my mother and daddy would pull on each side, about three rows. Then, after me and Billie got big enough, we pulled the down rows, and Mama pulled two on one side and Daddy pulled two on the other. He'd just tie the reins up over there close and them old mules just walk on down the row. They'd eat corn while they's going along, they's pretty contented, I reckon. Once in a while they'd pull a sneak and run away. Down rows were where the wagon went—it would knock the corn stalks down. We were little and short, so it wasn't hard for us to pull the down rows.

Pulling corn wasn't that bad. I mean, it was hot and that stuff would get all over you, but it wasn't hard on your legs or knees or back like picking cotton was. But one time my daddy was wearing overalls, and a scorpion got up his leg and was stinging him, and he run. You couldn't see where he went 'cause the corn was so tall, but he was trying to get out of them overalls.

### WILLIAM AKE POWELL

They raised some maize. They'd head it, cut the heads off, and it'd keep—put it in the barn and feed it like corn. And I've cut a lot of corn tops, tied them. You didn't cut them till a certain time. My daddy would make them strings, tie a loop end up, tie one around your waist, and put all them others on there. You first cut them and lay them on the ground and let them dry. Then you go gather up a bundle and tie you a string around them, and then you shock them in a shock. They stayed there three, four days, ever how long it took them to dry, then you hauled them in. Usually they made a stack outside where it'd be kind of waterproof. I've seen them stack them around poles, I sure have.

Yeah, I've cut them old corn tops, many a one of them. They made that fodder out of them. Used to cut them, shock them, haul them in, and stack them again. Had to handle that stuff quite a few times. Wasn't worth that much, but you had to do a whole lot to get it where it was going.

### ANDY GORDON WOLF

We didn't have grass hay back then. We used row binder to bundle [red-top] cane, we didn't have highgear and stuff like you got now. One of them bundles weigh forty, fifty pounds, and you shock it and season it out. You stack it heads up, like this, and when that got cured out, you taken it and put in the stock pile in a big stack—just layer it in there so it'll turn water.

You can just stack it heads together. You get two bundles and stack them up, they'll stand up, see? They're called shocks, and when it got cured out, on the inside of it, it'd keep its color. The outside may dry out, but the inside would be pretty green. I'm talking about sorghum [hay], red-topped cane.

### NORMAN RICKETTS HALL

Dad used to grow maize. Maize is not corn like some of the Yankees think, it's kind of like grain. He would plant three acres of that in a field by the house, and then we would have to go and harvest it. We'd grab the grain, took a butcher knife, and hit it, cut it off, and then you'd pile it in the middle of the rows. Well, no gloves, and always by the afternoon of the first day, I had blisters on my hands, so I wrapped a rag around the hand. Still used that butcher knife, threw that head down on the ground. Then, late in the afternoon, you went back and picked it up off the ground and put it in sacks. By then there was plenty of chance for a snake to crawl in under the pile. There were copperheads and rattlesnakes back then. I'd move the pile to make sure there wasn't a snake, so you can imagine how tedious it was. I was a sissy, but I hated it. I had rather pick cotton, I had rather gather corn.

I didn't want to go to college, my mother just sent me. I went to college, and I didn't like it. When school was out, I packed my footlocker, and I was coming home to stay. There was a fourteen-acre field on the other side of our house, and when I topped the rise, not only was a three-acre field planted, but that fourteen-acre field was planted in maize. So, when I got there, I told them, I said, "I can just stay overnight, I'm going back to summer school in the morning." I got a college degree because I didn't want to head maize.

### FLORENCE JOYCE HAEDGE

We had our own mill. It had an engine, gas engine. Daddy planted two rows of corn, then he skipped over and left two rows to plant something like black-eyed peas. We raised maize and highgear, and he took the maize and highgear and black-eyed peas and corn and some green stuff, millet, and he put that in his mill and grounded it up. Then he always got the chicken feed stuff in Gatesville or Copperas Cove, and that would be laying mash. And he would grind that grain up [in our mill] and mix that with laying mash and feed about three hundred chickens, and our dogs and cats would also eat laying mash. Yeah, that's what he done.

## Domestic Livestock

*Corn and cotton farming was in some ways a simple operation compared with managing the array of domestic animals so important to "living on your place." Most renter families had at least chickens and a milk cow or* two. *Most landowners had chickens, milk cows, hogs, and some beef stock. With a close or uncertain allegiance based on regular doles of corn, barnyard fowl ranged out from the farm every day to forage for most of their own food. These might include chickens, turkeys, guineas, geese, and ducks. Farm wives mostly masterminded this menagerie, with the excess animals or animal products sold or bartered for necessities at the store or for small luxuries from the passing peddler. In the right kind of wooded landscape, cash profits from autumn turkey sales might in some years surpass those from cotton.*

### JUANITA GRIFFIN DUNCAN

We had a barn that had one, two, three, four cribs in it, and had a hallway in it, and there was an open place on the north side where Daddy hung his harness off of his mules. We had chicken nests out there, and we had a chicken house out there—in fact, we had two chicken houses. We had one close to the house, and we had baby chickens out there in that.

We had an incubator that we set our own eggs in, which would be maybe 150 eggs in it. It was heated with a little kerosene lamp, and you had to get up and check it during the night to keep a certain temperature. And every day you turn the eggs like the hen does, you mark the "X" on one side and the "O" on the other, and you turn those eggs. It was just a kerosene lantern set in a about a two-foot-deep hole and covered with a piece of tin so the little chickens wouldn't fall in the hole. You put them in to keep them warm until morning, then they could come and go as they pleased.

Then we had a bigger chicken house that the hens roosted in. They didn't stay in it, they roosted out there. As we grew older, it came our time to clean out that chicken house about every Saturday. My younger sister said she guessed it was one of the best lessons she ever learned in her life. She despised doing that job, and [one day] she went out to clean the chicken house and set down and was crying because she had to do it, and fleas was getting on her, and she said, "Well, I just might as well get up and do this, I've got to do it." And she said, "I guess that was one of the most valuable lessons I learned, was that if you've got a bad job to do, do it!"

### H. P. BROOKSHIRE

Didn't sell no milk, but they'd always milk three, four cows, and they'd skim the cream off that milk. And if you'd carry it to town, you could sell it. And chickens, Mother would get three or four hundred baby chicks every spring, and we'd start eating fried chicken by the time you could tell the rooster from the pullets; you can tell by the combs [on their heads]. They'd be a little bit bigger than quail when we'd start eating them, and we'd eat fried chicken all summer and pork all winter.

They had a Winfield's Hatchery up there, and a lot of times if you'd buy your feed from them, they'd give you the baby chickens. When we had an old two-seated Model A car, when we'd start to town, it'd be cases of eggs tied to every fender, and when we'd start back it'd be chicken feed tied on there.

Mr. Zook [the Rawleigh man] come around maybe once a month and handled products like salve, herbs, or spices. Them old farmers always had chickens, and it didn't matter to him, he'd trade. Nobody had no money. He had a chicken coop or two on the back of his old car, and he might leave with it full of chickens.

They'd raise hogs from pigs—they'd keep a sow and they'd raise pigs. In the fall of the year, about the first cold spell, they'd start killing hogs, and when they killed hogs, that's what they done! Mr. Bigham shot them all, and there was Daddy and Uncle Ira and Uncle Bill, Grandpa, they done all the scraping and the cutting up, and all this that and the other. The women would clean the intestines to put the sausage in. They'd just go from place to place, and in two days I'd say that each family would probably have three or four hogs, and it'd be sausage by the washtubs full.

And then they cured that meat. They bought Martin's Sugar Cure, and basically it was just salt. Had boxes of salt, and they'd turn that meat every day. It was drawing the moisture out of it, was what it was doing. And my goodness, them old hams, they'd just hang them up out there in the smokehouse where they'd smoke them. You'd go out there and they'd look plumb green, and you'd just slice that off and carry it in and peel that green off of it, and in the skillet fry it up. A lot of times they would cook the sausage. They had five-gallon crocks, and they'd just put that sausage in there and pour the grease over it. Then they'd just go, scoop out sausage, grease and all, and put it in a skillet.

### ROBERT E. GAULT

We kept hogs, we'd butcher five or six a year, because we salt-cured. Them old hog pens, they used to have to drain them they'd get so nasty. I hated those things, but I sure did like the pork. Did you ever eat tenderloin from a hog? That's a strip up and down the backbone, and it's white meat, and, boy, it is delicious. When we butchered a hog, that's the first meat we ate— ate it fresh. And then the hams and bacon we cured with salt and used smoke. And then the sausage we ground up—the shoulders, usually, and some more lean meat, and made sausage out of it. Usually we used sacks made out of flour sacks sewed about that big around and stuffed them with that sausage. Then we'd take them out there and hang them in the smokehouse, and they'd cure. They had a different flavor. Now, the last several years, Mother got to where she was canning her sausage, most of it, in No. 2 cans.

It was all good. Farm life is the best life in the world, if you can make a living.

### FLORENCE JOYCE HAEDGE

We had a hog pen close to the barn, big enough pen to where there was one end for the hogs to sleep under their shed and one place for them to drink and eat. In the summertime, they had a place for them to wallow in the water. We fed them corn on the cob, we didn't shell their corn, and we had slop. That consisted of what's in the house and, besides that, always fixed up a bucket of milk and shorts, that was a feed, and gave that to them. We always only had two, two little pigs. We got them from my uncle, he raised them—Poland China, black-and-white striped. And when the green stuff come up, like cane or millet or highgear, we'd cut a bundle with a knife and carry it to them to eat something green. In the wintertime it was just corn, and we called it "mash"—that was milk and shorts and whatever else. Sometimes he'd put in that grain that we ground, black-eyed peas and all that. We raised them just for fattening—for pork, to kill.

### ERNEST ALLEN COLE

We had a hog pen on the north side of our house [at Okay], because the wind blew from the southeast. We had ten or fifteen hogs in there, a bunch of hogs. I was usually the one that got to shoot the hog with my .410. That was always my job. When it was hog-killing time, the first big norther came in, Daddy says, "Well, we're going to have to kill a hog. Get up at daylight." We had a fifty-five-gallon drum open at the top. We'd fill that thing about half full of water and build a big fire around it until it was boiling. And then you'd lead the hog down there, usually put a rope around his foot and just beat him down there, and I'd shoot him.

It's down by the blacksmith shop, and we had a block and tackle there. We'd take a singletree on his back feet, and that water's boiling, and dump him down in there, up and down. They had the table out there, and they had big old butcher knives, a lot of butcher knives, and we'd take and scrape the hog and gut him. And I don't know how they knew it, but these sharecroppers, one of them or two of them, always showed up the minute you killed a hog. Their take was the heart, the liver, the kidneys, that sort of thing. That was usually the deal. Usually somebody would get the head, but, if I shot him, it didn't leave much brains to make brains and eggs out of.

We had a smokehouse, and in there Daddy had a box about six feet long, and he kept a whole bunch of rock salt in it. You'd take all of your meat and put it in there till it drew the water out of it. [Then] you'd take the hams and smoke them or rub them, rub them with a bunch of stuff, and cure the hams up in the ceiling, and bacon the same way. But usually, by June or July, they'd get wooly worms on them.

Made a lot of sausage—for a long time we'd make sausage and hang it up and smoke it, but it didn't keep too good. We got ten-gallon crocks, and when we rendered the lard we put about an inch of lard in there, and then Mother'd make sausage patties and cook them, not completely done but pretty done, and we'd put a layer of sausage patties in there, might fill it up with sausage patties, and then pour grease over the top. Then we'd put a lid on it where nothing could get in it and put it down in the storm house. We might have two or three of those [crocks] before it was over. That gave me something for my lunch. I usually had a cold biscuit with a sausage patty in it.

### CLEMENTS W. "SPEEDY" DUNCAN

My grandpa had a crippled boy that never did marry, named Jess, a bad cripple. Doctors operated on him before 1900 over here at Oakalla, just two sheep-herding doctors, I think. One of them had been a herder, herding sheep. But they operated on his leg and it was way short. Anyway, [Grandpa] had a hog pen off from the house, [and] when they killed a hog, of course my daddy and I had to go do it.

They put a rope on the hind leg of that hog, and my old crippled uncle walked on a walking stick, and he'd drive that hog—it couldn't get away from him—to where we killed them.

By that time I'd killed hogs for years. Fortunately, I'd never made one squeal. You hit a hog just right, he won't squeal; it's a dead X between his ears and his eyes. It don't work on a beef, their brain is off to the side. I was going to shoot the hog, [but] my grandpa had raised this crippled grandson from childhood up, and he was the one that had to do the killing of the hog. So he grabbed my gun and shot the old hog, a big old hog, and didn't hit him right.

A shot hog will go kind of crazy. My dad was holding him with the rope, and I'm perturbed because my cousin throwed my gun down, and I was perturbed about my gun, and that cousin and I had a few words, and he took off to the house. My old grandpa had a little black and white dog that rode on the saddle on a horse or a mule. Whatever he rode, that dog would set up on the horse. This old crippled uncle saw the dog was barking and biting at the hog, and he threw his walking stick at him and knocked the dog unconscious, and my grandpa was about to kill my uncle for killing his dog.

My daddy yelled at me, "Get over on this rope, son!" And I knew to get on that rope. I didn't know whether I could hold that old hog or not, but I knew I had to get on that rope. And my daddy grabs up an old single-bit ax and settled that old hog, knocked him in the head. And everything quieted down. The dog come back to, and everything got back to normal.

### WILLIAM AKE POWELL

When they'd kill a beef, somebody would kill one, they always give part of it to the neighbors. They was real good about that. Some places had what they called a "beef club." Whenever one person killed a beef, they divided with all of the neighbors. Then, later on, it was time for another one to do that, and he did the same thing. They didn't have places to freeze it and put it, so when they did it they just divided it with all of the people.

### JOE D. INSALL

I remember back, they had a kind of beef thing. We didn't have refrigeration, and most people didn't have electricity. There was a beef club, and they would kill this beef, and everybody'd come over there and get them a chunk of meat that belonged to it. Then the next week, it would be somebody else's turn to kill one, and then just go on and on. I don't know if it went round or just a certain time of year. We didn't belong to it, 'cause we didn't ever have no beef.

### NORMAN RICKETTS HALL

We processed milk. Do you know what a milk cooler is? They came up about six feet, and there was a trough that held water, and inside of that there was a deal made of metal, two or three shelves, and on top of that was another pan of water. You put a sheet all the way around, and then you put water in the top and water in the bottom, and water just kept blowing back and forth. It kept the inside cool. You kept milk and anything like butter and vegetables—it didn't preserve it long, but it helped.

Then, if you had milk, you could let it go to clabber, and a lot of people like clabber, cornbread and clabber, and it was a meal. Or you fed it to the animals. Then we got real modern, probably while I was in high school. You could buy an icebox, and an iceman came around every other day. You could get twenty-five pounds of ice. Or you could get fifty pounds, if you were pretty well off in the money. It was a common occurrence for the lady to meet the iceman and say, "There's a chip off that twenty-five-pound block of ice, I want the chip." The box was insulated and did preserve food for a while, much longer than the cooler.

Milk cows were always big, [we] had five or six. But they'd hear these stories about somebody over here had a milk cow that'd give three gallons of milk a day, and here we had this one giving just three quarts. So my dad would go buy this one, bring it back home. Well, sure enough, it'd give three gallons there for about a week, then production would decline to three quarts. My folks couldn't understand what was the matter. 'Course, when I took agriculture, I found out. My dad would take a coffee can and feed the cow cottonseed cake or cottonseed, and they'd go out in the pasture and eat grass. The place they had come from had probably been giving a gallon or two gallons of cottonseed. We were just starving the cows to death! I was never able to convince my folks. [Dad would say,] "Well, I don't know, that's pretty expensive. You can't just put that money in a cow."

I always felt like my parents really loved me, but I didn't realize until years later how much they had sacrificed to send me to college. I didn't want to go to college, but I didn't think I had a choice. But when I did go to school, I fell in with what they do, and I'm sure I was spending quite a lot of money going to shows, doing this and that. If a new coat came out, the kids would buy it, and I wanted a new coat, too. I highwayed it home in my freshman year, I would usually get there Friday afternoon, and I had a cousin that was the bookkeeper for the big store, the department store [in Killeen]. He told me one time, said, "Norm, come on over, I want to show you something." In Killeen, not fifty yards away, was the stock pens, where you loaded cattle. And he walked up there and said, "You see that milk cow there?" I said, "Yeah." And he said, "Look familiar?" And I said, "No." He said, "Well, it should. The last time you asked for money, your dad sold that milk cow. They only have one left, you've gone through four."

Boy, that was hard! I went back to college, got a job in a dining hall, worked for the rest of the time I was in school. They never said a word, they just did it.

# Fishing, Hunting, Trapping, and Gathering

*Frontier skills of hunting, trapping, fishing, and foraging still were prac-*
*ticed at the settlements that became Fort Hood. People sought wild foods*
*for the pot and as recreation from the hardships of the farmer's inexorable*
*round of labors. They went fishing after crops were "laid by" in early sum-*
*mer and hunting and trapping in the winter downtime. When things grew*
*especially hard, these fishing, hunting, and foraging pursuits took on a*
*desperate quality. Shot and caught and consumed by many, Texas wildlife*
*populations reached their lowest levels during the Great Depression. Even*
*nine-banded armadillos, the animal some called "grave robbers," became*
*known as "Hoover hogs."*

### ERNEST ALLEN COLE

One of these little creeks [near Okay] went down into Clear Creek, and in
the springtime I'd go down there. [I'd catch] little old perch about this long
and minnows. I carried my worms in a Prince Albert can and take the stopper out of a medicine bottle and get some string off something they wrapped
up at the grocery store and cut me a willow pole.

### JOE D. INSALL

We would go fishing on Cottonwood Creek and the Cowhouse [Creek]. Get
us a Prince Albert tobacco can and dig a few worms, stick it in our pocket.
The only store-bought thing on it was a hook. They used to wrap things in
paper and tie string around them; they didn't have paper bags. We'd save the
longest strings we'd get and tie them together and rub beeswax on them. Tie
that hook on there, and find a piece of lead off a roofing nail or something,
and beat it flat, and roll it on the string for a sinker, and find us a cork that
come out of a bottle, put that on, and then we'd adjust it in a rainwater barrel
to see if it worked. We'd hook the hook in the cork and wrap the string and
stick it in our pocket, and we was ready, 'cause we'd cut the poles when we
got to the river. Never did catch nothing much over ten inches long.

### WILLIAM AKE POWELL

There was several creeks around that was within wagon-going that had fish
in them. Almost any creek, if it had big holes of water, had fish in it. If it
rained too much, and it's on the Fourth of July, and everything was caught
up, we could go a-fishing. Us kids used to fish on Owl Creek and all the
branches and everything, just with a pole, cork, and hook. I remember my

mother used to like the perch, the big old perch, she liked those things fried. Man, fried real brown, that was her favorite. And you could catch them out of nearly every little old creek.

### ANDY GORDON WOLF

Ever year my dad and us would load the wagon, and we'd go and take a seine and seine fish and have a big fish fry for three or four days, maybe a week. Paw would say, "Let's get through the work, boys, and we'll go fishing." So we'd all load up there, my mother would make molasses cake and molasses cookies and things. We set lines out, had to go by hand, you wouldn't have a boat or anything. Generally, we'd wade the water and we'd seine. You'd just seine a hole of water and catch round suckers and things like that, and sometimes catfish. Them old round suckers was bony but they's awful good, had a good taste.

### ROBERT E. GAULT

We never did go to town in the summertime. From the time school was out till it started again, I didn't go till we went to get me some school clothes. I didn't mind that a bit. If we had to work too hard, about Saturday evening we'd go talking to Dad about fishing, and we'd go set out the trotlines.

Lots of people used to trap them, and that was always illegal. You can take an old net-wire trap, with a funnel entrance to it, and you can take some cottonseed cake in a sack and put in there, and them old catfish would come to it. And they couldn't get out then, you see, couldn't find a way out. There's lots of people trapped that way, but we didn't do that.

We always figured if it's worth eating, it's worth getting out and hustling for. 'Course, Dad kept us burned out on fish, he caught so many with pole and line. He never used a rod and reel, he used an old bamboo pole. And he'd rig that up, and he caught 12- or 15-pound catfish on that thing. He fished year round if the weather's decent, he just loved to fish, and those days the creeks had lots of fish in them. We had hollow banks, which was a harbor for catfish. My first memories of fishing, I'd get to go with him, and I'd fish for perch for his bait.

Oh, we used to catch them! We went down there one time, and we couldn't get minnows. We finally took a minnow seine and got crawfish out of a little old creek running across our pasture. I guess we got five gallon of crawfish. We went down there and set those trotlines out with crawfish. Dad says it'll be a good night to fish, 'cause there's clouds threatening. Says, "There's a cloud coming up. It's an instinct with fish, they're afraid that water's gonna get muddy and they won't feed." And it worked that way, the next morning we had catfish on twenty-something hooks out of fifty. I'm telling you, it's the best I ever saw.

'Course, we have lost trotlines when clouds come up, too. Those old creeks like Cowhouse there, it was swift. Boy, it come down swift when you got a rise! It would come down.

My brother Frank used to gig fish in cold weather. They're sluggish in cold weather, and you could get them with a gig, what they called a "frog gig." He'd put a handle in there about ten foot long, put a cord on it case you had to throw it. He'd get out there in that boat in real cold weather, and go along there and see them, and get just right over them, and come down on them and get them. He got a lot of fish that way. I've rode a boat with him fishing when ice would form on the handle of the gig.

When it's freezing cold, they just don't move as fast. You can take a carbide headlight and shine it down there and get them, which is illegal, too. But we were just getting what we ate, you know, and it's lots of fun, if you didn't freeze to death at it.

And did you ever see any "grabbing" done— what they called "grabbing"? That's where you put a big treble hook on your line, and you let your line lay down on the bottom, and when the fish go across there, you jerk your pole. Those grab hooks will catch fish, you see. That's the way they used to catch suckers in the wintertime. Real cold weather, that water gets clear. Dad used to go over in House Creek and do a lot of that, it was clearer than Cowhouse. It was really something to do that. I used to get to go up there and scare the fish back when he got set up, I'd go up above him and scare them back, make a racket or something where they'd move.

Those big old yellow cat bedded in dark holes in the bank. You talk about fishing for them, some of them old-timers would take a pole and put a big hook on it and a red bandanna, a red flag, on there. You run that back in there, and you can catch them big old cat on their beds. They're fighting, then, and they'll attack that thing. A fish like everything else that's got a bed of eggs in there, they're combative. We never did do that, 'cause Dad was strict on it, but I've heard of people that did.

My brother Frank used to go under the bank after them. I didn't have the guts to go under there myself, but he'd go under there and grab those fish and bring them out. They called that "grappling." That's illegal, too. He caught them in the gills, mostly. I knew a boy at Killeen that run his hand down in their mouth, and I've seen his arm all just skinned up all in here. I've seen Frank pretty skinned up from them, too.

Right back of our field down there, I saw him pull a forty-seven-pound cat out from under there, one day. He'd scare me to death. Seem like he'd be gone five minutes before he'd come out. What he'd tell me was that there's usually, back under the bank, there's an air space, you see, and he'd raise up there and breathe a little bit and then go on under. He caught a lot of fish that way, and he caught a lot of them out in the holes where there are a lot of rocks. You can get blue cat from them, you know.

Now, my dad wouldn't let anybody seine on our place. He said they got too many game fish when they went to seining. But Frank's grappling, he didn't mind that. He thought anybody's fool enough to go under there and get them, they ought to have them.

I got in trouble one time. I was blocking a hole for Frank, he went under the bank for one, and that dang fish hit my leg. He drove it back there, and I couldn't stay. I was about eleven, twelve years old, and shoot, that fish hit me, I jumped! Frank come on out and give me heck for that, but I couldn't stay there.

### H. P. BROOKSHIRE

When my cousin Phelps would come up—he trapped back then, had a trap line, and he'd stay with us for the winter—I'd go with him hunting. I got my first .22 when I was eight years old, and I still got it. He trapped coons, fox, skunk, possum, and ringtail. Back then, them furs, they'd bring six, seven dollars, and that was a lot of money. He'd bundle them all up, mail them to up there to Paris, Texas. Then they'd grade them and he'd get a check back. A dime back then was big as a wagon wheel now.

### ERNEST ALLEN COLE

In the wintertime, kids would gather, and each of us had a dog, and we'd go up in the coves of these mountains, and we'd hunt that night, go overnight hunting. The main thing we caught was possums and coons. There was a mountain persimmon up there, blue or black, a persimmon about the size of my thumb, and the coons and possums loved those things. So that's where we'd usually catch them, and in the cove of the mountains, too, where there'd be blackhaws. We'd skin them and turn them wrong side out. We'd get a forked stick and put them on that and stretch them and then rub the salt on the outside of them and then dry them. And when they got good and dry and hard, then you could take them in and sell them. But they wouldn't buy them when they were green, they wouldn't buy a green hide. For a possum I think we got a dollar a hide, and for coon, I think it would be two dollars or two-fifty. That was our winter money.

When I was five years old, my Christmas present was a BB gun, and on my seventh birthday, Dad ordered me a .410 shotgun from Montgomery Ward and two boxes of shells. I had to show him [that I knew] how to load it, and he says, "Now, go hunting." The first day I got it, I went out to the woods and killed five rabbits. I remember Mother said, "Look at that boy coming, he's dragging a whole bunch of rabbits!"

That's what Grandpa and I'd do when we'd go up on the mountain. I'd take my gun and kill a rabbit. He'd take a rabbit and split it and skin it, no hairs on it, gut it. He'd take and run a stick through it, and he'd take two forked sticks and build a fire and put the rabbit up here and cook it. No salt or anything, but he thought that was good eating.

My dad loved half-grown jackrabbits. In the springtime, where this woods was, there was a fence and then a cotton patch. These doggoned jackrabbits would come out of the woods and go in there, and they'd just clip off the cotton. Dad would send me out there with my .410, usually late in the afternoon or early in the morning about daylight, and these rabbits would come out. I'd lay there and shoot them. The half-grown ones, he'd take them and skin them and cut them up like chicken. And Mother would fry them, and that was good, we ate that. And down on the river, we killed squirrels, we'd eat squirrels.

During the Depression, a lot of these people, they ate what was called a "Hoover hog." That's armadillos. They migrated out of Mexico, and they were just getting up in our part of the country. Their common name in that part was "grave robber" because they always seemed to dig holes in the graves. I remember when an old man died at Okay, we took him down to the graveyard, and some of the graves had holes in them, and they said the grave robbers had been in there. 'Course, the armadillos were after worms and stuff like that, just rooting around. But people would kill them for that reason.

### JOE D. INSALL

Them old pioneer farmers, they'd eat anything running loose. I had this little bitty trap I could set. I wasn't very old, I don't know how old I was. I'd spent half a day trying to catch a mouse for bait, and I'd tie him on a string and hang him on a tree limb where he hung down. And I'd put this little trap under it and tie it to a tree or something with a piece of baling wire. Next morning, I couldn't wait until it got daylight and go check my trap, and I'd have a little old possum in it. Just thrilled me to death, cause that was about a dime, fifteen cents. I'm going to make a bunch of trips to Antelope store. I'd get my dad to skin it for me. I'd be bragging about it, I'd go tell my grandma. She'd sit there, and she'd say, "Is he a fat one?" I'd say,

"Yeah." "Is he a young, tender one?" I'd say, "Yeah." She'd say, "Well, tell your mama to cook it for me."

That's about like eating a buzzard, 'cause they're scavengers, but them old-timers done it. I've heard them tell they'd put them in a pen and feed them good groceries for a while so they wouldn't have all that old stuff in them, but you can find a dead cow and kick it and there'll be a lot of possums run out of it. There's a lot of that stuff that's not too good groceries.

### ROBERT E. GAULT

My brother trapped all the time. He got lots of raccoons down there [on Cowhouse Creek], got fox, got skunks, possums. And when I got up older, I trapped up at Turnersville, I trapped with my brother. I learned a lot down there. He had a cave he went down in, it went back about forty foot. You could get a skunk in there all the time, but there's rattlesnakes in it, and those rattlesnakes would throw our traps—you couldn't hardly catch one in one. But those old skunks and rattlesnakes lived right there together. We'd get skunks in there, and then you stunk for a week after you killed one.

Skunks were a beautiful animal, a clean animal. The blacker the pelt, the better it was. White damaged them, but a good, narrow-striped skunk used to bring four or five dollars back when that was a lot of money.

You could take a can of sardines and put it in a jar or something and leave it about half open and let them go ahead and ferment and get stinking. You'd set your trap out and put a little bit of that on the trigger and pretty well submerge the trap in leaves or something, and you could catch a skunk good. Now, if you wanted raccoons, we'd put our trap in the water, even in the mud, and we'd put some bright feathers or something. They're real curious [animals]. You could take redbird feathers, things like that, and put up there, and a doggone raccoon would go in there and see what it was. You catch them that way, anything that calls them over there, they'll get over and look at it. And fox and things like that, they go on scent. You use female scent to draw an old fox, more than anything else.

You turned [the hides] wrong side out and put them on a stretcher where they fit pretty tight, and you scrape them down and let them dry good, and then you just bundle them up and send them in to Sears and Roebuck. Wrap them in burlap. They took possums, but they never did bring any money. But a good prime skunk ran from two to three dollars, and a raccoon was worth about ten.

**T. A. WILHITE**

Daddy killed the last deer there was in that country there around Fort Hood, a great big old buck. And he killed him and brought him home, and we eat him. And there's nobody ever saw another'n.

I hunted all the time, fished a lot. Lived right there on the Cowhouse River. When I was a little old kid, I hunted. When I was seven years old, I was going all over them mountains by myself. I had some good dogs. One time I broke the lamp globe up in a tree a-trying to find out what the dogs had treed, I broke that globe and didn't have no light. The rattlesnakes was just singing like everything down under there, and I waited till they settled down and eased down and went on and got out of there. These snakes had a den there on the ground, back in under a little bluff. I don't know how in the world I got out of there without getting bit, but I did.

I made expenses all winter hunting possums, ringtails, and coons. I had some good dogs, and they'd tree everything that come along. I was selling the hides and making pretty good money. Had places here in Belton, one or two, that they'd buy them. Ringtails was worth around six dollars, and possums was worth seventy-five cents.

I trapped, too. Lots of them, if there's a little old spring running out of the ground over there in one hollow, and that's all the water that was there, well, they'd come there to drink, you know. I was baiting this trap there, and I'd catch them—ringtails, possums—whatever come along, I'd catch him.

One old fellow lived up there above me a little piece, and he had a big log barn. And there's a place around at the back where there's a pretty good hole. And he noticed his corn was getting out of there. So he got a big wolf trap and set it in there. This fellow come that night, and it happened to be his closest neighbor. He's reaching into that hole to get some corn ever night to take over to feed his horses, and he stuck his hand into that trap, and he couldn't get it out. The fellow had the trap set where he couldn't pull it outside. And hell, he had to stay there all night. I don't see how he stood it, but he did.

When he got a-loose, he told that old man, he says, "If you ever tell this on me, I'll kill you." The old man didn't tell it till after he died. After he died, why, then he told about it.

**ROBERT E. GAULT**

When I was about nine, ten years old, I got me a .22, and I'd go out and get fifteen or twenty squirrels in a little while, shoot them out of those big trees. I'd take that old dog, and he'd tree them just right up and down there. We'd be home [in a] couple of hours, always. I had an old .22 Winchester single-shot, and that was the most accurate gun you ever saw. If I didn't shoot one through the head, I didn't take it home, 'cause Dad would whip me. He didn't want them shot anywhere except through the head.

Did you ever hear of people hunting robins? They roosted in cedar trees by the hundreds in the wintertime. They were sluggish in the wintertime, you know how anything [is] when it goes to roost or goes to sleep. And you go out there and take you a torch and take you a switch or a paddle or something like that. And when they flew up, just knock them down and pick them up. They were good eating. You made robin pies out of them, kind of like chicken and dumplings.

### KYLE HILLIARD

During the Depression, there were quite a number of people that would kill swamp rabbits and eat them. In fact, a time or two we ate just a plain old cottontail rabbit, and it's somewhat like chicken. We didn't really want to, but we did it sometimes.

We had this thicket—underbrush, post oak and live oak trees and Spanish oak trees—it was a pretty thick thicket. In the wintertime robins would come in and roost in that thicket. It would be in February. Cold and rainy weather was what you were looking for—not necessarily freezing but cold and rainy weather. I can remember that we had good friends that lived down on Union Hill above the Sparta bluff, and they knew that the robins were in there better than we did. They were roosting there at night. So these three grown men came to our house one night just about dark and asked if they could go robin hunting out there. They way they did it, they had a stick, a club, and they would just knock them out, maybe two or three at a time, and fill up a game bag full of robins. It was a slaughter, but they ate them just like you would eat chicken.

### NORMAN RICKETTS HALL

Killeen was a dry town, but my cousins and my dad had mustang grapes out in a pasture. They'd go pull mustang grapes, and usually without Mother knowing it, either in the smokehouse or out in the barn, would start the process of making wine. And they'd make it and they'd bottle it. I thought it was grape juice, I thought I really liked it.

### ROBERT E. GAULT

Mother made preserves, and preserves in those days was preserves—half sugar and half fruit. They'd turn black, but they was good. We kept grape juice all the time. We used mustang and those little winter grapes, both of them. She had old whiskey bottles that somebody had got somewhere. She'd fill them with that grape juice and then put a cork on there and pour hot paraffin over it and seal them. She always had a bunch of that on hand. I'll tell you, the old mustang grapes made awful good grape juice, and they made good grape jam. You can make jam out of what you have left. They didn't waste anything. Now, plum jelly, you can't hardly beat that. Them old wild plums, "hog plums," we called them—little bushes, you know— that was the best jelly you ever saw. And they had a tree plum that grew wild out in the pasture, it was an awful good plum. "Choctaw plum," or something. She always picked them off the trees out there.

### JAMES W. CALHOUN
Grandma always dipped snuff. She'd take them old redbud roots, she'd chew on them, and then she'd put it down in that snuff box, stick it back in her jaw. I remember her [saying], "Jimmy, would you go out and dig me some redbud root?" I went out there when I was just a little old kid and dig around under them redbud trees, dig down and find them little roots, cut them roots off. She never did call me James, always Jimmy.

### MARY EDWARDS GROVES
What amazes me [is] some of the food we had those days. We had [wild] onions along the banks of the Cowhouse, and when they would get really good, we had one little area that Daddy would always close off because he didn't want the milk cow to get in there. If the cow ate those onions, you couldn't use the milk, it was terrible. The onions would get nice size, and I've seen [Daddy] come in with a towsack just as full as he could get it with those onions. How in the world did we ever get enough peeled and ready? But Mother would take those onions in a huge skillet, and she would make cooked onions for a family of six, and I can just taste those onions right now. Of course, they were sautéed—we'll use the modern term—in bacon drippings. We always had cornbread.

### ALLEN COLE
There was a bush that grew right by the side of our outhouse. It had thorns on it, and the leaves were kind of a light green. We called it a "tickle-tongue bush," chew the leaves and tickle your tongue. It'd numb it, you know. For [chewing] gum, kids would go to one of these coves in the mountain, and there was a vine in there called a stretchberry vine. We'd gather

stretchberries, and they were about the size of a buckshot, about a quarter of an inch in diameter. You pulled that hull off, and the round seed had a rubbery sheet around that. You take that and put it in there with the gum, put about six or seven stretchberries in there and chew that gum, and you could blow bubbles better than bubble gum kids do now. You didn't want to destroy this, because it was pretty valuable, it was hard to get. So we'd stick it behind the door facings or under the kitchen table. Everywhere you went, you'd need some gum, you could find some.

### LOUIS TOMASTIK

When it rained in the fall or spring, [mushrooms] would be in the pastures. Our pasture had a lot of places thick with live oak, and there was a lot of leaves on the ground, and when it rained a lot, that was when the mushrooms were around trees or where the leaves were. The good mushrooms were thicker and kind of a different color, too. The poison ones were thinner, and they had that little comb. There was a lot of difference in looks. Daddy and Mother [had] learned it from the old country, their grandmother and grandfather taught them. And, oh, those mushrooms, when they're fresh like that, they're delicious, sometimes kind of like fried okra. Most times you'd stew them, and then you'd use them with other foods a lot of times.

## Medical Self-Help and Town Doctors

*The "medical" approach to illness did not entirely dominate the countryside before World War II. Many people believed they could not afford medical doctors, and others distrusted them, preferring instead to rely on herbal remedies passed down from older relatives, patent medicines purchased off the shelf, or various home concoctions based on the old standbys of coal oil, turpentine, and whiskey. Midwives delivered most rural babies. Families treated their own illnesses, often calling in the town doctor only when all else had failed. Sometimes they waited too late.*

### DORIS LEE WHITE THOMAS

Every fall and every spring Mother gave me calamine tablets, and then she'd say, "You have to take this castor oil," or I would die. This was to clean out your system. We had to get ready for the winter and get rid of the winter in the spring. Whew, isn't that far-out? That's what Grandma did, I guess, I don't know. [The castor oil] made me sick. Anything oily I could never take. I'd always get sick, and it'd all come up, then you'll have to take some more or you'll die. By that time I was limp as a dishrag.

I know they used a lot of sulfur to rub on you for something. Mother bathed me in lye soap. Kids would get skin diseases back then, but she'd bathe me in lye soap. Nothing could live through that.

### MARGARET BERT WILHITE BOUNDS

You ever hear of asafetida? That's supposed to keep you from having anything. My mother would tie asafetida bags on us, and we'd get out of sight and we'd tie them on the end of the turnrow fence. Then, that evening, when we come back, we'd put them back on like we'd been wearing them all day. We had mumps and measles and all the kids' diseases that went around that year, I imagine she wondered how we got them. Ooooh! I would have hated to have been the teacher, all warm [in the schoolroom] and those things get to smelling.

We treated ourselves. One time when my mother was a kid, her and her brothers and sisters was running and playing, and she run into a clothesline and cut a gash right there in her eyebrow. My grandmother put soot in it, and she always had a black scar there, but it stopped the bleeding. I was washing a glass, and it cut right under there. You can see that scar now. I probably should have had stitches, but I called my husband, I walked out on the front porch and just laid down and passed out. I had to put a cup towel on there so it'd stop bleeding, and I's trying to hold it till it quit, but it just kept bleeding and bleeding and bleeding, seem to me like, so he put flour on it. I've got a white scar there where he put that flour.

We had to have a tonic every spring, and if you stuck a nail or cut your foot, soak it in coal oil. We didn't know what a tetanus shot was. Did you ever use a poultice? Like if you cut your foot, you mix up flour and water and put it in an old sock and put another sock over it so that dough wouldn't seep through the sock. That kept it open, I guess, and soft, and infection wouldn't set up.

### JOE D. INSALL

I don't know how we survived. I was pretty little, my grandma sat in the middle of the wagon in a stiff-backed chair, and we were traveling along at a pretty good little clip of speed. And we run over a red ant mound about a foot high, it tilted the wagon, and she fell out and broke her hip. She never did go to the doctor. I'm pretty sure it broke her hip, because she was crippled the rest of her life. Didn't have no walker, so she used that straight-backed chair to push in front of her. That's the way she traveled from the bedroom to the living room. She'd sit there in the rocking chair all day. I carried her many glasses of water, she'd always holler at me, and she left me a trunk and a bedstead when she passed on. She was ninety-four.

Then we had a neighbor that lived in this place where my Uncle John lived, and he got appendicitis. Of course, they waited until he was about dead before they did anything. His dad had a wagon that was made out of a car frame, I guess it had rubber tires on it, pretty smooth-riding wagons, and down the road about a mile Jack Scott had a car. They took him down there and loaded him in the car. Then they took him to Gatesville, took out his appendix, brought him back home, and he must have busted a stitch or something. I think they was killing rats in the barn, were jumping around there, and he got an infection and died.

They didn't have much for anything then. We'd step on rusted nails all the time, never did know what a tetanus shot was. Mama would put a little kerosene on it and tie a rag on it. Said, "That'll take the soreness out."

One time I was cutting posts on a hillside. Usually I'm pretty careful, but my foot was where it shouldn't have been. I had on some old brogan shoes, and it went right down the side of them. Didn't hit a bone, but it cut a big blood vein. I walked to the house, bleeding, and it was raining, and you couldn't travel the road to town because it was too muddy. We had a bed on the front porch, and I laid on the bed and propped my foot up and got it to quit bleeding. It started raining again, and I got up and walked on it again to go in the house, and it got to bleeding again, and when it stopped I'd done lost a lot of blood. I knew better than to put it on the ground again, 'cause never did get it sewed up. Old Jake Heiner said, "You ought to have hollered, I'd come and sewed it up." And he would have, like he does a hound dog. I run around there on one foot for about a week. I could ride a horse or use a walking stick, you know, and hop.

### NORMAN RICKETTS HALL

There were two doctors in Killeen, and it almost caused a revolution when they said they were going to start charging a dollar for every time you came to see the doctor. [People] said, "Now, this is beyond all reason, a dollar for talking to the doctor!" Usually it had been free. Like, when women had babies, the doctor would come to the house, but both of the doctors that were in Killeen owned drugstores, and they were there for doctor visits. They usually had soda fountains in the drugstore, and that was a big part of town. The doctors were real pillars in the community.

### ROBERT E. GAULT

Dr. D. L. Woods was at Killeen, he delivered several thousand babies. He lived until 1944. He delivered all of us. He come out there on the farm, did a real good job. I think it's ten dollars he charged for a maternity case in those days. My sister had typhoid fever once, and he come out there and took care of her. He gave me five typhoid shots during that time, and boy, those things hurt in those days—those old unrefined shots. I run and I hid under the bed one time, and they drug me out by the feet.

Dad would always take me in to [Dr. Woods's drugstore] to have a checkup in the spring of the year, and old Dr. Woods would examine me, and if I needed anything he'd fix me up a tonic. It's twenty-five cents, then he'd go in and buy me an ice cream cone. Big old gruff guy, you know.

Heck, we was out in the weather all the time, we were healthy, we didn't have no reason not to be. My feet would get cold, and my ears would get cold, and that was all that ever hurt me.

### MURREL L. THOMPSON

We used kerosene a whole lot, and Mama gave me castor oil sometimes. When I had the croup, she'd mix kerosene oil and sugar and give it to me in a spoon. And when you stepped on a nail or something, barefooted, we soaked our foot in kerosene.

Then, if you had a splinter, they'd take a piece of hog fat and place it over where the splinter was and somehow tie it there and leave it overnight. The next morning, there was the splinter out of the flesh laying on the fat. The fat had drawn the splinter out.

There were not many doctors in our area. Dr. Woods in Killeen [was] the only doctor I ever went to. One night I was just about to die with the croup, couldn't breathe. I was just little bitty, trying to breathe, and I got scared. Dad and Mama got upset, and they called Dr. Woods at his home. The weather was bad, cold and rainy. We couldn't go into Killeen, nor could Dr. Woods come to us because the roads were so muddy a car would get stuck. He told Mama on the phone to give me a spoonful of sugar with kerosene on it. And they heated up Vicks salve, had me lean over it with a cloth over my head so I would breathe in the fumes from the Vicks salve. That was supposed to open up my head and maybe my lungs. I made it, somehow or another.

### KYLE HILLIARD

I was sick a lot, and when I was nine years old I had pneumonia. The year before, in 1934, my twenty-four-year-old uncle, who [had] regularly picked

400 pounds of cotton a day the summer before, which is big-league when it comes to picking cotton, had died of pneumonia. So it scared my mother and dad to death.

We had an ace in the hole, our family doctor, D. L. Woods of Killeen, Texas, who was an absolutely superb doctor for those days. They got Dr. Woods, I can remember him coming out to our house when I had pneumonia. He didn't lose a pneumonia patient unless he got them way too late in the week they had it. He said, "I want him to drink about a gallon of water every hour." He didn't mean that literally, but he meant for me to drink lots of liquid, lots of water. A simple thing, but it's very, very important.

He looked around this old house we lived in. It wasn't as bad as that one down in the pasture for day labor, but the wallpaper was not stuck to the walls like it was supposed to be, and that high winter north wind would blow, and it would billow out and then come back and cling to the wall. Dr. Woods looked around and saw how the house wasn't very tight. The wind was coming everywhere and the windows and the fireplace, too, and he said, "I see he'll get plenty of fresh air in this house!"

They said I was unconscious some of the time. Had a real high fever, and they were putting those ice packs on me. I didn't know what was going on for two or three days there, but I got all right.

### ANDY GORDON WOLF

In the early thirties Pa got an old Model T. I don't know how he got the Model T, but he did. And my youngest brother, William, come down with pneumonia, and he's two years old. That was 1932, he's born in '29. It had been raining like it is now, except that it just had dirt roads. Pa had to take a four-mule team and pull that Model T out three miles to where this road's solid enough to run this Model T on. We went to town and got old Dr. Brown, and Dr. Brown come out there [to Wolf Valley] and stayed three days and nights until the boy's fever broke. 'Course, the neighbors come in and helped set up with him and all that.

We didn't have no telephones and no way of communicating with anybody. In 1929 one of my uncles died [with] a burst appendix. There wasn't no way to get him to town to the doctor. You can imagine if you have appendicitis, and they put you in a wagon and haul you twenty miles to town what's going to happen. You never would make it. We had doctors we could depend on then. If we hadn't, I guess a whole lot of us would have died. My aunt, she had ten or twelve kids, and I don't know how many she had before the doctor got there. 'Course, they'd come to see about her, but too late. She'd had a baby before they got there. We had some midwives around. Mrs. Baker was a pretty good medical person. Of course, you wouldn't want your life to depend on her.

I was two years old when my uncle died, and I remember him being in bed. He was eighteen years old. Now it probably wouldn't have amounted to anything. He had an old paint horse that he called Old Bess, and they kept her until she died. That was his horse.

### JOHN DANIEL WOLF

We lived in Wolf Hollow, the last house up in the hollow, and if it rained as much as an inch or two, there was no getting out for a day or two. You just waited until it dried up a little bit so you could travel out.

On my mother's side, I had an uncle to die of appendicitis. They couldn't get him to the doctor. When I was a little kid, my Aunt Edith was twelve or thirteen years old. They got word to us that she had appendicitis, [we] were about five miles apart, and we immediately got in the buggy and took off. We got there, and my dad said, "You got to get her to the doctor." [They] said, "We don't have any way of getting a doctor." My dad said, "You damn sure do! Charlie lives down the road and he's got a car. I'll be back with him in a few minutes."

They had had words with Charlie, they were cross with him, but Dad went over and said, "Charlie, we need to take that girl to the doctor, she's gonna die." They both jumped in the car and came back and got her and took her to Gatesville. Her appendix bursted, but they pumped that poison out and saved her.

### GLADYS MERLE KEENER CHASTAIN

My sister Linda, the third sister down, she took the "bloody flux." Mother did everything in the world to cure her, she was just a little bitty thing, and [Mother] wouldn't let us eat around her, we'd go outside to eat. Daddy walked to Killeen, which was ten miles, to get medicine for my sister Linda, and I remember Daddy crying and Mother crying, both trying to cure her of this. A lot of people back in those days died of the bloody flux, or something. Today it's diarrhea to us and not that big a deal. She might have been between one and two years old, and it was really bad. We thought we were going to lose her. I remember Dad crying about it.

My Aunt Lucy had a son that she lost with the bloody flux when he was about four or five years old. I know she kept all of his clothes, and when you'd go to her house you'd see that little cedar chest with all of little Buddy's things.

### JAMES W. CALHOUN

Talk about doctoring, Daddy used to buy a new can of Red Top Axle Grease, and first thing done when he got home, Mama'd take the lid off and have some empty Vicks bottles, and she'd starting scraping that stuff off and putting it in the Vicks bottles. That's what we doctored sore toes with, Red Top Axle Grease. And coal oil was big. Somebody got a cut or something, first thing they'd do is slap it in a pan of coal oil. It killed infection.

But our oldest sister had an abscess on her hip bone about 1932, '33, and it was swelled up big. It was giving her a hard time. She'd probably have died from infection if they hadn't done something about it, but hospitals were nonexistent. Dad's brother was a medical doctor in Dallas. Dad went to Gatesville and called him, and him and one of his doctor associates that was a surgeon came down, and they did surgery on Dorotha on the dining table.

### MELBA GOODWIN BENNETT

My first year [at Stampede School], my sister took the flu and I had to help her get home. We liked to have never crawled through the rock fence and the barbed wire fence to cut across and get her home, 'cause she was so ill.

I can remember another time when my entire family was ill. My grandfather, my mother's father, Grandfather Cleveland, came from Oakalla to live with us. Everyone in my family—my mother and dad, my grandfather, and six kids—were ill with flu, and I was not sick. I was between six and seven, because we were living on the Sadler place. I made soup. My mother said, "Oh, put this in, put a handful of that and a little dab of this." This is the way she instructed me to make soup. I had to feed them all, because I did not have the flu. I was never sick.

### GLADYS MERLE KEENER CHASTAIN

Dad, he had all the neighborhood, everybody [to dinner]. He seen anybody walking down the road, "Come eat dinner with me! Come eat supper with me!" Poor Mom's cooked for more strangers than most people ever know.

My mother was a caregiver. There was always people coming to stay, and when I was reading my diary, I thought, Where did all of those people sleep? Mother had a sister, Una, and she had polio. They said at the time they thought she ate too many green peaches, but it made her crippled, she had a crippled arm. Back then they didn't have any walkers. Even up until she died, she pushed a cane-bottomed chair around. When we were living at Silver City, Aunt Una and Uncle John were always coming to stay with

Mama. Mother and Dad took everybody in. My aunt fell and hit that arm, her crippled arm, on the sewing machine and broke it, and they had to amputate. Mother looked after Aunt Una forever, and then she had a brother named Richard that lived with them towards the end. Mother was just a caregiver.

My Grandfather Hopson lived with us [and slept on the bed inside]. Mom and Dad slept out in the yard under a tree, and every night she'd have to take the sheet and shake the leaves off it before her and Dad could go to bed. My sister and I were sleeping on the front porch, and I heard my grandfather when he give his death gurgle. I hollered at Mom and Dad. I can remember it to this day.

### CLEMENTS W. "SPEEDY" DUNCAN

When I was a little boy and a curious little kid, my mother had an old trunk, and down in the bottom, the very bottom of that old trunk—I only got to see it a time or two—was a pint of whiskey, sealed up, a full pint.

My daddy got bit by a copperhead, and when my daddy got snakebit, my mother walked on a walking stick on the wooden floor, and I could hear her going. I knew where Mama was going, she was going to that trunk. She came back with a pint of whiskey, and we got it open, and Pa drank half of it. He wasn't a drinker, you know. Had to call a neighbor to come get him in a car, we didn't have one, the neighbor got him and took him to Killeen. Then they couldn't get him to go the doctor. He'd drank the rest of that whiskey, and he didn't want to see no doctor!

They had one old doctor that'd delivered all the kids within many miles of Killeen, his name was Woods. They finally talked him into going to see Dr. Woods, and he looked at him, says, "Yeah, just go on home and die." He was a gross-talking old doctor. I loved him, he had delivered me in 1923, but he just said, "You damned idiot, go home and die!" He almost did, too, he almost died. I had an older brother that had kids my age, and he says that whiskey was in that trunk when he was a little boy, he could remember. That's how long that whiskey had been in that trunk for snake bites. And that's the worst thing in the world to do [for snake bite], is drink whiskey.

### JUANITA GRIFFIN DUNCAN

We fed the food scraps to the dogs and cats, because we always had dogs and cats. Everybody in our [Brookhaven] neighborhood had them. We had a Collie-like dog, and we had lots of rattlesnakes in the area where I was raised, and that dog was real good at finding the rattlesnakes before we did.

I'm sure he kept us kids from getting bit more times than one. He got bit quite a few times, and my mom always felt sorry for him. She had been bit by a rattlesnake when she was pregnant with my oldest brother.

Her and my older sister was up there picking peaches, and she reached under a cedar bush where one had fell, and the snake bit her. It evidently was a great big one, because the fangs reached completely across her hand. They wrapped her hand with a rope, they were in a buggy, and went back to my grandmother's house. They called the doctor, but she got really sick. She had scars, of course, on her hand.

She had three brothers, my three uncles, and all of them were snakebit, and my grandfather died from a rattlesnake bite. He went out to the barn to feed his mules, he reached to get some corn or some hay, and one bit him. He lived about two days.

So we kind of knew what it was to live among the rattlesnakes. Of course, we were taught to be careful and watch for snakes, which we did, but that dog was a very important part of our life.

### WILMA EARL COLVIN EDWARDS

My mother's father was so crippled. He had osteomyelitis when he was four years old, and it had damaged his bones. Of course, he lived in the horse-and-buggy days, and he had lots of accidents, and teams would run away with him. He had to quit farming because he was already crippled so, and his field work was too hard. So he bought the Tama store, and he owned the gin for a while, and he then he had a blacksmith shop. He was postmaster of Tama from 1906 to 1918. He was a responsible businessman of his community.

He had a dray service, hauling stuff from Killeen to his store for people to purchase. He was coming back from Killeen with this load of lumber, and there is a place on the Killeen-to-Gatesville road that crosses the Cowhouse [Creek] called Gap of the Mountain. Something frightened the horses, and they ran away with him. He fell off of this dray wagon and caught his leg in the spokes. It ran two miles with him like that. It even broke spokes out of that wagon wheel.

When everybody found the horses, he was just a bloody wreck, he was terrible, but they recognized who he was. They sent the Webb's son to Belton to get a doctor, and another son went eight or nine more miles up to where my grandmother lived to get her and bring her here.

Two doctors came, and they decided that they would have to amputate his legs. 'Cause Grandmother was crying and they had a lady to fix her table with sheets for surgery, he caught on to what was going on. He told Grandmother to bring his pants to him, and she said, "What for?" And he said, "I want my pocket knife." He was a very firm person, and there was no amputating his legs. He got his pocket knife, and he said, "I'll kill them before they cut my legs off." He wouldn't let them put him to sleep, because he thought they would amputate. They put a stick in his mouth to keep him from chewing his tongue. They couldn't set his legs very well, being such compound fractures. Both legs were broken, one of them two times and one of them three times between the knee and the feet—compound [fractures] and drug in that dirt and everything. So I don't know how they ever saved his legs, but he did not get gangrene.

The Webbs kept him there six weeks or two months, because it took that long for him to heal. They were a real close community down in there, and everybody heard about it, and they all came to see what they could do to help. They finished his crop out, and they helped him that way, and they had their garden and all that kind of thing. So he finally survived enough to get home.

It was really hard on my grandmother, because she had to do all the work. They had cows and chickens and horses, and then she had the garden coming on. Mother said he would, when he got to where he could walk at all, he would put one of his knees somehow on a chair and just drag around like that to walk a little bit. She would take things to him. He would peel and snap the beans. He helped her in every way he could. He finally recovered, but he was very crippled from then on, and he never walked without a cane. Everybody loved him, and he never complained.

Then my Grandfather Colvin was ten years old when his mother died, and she had six living children and a set of twins that had died during that time. Can you believe that? She had a little son that was six weeks old, and she had gone to help her husband clean out a dug well that they had to get the debris out of because they had to use that water. He was in the well, filling these buckets, and she was pulling it up and dumping it out on the ground. She dropped dead and fell in his arms, and he held her out of that water for several hours before anybody heard him screaming for help. They got her out and of course she was dead, had been all that time. I think that's so sad that he had to hold her there like that.

He married again in less than two years, and he had two more children, and that lady died. Then he married another lady named Molly Raines Keele, and they in turn had nine children. He was the father of nineteen children, seventeen who lived!

# CHAPTER THREE

# Money Crops

## Cotton and Other Crops

*As an old farmer once told me, "Without cotton, son, you was just blowed up!" No matter how diligently you lived off your place, you needed some money for food you could not raise, clothing you could not make yourself, kerosene for lamps, and payments for taxes and debts to the bank or the mercantile store. Despite admonitions of "book farmers," county agents, and newspaper editors urging "diversification," most area farmers relied on cotton as their cash crop until the government changed the rules of the game during the Great Depression. Family farms in the area often produced only a few bales of cotton, yielding one hundred to three hundred dollars of profit, and in this hardscrabble place, everybody knew a few one-bale-a-year cotton farmers. Work stock, cotton, and cash flow were closely related, but no work stock helped in the picking of cotton. Seed cotton hung from the bolls in the field, exposed to the destructive winds and rain of late-summer thunderstorms. People forgot many things about the farming life, but not picking cotton—not the long, hot, sometimes desperate days bending or kneeling down long rows shimmering in the heat. No wonder that some area farmers developed alternative money crops to the white staple: syrup cane, small grains, broomcorn, and others.*

### J. W. SHULTS

Everybody was pretty much the same. They farmed, they raised cotton and corn and some kind of crop to feed their animals through the winter. People could shear the goats twice a year and sell the hair. Sheared the sheep once a year, sell the wool. And we milked the cows, and whenever the calves get big enough to sell, we'd sell them. Then in the fall we'd have a couple, maybe three, bales of cotton.

That was our money crops, but up until '42 there wasn't anybody that had any money. There just wasn't any money, everybody was in the same predicament. They didn't anybody have anything more than another one, and everybody was happy. We had a lot of fun, and most of the toys we got at Christmas were homemade, as was most of our clothes.

### MURREL L. THOMPSON

We grew cotton, corn, oats, maize, and cane. We had four mules that we used all the time. We raised nearly everything that we ate. I remember when we'd sell some crop, or portion of a crop, we might have a hundred dollars, and I remember Daddy saying, "Maybe we can make it another year." A hundred dollars was pretty good.

We had a cultivator and a team, and my daddy had me plowing when I was just barely old enough to reach those pedals that kept you from running over the corn. I was six or seven years old. We had cultivators, breaking plows like a double disk, and a triple disk for breaking land, a grain drill to drill the oats in, and then a reaper to cut oats.

We eventually got an old Fordson tractor, and in breaking the oat stubble I would drive that occasionally. I probably was ten years old when I drove that tractor and broke the stubble with it. When we headed and gathered maize or pulled corn, I drove the team, pulling the wagon alongside the boys gathering whatever, and they'd throw it in the wagon. I guess I was about six years old when I started driving the team and working in the field.

I always liked to go with Daddy. We'd take the wagon with a [load] of cotton, go to Copperas Cove to the cotton gin, leave early in the morning before daylight. It was about seven or eight miles there. After the cotton was ginned, we'd leave the bale of cotton there to be sold, but the cottonseed was put back in the wagon, and we brought it home. I'd play in the cottonseed and sometimes went to sleep in it on the way back home. We mixed some feed with it and fed it to the milk cow. That was one of my other jobs.

### NORMAN RICKETTS HALL

When the other people went to tractors, Dad never worried about that. He stayed with mules. He might have had six at one time, and he'd work four real hard one day, and then he would change and work the others the next day.

Back then, one of the dangers was a mule being bitten by a rattlesnake, 'cause if that happened, it was very likely that they would die.

Dogs were bitten by rattlesnakes real often, and they'd usually die. But if they were bitten in the head, sometimes you could feed them lard, and that would 'cause them to sweat. They said back then it "sweated the poison out." But if they were bitten on the leg or body, it was just a matter of time.

Once, my dad was going to the field with his mules. He had gone through a gate and parked, and a rattlesnake bit one of his mules. First of all, he called this man in town on the phone, and he said, "Well, you take a chicken and tear it right in half and put that on the wound until I get there." So they got a chicken and put that over the bite. When he got there, he looked and everything and lanced the bite. You couldn't do much, 'cause the mule's not going to stand for it. Then he said, "Go get a bucket of milk." We got the milk. The bite was just above what you call the ankle, and he placed that in the milk bucket. I didn't know what was going on, but the mule did live. That enhanced that old boy's reputation quite a bit in the community. Chickens didn't think very much of him.

### CLEMENTS W. "SPEEDY" DUNCAN

A lot of people never think about it, but mules made the United States. They built all the railroads, and they did all the farming, and they pulled them wagon trains across the country. They don't get their just credit, the mule don't. He's the most unappreciated thing that ever happened to this country—the cotton-picking old mule.

Dad married in 1900, just over that hill right around there, and him and my mother lived in a covered wagon. He made his living breaking horses and mules. Work or ride, it didn't matter. Whether it was a mule or a horse, he broke them to work with a collar on and a harness or broke them to ride. It didn't matter to him, just what they wanted. That's the way he made a living, breaking them, so I'd say he knew them pretty good.

I enjoyed driving mules. I was a grown man, I guess ten years old, I was driving mules. Had an old leather line, and I was playing a little tune on them mules. My daddy reached over and liked to have tore my little old hands off, jerked them lines out of my hand. "No, no! When you get grown and get a team of your own, you can make deadheads of them, but you ain't going to ruin my mules!" My daddy and I were taking a bale of cotton to Killeen one time, and said, "Son, look a-yonder." There was a wonderful span of mules, and the old guy was whipping them all the time with the lines. He said, "Them mules won't ever be worth nothing," says, "They're just making deadheads out of them." He taught me that when I was awful young. You could whip them with those lines, and they'll just get immune to it.

In reality, kids are a lot like mules. An old mule will get by with what he can if you don't watch him. I've had people come here and never quit hollering at their children. Don't fall off of that! Don't do this! Just continually hollering at them, and it wearies me.

My pappy still worked mules in South Texas. We used mules to pull cotton wagons to the gin, and down there is a large farming country and there'd be people heading for the gin in their wagon behind the tractor, pulling maybe a five-bale wagon behind a tractor. We just had one-bale wagons, homemade jobs, but them mules would outrun them tractors so bad we like to got in trouble! They could pull a bale of cotton running, and maybe a hundred wagons coming in, and in flat country you can see forever! Some of those old guys on the wagons would get there, and [we'd] just about have a fight on account of because we cut ahead of them.

### ERNEST ALLEN COLE

Daddy had a tractor later, [but at Okay] we used mules. You raised your own mules. There was an old boy came around about once a year with a great big old black donkey. He was big as a mule, and he bred the horse mares. He was a pretty big animal for a jackass, [but] we had a pit about two feet deep with a fence on both sides so the mare couldn't get out, and he'd breed the mares. Then, every year, you'd have one or two mule colts.

You raised your own mules, and nearly everybody plowed with a mule. The mules had one advantage, they never foundered. You put a horse where there's lots of food, and they'll eat until they bloat. But you put a mule out there, and he gets full, he quits. And the mule had more stamina, they could stand more hard work than a horse could. I can remember you had to be careful when you were hooking them up, or they'd kick you halfway across the barn, but they were a better work animal than a horse was. The mules produced with this old stud, this old black donkey stud, were big mules, big heavy mules.

### MARGARET HUNT CARROLL

Daddy was a horse trader. First Monday on the square at Belton, that was the trade square, and everybody took their stuff to town on First Monday. They'd go to town, and they'd trade horses [and mules], whatever you had to take to town. They'd always be horse trading, and Daddy would always go down and trade horses.

We had mules and horses. Whoever broke them to begin with, from an unridden or unused horse, you had to break them and teach them how to pull a wagon, pull a plow, whatever. And however you hitched them up when you were training them, you broke them for the right-hand or the left-hand [side]. Some of them, after they got older, you could do anything, but they could do better if they was hitched up as they originally learned. Just like you, if you learned to do something left-handed or right-handed, there you'd be.

So Old Kit went on the left side, Kate-Kate went on the right side, that's the way it was. You train them to walk on the right side of the row when they're plowing. They know where to walk, [but] we got a horse one time that had been broke to a double-shovel that, to work him, you had to plow backwards! Instead of going around this-a-way, you went this-a-way! It was the same difference, but the horse, he would be so miserable. He'd step on the stuff, and you'd get him straightened out, and he'd go for a minute, and directly he'd be trying to cross over and walk on the other side, and before you could realize it, you'd plowed up some stuff. And so Daddy just turned and went the other way.

Whenever you got one trained to do something, you didn't have any trouble with them later. Daddy had a young team of mules when he got married. Old Kit died on Christmas Day when he was thirty-one. He was standing by the gate.

### ROBERT E. GAULT

I learned to hoe real young. I was always good with a hoe, I liked it. It was something I could make a showing on, you know. I'm kind of an impatient person, and I liked that. Usually when you're chopping [the cotton], you're riding it up with the cultivator first, that gets a lot of the grass out of the way. Then, when you chop, the way we did, [we'd keep] the width of the hoe between stalks. We took everything out but that one stalk every time. Then, the last hoeing, usually, when the grass got to coming back, we'd come in there and hoe everything and then plow it. Plow it last and lay it by. We didn't have any Johnson grass, Dad wouldn't have that, no cockleburs and no Johnson grass. If you saw one and you didn't pull it, you was out of luck. I've hoed in the summertime barefooted, and you have to get over in the other row in the shade of those stalks. That's the only way you could stand it.

### DORIS LEE WHITE THOMAS

I never did have to pick any cotton, but I had to go to the field with them [at Spring Hill]. I never could take the sun. I'd get so hot, and I'd get sick at my stomach. I'd sit under the wagon in the shade. One day Daddy caught a little rabbit, a little cottontail rabbit, and brought it to me and tied it to the wagon wheel. He went on back to pick cotton. And that little sucker went to jumping and a-squealing, and I went to hollering, "Daddy! Daddy!" He had to come and get me quieted down, but he didn't do away with it until later on.

Once, at Peabody, my teacher had a younger sister that was just about a year older than me, and we played together a lot. One day they were picking cotton for Daddy. I decided, well, I'll go out there and pick, too. I guess I was eight years old. I just went lickety-split down that row, picking now and then to get up close to her. Daddy said, "Now, turn around and go back down that row and pick it right." By that time they had turned around on other rows, and she was far away from me. So that didn't work. But he never did get on me hard.

### MARGARET HUNT CARROLL

That was farming country, we raised cotton, corn, and cane. I was the oldest "boy," I had to [help out]! I started driving a team when I was eleven, whenever I started helping my daddy. He'd do the plowing, and then I'd come along with the planter and a mule. I was so little that when I pulled around at the end, I had to put the plow handles up on my shoulders to get the plow out of the ground enough to where I could follow the horse around and put him back where he belonged. Then [I] dropped the plow back down, and we'd go again.

That seed planter was all I was big enough to do for a while. Then when I got bigger, plowing was my job—or whatever, driving a team. I didn't help to wash dishes. See, everybody had a job. You gather the vegetables, help prepare them for canning, peel peaches until you dropped, make preserves.

Planting was the first job of the season, and when it come up, then everybody, everybody grabbed a hoe and went to the field to hoe. These rows was planted, and you chopped between all this stuff. You planted the cotton heavy, and then you'd go down the row [with the chopping hoe] and you'd swing, swing, and you'd leave about three or four stalks—whack, whack, whack, whack—when it was real little. Then they'd come along with the plow between each row and put the dirt back to it.

Then, as time went on, as it rains, everything grows, weeds most especially. You'd go hoe all this kind of stuff, and when you'd hoe it all out, you'd take a team and a plow and go back and dirt it up again with a double-shovel. Little stuff you did with a double-shovel. It had two little sweeps, little buzzard-wing sweeps on it. You used this double-shovel to plow [the cotton] when it was little, because it had little sweeps on it, and it didn't cover it up. As it got bigger, then you swapped to a big buzzard-wing for the middles.

That was my job, but whenever I got through plowing, I helped hoe, too. And the best time about it is when you pick the cotton, because [after] all this work, you could take the cotton and sell it, and then you got paid! You worked all year long before you got paid. I loved the cotton-picking season, because I got money! I didn't know any better, I liked doing that. I would rather do anything than wash dishes, and my sisters had to wash dishes.

### MELBA GOODWIN BENNETT

My mother's father had no place to go once his family married and his wife died. When she died, he broke up housekeeping and came to live with us. Granddad worked very hard with Dad, he rode a three-wheeled plow. Granddad made rows for the corn, rows for cotton, and everything. He always plowed for Dad. I can remember my grandfather living with us until he died at eighty-four. I had to trim my grandfather's mustache all the time when I was a little girl growing up. He wouldn't let anyone else do it.

### R. E. GAULT

Our school used to start October 12, about that late, for cotton. I was sure glad to go back to school [after] that cotton picking. On forty acres, [we'd] have from ten to twenty [bales]—probably fifteen average. Around a third of a bale to the acre probably. We had good yield most of the time. We [picked] it ourselves, and I'm telling you, I didn't like it. The year I went to California, I come back in time for picking cotton. I was down at Oenaville, on some of that blackland. My mother and dad was living down there, so we went down there and stayed and picked cotton that fall. They had a black crew from Welder out there, and had an old boy that sang all day and picked 1,100 pounds of cotton a day. He was out there at daylight and didn't go in till dark, and they'd bring him an orange at noon, and he'd eat that orange and just keep going, sing all day long. He told me he got the most pleasure out of that than anything in the world. But he was so dang good!

I was picking cotton one day [when] I was twelve years old, and you know how a kid daydreams. I reached down, and I felt something soft, and I looked down, and a big old rattlesnake was coiled around under that stalk in the shade. I guess it was asleep, but it sure scared the heck out of me. I backed up and got out of my sack and hollered, "Pa!" He come up and took a club and killed that rattlesnake. It was a big old thing, about like my arm. Had twelve rattlers.

### GLADYS KEENER CHASTAIN

I remember cotton picking. You'd get so hot, you wore an old bonnet, and you'd look around to see if a whirlwind was coming where you'd take your bonnet off and get a breath of air. That's a pretty strong memory with me, how hot it was. My sister said, "Oh, wish a whirlwind'd come along!"

Daddy could pick more cotton than anybody. Everyone in the neighborhood knew Daddy was the best cotton picker. Then after you'd pick cotton, you'd go back and scrap the bolls. That's what would hurt, the bolls would hurt the ends of your fingers.

That was scrapping cotton—nothing wasted, nothing wasted. And all the wives would take their babies and lay them on pallets to help the husbands pull cotton and pick cotton. They didn't stay at home and listen to the radio, I'll tell you.

Back in those days I had nosebleeds really bad, and Mom would try everything to stop the nosebleed. I was the one that learned to cook first and would stay in and cook the meal—very, very young—because I'd have nosebleed when I'd get out in the heat picking cotton. Faye would always say, "Yeah, you just got nosebleed where you wouldn't have to pick the cotton."

### MARGARET BERT WILHITE BOUNDS

Daddy probably made about ten bales a year. Daddy wasn't hard on us, everybody was doing that, all the kids our age was working in the field and helping out. Now, kids'd probably say it was child abuse if they had to get out and work in the hot like that. But you know, you never thought of nothing like that. That's just the way of life, and you do it.

The first time I remember picking cotton, I picked in a towsack, and [Mama] sewed a strap on it, 'cause I wasn't very high up from the ground. It was all I can do to drag it, and Mama'd say, "You don't have to pick that much, you don't need to be dragging that much cotton." But you needed to finish the row out, so you dragged just a little harder.

When I was little I [picked one row], but when I got bigger I picked two rows. Daddy would pick two, and Mama would pick two, and usually there was other people helping us. Sometimes some of the farmers would have their kids to come help us. [They got] so much a pound, and Mama would keep weights. She'd have a little book, and everybody had a page [for] whatever they picked, and then on Saturday they got paid.

Our mother went in the field, too. How she cooked dinner [I don't know], I guess she cooked beans the night before, and she'd fix cornbread. She might quit just a little earlier than we did for dinner, but she'd have beans and cornbread and fried potatoes and onions and all that good stuff ready when we got there. We had a swing on the porch, and Daddy would lay down and take him about a five-minute nap. And she'd be in there washing dishes!

Picking cotton, they would have the wagon sitting in a designated spot, and you would pick cotton and go to the scales there by the wagon and weigh. We had jugs of water, and they were wrapped in towsacks, because you didn't have ice that much. You'd wet those towsacks, it may be wrapped around there two or three times, and that was our thermos jug. Mama thought we ought to be covered up. We'd have long cotton jackets and lots of times gloves and bonnets.

My oldest sister, she snagged it, but she could get that cotton. She'd go faster down that row than I could. I'd think, I'm picking as hard as she is, but she'd get more cotton. I couldn't get what my older sister got, but she'd snag hers, she'd leave little [tufts in the bolls], and I'd pick mine clean. I wanted all that cotton out of that boll. Daddy never told us how much we had to pick. He'd say, "Now, do your best."

In picking, if you bent over and picked, then you had a sore back after the first day, and if you crawled on your knees, then your knees was sore. Oh, that second day you couldn't hardly get out of bed! But you did.

We lived close to a neighbor [at Sparta], and their cotton field was on one side of the road, and ours was on the other. My nephew got sick one day, so he went over and laid down on the neighbor lady's porch, and she let him get by with it. Well, the next day, he was sick again, and her son about the same age got sick, too. So she gave them a dose of castor oil, and they wasn't sick anymore after that. That dose of castor oil changed both of them's minds, they decided picking cotton wasn't so bad.

### ZELL KINSEY COPELAND

When my daddy died, a lot of people wanted Mother to put us in an orphans' home, which I can understand, and probably thought, How in the world is she going to do this? But she was determined not to, and she didn't.

We tried to make at least a bale a year on the places we rented. When we were on Mr. Hord's and Mr. Jones's places [at Friendship], after all the cotton was picked, they would let us go through and scrap what was left in the bolls, there's always some left, and that's what we made our quilts and mattresses out of. I'm sure that they got that out of the Bible, because that's what it says, let the widow glean. They were good Christian people. I definitely think they were nicer to us on account of Mother being a widow.

I didn't like to pick cotton! In the cotton patch we wore overalls and slat bonnets and gloves over our hands and all up our arms, so we wouldn't brown. You didn't want to be brown. I got up to 200 pounds [a day] in my later years, not when I was so young. You didn't leave and go get you a drink of water when you got thirsty, you waited until you got back to where the wagon was. I remember that I was barefooted, many of us were, and that ground would be so hot you'd try to step in the shade of the cotton stalk.

Really, what was harder for me than anything else, part of the time we had to empty our own sack, and that's not easy. I remember weighing out forty pounds that I drug in the sack. You're standing in the middle of this cotton, in the wagon, or they might have it piled on a tarp, trying to empty your sack. Your back would hurt 'cause you stoop over so long and you crawl a lot. We all had kneepads. When I got up the next morning, my back was still hurting.

And my family killed a lot of rattlesnakes! One time we were picking cotton there. 'Course, we all wore leather kneepads, and a rattlesnake struck my oldest brother on the kneepad.

We did not start to school when everybody else started, we had to stay out about two weeks because that was cotton-picking time, and we had to finish picking that cotton. We had to pick as long as there was cotton to pick, because that was our money, and it was our food. I remember being in the cotton patch and seeing the kids pass by going to school. I didn't like that.

### WILLIAM AKE POWELL

I got an aunt that I lived with them a couple of years. They farmed a big old place, and my aunt liked to work me to death trying to pick as much cotton as she could. It took about 1,200 to 1,400 pounds to make a bale, depending on the kind of cotton, and, damn, I had to pick that cotton, and ever other day you took a bale to the gin then. My uncle, he done the farming, but he didn't do no cotton picking, and me and my aunt picked a bale of cotton ever other day. It wasn't anything unusual, if the cotton was good, for her to pick 400 pounds a day.

We went out there and stayed all day. We'd carry the lunch with us. My uncle, he'd get up early and go out to the barn and kill two or three chickens and dress them and bring them, and my aunt would fry those chickens, make a big bunch of biscuits and a big bunch of gravy. We had them for breakfast sometimes. I used to try to pick as much cotton as she could, and, boy, it just killed me, but I don't think I ever did. She'd fix lunch, carry it with us, sit down for a little time at dinnertime and eat, then hook up that cotton sack and go again.

### T. A. WILHITE

My daddy had eleven children on 125 acres. We raised cotton, and when we got our place cleaned out, we headed to get a job and make some money, chopping. See, cotton made our clothes, the school clothes and stuff. That's the way we got school clothes. Every year, Daddy borrowed twenty-five dollars. I got the notes out there in the barn. In 1925 there was a drought, and two or three carloads of us went to West Texas, I was in the bunch. You had a crop failure, you had a hard road to climb.

### MELBA GOODWIN BENNETT

We were in a German community, everybody there was German. I say this with all fairness to them, because they're good friends of mine now, we were looked down on somewhat when we went to school. They would call us "stinkouta," means polecat. That's the only words that I learned in German.

I never saw a Negro until I was at Plainview, and my dad had to hire some Negroes to come in and pick cotton for us one time. I'll never forget this as long as I live. I was scared, very scared. I could not pick cotton and be in front of them, I always had to be behind so I could watch as I was scared of them. My dad assured me there would be no problems or anything, but I did have that horror. Yet we learned to know them. They moved in a house not too far away from us. It was the only family in the community that was colored, or black.

### ERNEST ALLEN COLE

We had a family that every fall, when cotton-picking time came [at Okay community], they drove up in a covered wagon pulled by two mules to pick cotton. There was a boy about fifteen, the girl's about thirteen, and they could pick more cotton than anybody I ever saw. I was a little old kid, and I was curious, so I'd talk to them. When the cotton was gone, they left, of course, and I asked him where he spent the winter. He says, "Well, I spend it up on the Trinity River between Fort Worth and Dallas. I sleep on a *Fort Worth Star Telegram* and cover up with a *Dallas Morning News*." He said, "We pick pecans and sell them and eat them, too. We fish, and we catch possums and coons and sell hides and shoot squirrels."

Grandpa ground corn on the halves, and everybody brought their corn over there. That's what most of his sharecroppers ate, cornbread—cornbread and sowbelly. Sharecroppers were usually Mexican people, and sometimes they'd stay three or four years, and sometimes they wouldn't. Right east of us was a family called the Rileys, and they had a sharecropper house up there. One of these kids that lived there one time stuck a cottonseed up her nose. It started swelling up and sprouting, so they had to carry her to the doctor and get the thing pulled out.

On this farm right north of us, one time a preacher lived there. He was a sharecropper preacher—preached on Sunday and hoped to get a donation or something. He had two boys about my age, and Mother every once in a while invited the preacher in to eat fried chicken on Sunday. I didn't care much for these boys, even though they didn't live but a mile from us, but she insisted I invite them to Sunday lunch. So I did, and when they got there, Mother asked them if they didn't want to wash their hands, so they finally did. And she said, "Don't you boys want to comb?" Says, "Oh, no, ma'm, we better not. Things fall out of our hair sometimes when we comb it!" That was the last time I had to do that.

### MARY EDWARDS GROVES

We'd have baked sweet potatoes. I remember when the guys would be work-ing in the fields, our mother would take a huge baking pan that fit in the oven in the wood stove and bake sweet potatoes. It would the mid-after-noon snack for guys that were working in our fields, carry that pan of baked potatoes down there in the middle of the afternoon. Can you imagine, now, there would be anyone that would be working for you, and you would go out and take them baked sweet potatoes in the middle of the afternoon?

### CLEMENTS W. "SPEEDY" DUNCAN

They'd always leave one wagon back in the field to put more cotton on. It would be one wagon full, and by the time you got back [from the gin] you needed another one—if you had a lot of acres. I was picking cotton and picked up one great big old rattlesnake. I wanted to make a scene out of it, but Papa grabbed me and said, "Shut up! Shut up! Shut up!" He was an extra strong man, and jerked up that cotton stalk and killed that snake. He says, "Son, be quiet! Half of these pickers will leave the field and we need to pick this cotton!" Of course, they all knew there were snakes in the area. It sure wasn't no secret.

### NORMAN RICKETTS HALL

We had 700 acres of pasture and 110 acres of cultivated land. We raised cotton, and that was a money crop. One time my dad made quite a bit of cotton. In fact, he had fifty-one bales, and he didn't sell it to the gin, he had it delivered back out to the farm. Cotton was forty-two cents a pound, and he was gonna get fifty. Well, that was in 1929, when the Depression hit, and he sold it for three cents a pound. He said Mother never let him forget that. Every time she got mad at him, she would say, "Well, you remember the forty-two-cent cotton?"

### KYLE HILLIARD

I was born in the Palo Alto community in 1925. Grandpa had a good, big farm. He had several boys who would help him with labor, and in 1922, especially, he had a great crop of cotton. He made a bale to the acre without fertilizing and without irrigating—just planting it and hoeing it and plowing. Cotton is labor-intensive at the very best. There were no boll weevils back then, they hadn't arrived yet, and he didn't have to poison, and so he made a bale to the acre. This was post–World War I, and he got forty cents a pound for that cotton. He practically was able to pay off his place with that wonderful 1922 cotton crop.

His sons, including my dad, saw that happen, so they were all cotton farmers, as was nearly everybody else in this Fort Hood area. We had cotton fever, it was in our main crop, but in the 1930s the Depression came along and the situation changed considerably. Ten years later Daddy was trying to raise three kids on a 103-acre farm, and the price of cotton was five cents a pound in 1932, and by that time the boll weevils and other insects had arrived, and the land was much more worn out after farming cotton on it for ten years. So instead of making a bale to the acre, we would do well to make a bale to three or four acres. We nearly starved to death during the Depression trying to make a living growing cotton.

We stayed there. Our landlord would've had reason to get us to move. We didn't have very good equipment, didn't have very good mules, but the owner was from West, near Waco, and he wasn't trying very hard to make any money out of that farming during the Depression. He knew there was a family with three kids living on this farm, and prices were extremely low. Cotton was five cents a pound. We were supposed to give our landlord a fourth of everything we grew. We didn't do that at all, and he didn't complain.

It was very difficult, 103 acres just wasn't enough land to support a family. My dad was the next to the youngest child, and by the time that Daddy got grown, Grandpa was old and tired. He had helped some of the older boys when they first got married, and he knew the names of their children. He didn't even really know my name. He didn't pay any attention to any of us, and he didn't worry about us at all.

There were quite a few people who just rented the farms, and then there were some—the Halls and the Ramms and Jim Brown and my Grandpa Hilliard—who were the well-to-do farmers. In our close proximity those were the good, going-concern farms. Then there were quite a few like we who had smaller, less desirable places [where] at least you had a place to call your own, and you didn't have to pay rent, and you had a place to grow a garden and to keep cows and chickens and all that sort of thing as well as the land, and you were supposed to be able to give a fourth of what you got off the land to the owner.

So, it could have been worse, and it was worse. Between us and the Ramms, somebody that had owned the place before Mr. Ramm had built a two-room house. Not two bedrooms, a two-room house, sort of a shack. Mr. Ramm let people who were looking for a place to live, that had nothing, live there. Just a place to live, not beside or under a bridge, he would let them live there for nothing. They would work for him if he had labor to do, such as picking cotton in the fall or chopping cotton in spring and summer. Maybe doing other farm labor. Seven people lived there in that little two-room house, and the only cash that they got was what they could get picking cotton for sixty cents per hundred pounds picked or chopping cotton or doing other labor for twelve and a half cents an hour. They were worse off than we were by quite a bit.

### ANDY GORDON WOLF

It never was a good cotton country [around Silver City]. You might take ten acres and make a bale of cotton. I had two uncles, Oscar and O. C. Hill, when they's growing up they left home and went down on the old Cooper place, which was an old house that's setting down there where Coopers had lived at one time. They lived there for a year and had ten acres, and they made one bale of cotton, and they lived for a year off that bale. It might have brought twenty-five dollars, so you can just imagine. 'Course, they had chickens and a milk cow and everything. So that's just the way you got by, everybody did, and you was just blowed up if you didn't have a milk cow or something.

Let me tell you a little story. Back in the early thirties, we's living back up in Wolf Hollow on the old Henry Wolf place, and I was four or five years old. Had a lane that went through there and big bloodweeds on both sides of the road, and I's walking up that road, and I met this fellow that had come across the mountain. It was old mountain trails up there that people had used always, they'd always been there. And this fellow was leading an old sway-backed horse, had an old oat sack throwed across the old horse, and his wife was riding that horse. He's leading it, and he's barefoot. I thought that was funny because I'd never seen a grown man that didn't have shoes on. I said, "Feller, where is your shoes?" He said, "Son, I don't have no shoes." That shows you what the thirties were like. They's a lot of people like that.

### CECIL L. NEWTON

In 1919 my daddy bought half-interest in the [Pidcoke] gin, and at that time it became Perryman and Newton Gin. The gin operated each fall to gin cotton. My father passed away in 1930, and one of my older brothers, Akard, took over the operation for the gin. I worked for him for several years, 1933 to 1938. That was when the gin ginned its last bale of cotton, in 1938.

I can remember I used to help get cordwood for the thing back in the summer months. It'd be hot, and we'd be getting the wood that would furnish the heat, the steam, and that would start in the hot months. I imagine we cut 200 or 300 cords and stacked it out on that gin lot out there. It'd be in rows, and the wagons would have to come through the rows of cordwood. There was a lot of wood out there.

A regular ginning season was slower, then. The cotton was brought in by wagons, wagons and teams. It took longer to get the cotton out of the field. They had to pick it by hand, and the ginning season would be longer. Maybe twenty or thirty wagons would be lined up at the gin at one time. Most of the time, [the farmers] would sit and wait. I believe each one just lined up and kind of knew where they were in line. Then, if they brought their children with them to the gin, they'd all go to that swimming hole [on Bee House Creek], the kids would all go to the creek. I guess it'd take at least an hour to take the cotton from the wagon and run it through the gin.

There'd be a strong suction line from a big fan, it'd suck the cotton off that wagon. A hand would have to operate the suction pipe that would suck cotton off of the wagons. Then the cotton would go through the gins and be separated from the seeds. The seeds would go into this one building, and the cotton would go into what they called a bale of cotton. It'd be a 500–pound bale.

It's hard for me to describe that noise. The gin was noisy. It'd be three gin stands that separated the cotton from the seed. Those three sections would take up maybe fifty feet, and they were the noisiest parts. Those things whirled so fast to separate the cotton from the seed. That's where most of the noise came from, it was a humming sound.

That engine room down there, it had a big engine and it turned all the drives, the drives that went all the way through the gin. It was a large shaft about four inches in diameter that went all the way through, it had pulleys coming off that would power the gins.

There was a big pipe, maybe three feet in diameter, that'd carry that cotton from the gin to the press box. It was rolling there with high-pressure air—it had a big fan that would blow all that cotton from the ginning in the gin up to the press box. Then, after you had your full bale there, then you'd put on this compressor and bring it into a 500–pound bale. It'd be a hydraulic pump that would compress that cotton. Then you'd wrap it with what you called bagging and ties—you'd tie it off, you'd use about six or seven ties. Then you'd open this box, which was built real strong, and you'd throw the bale out. You can handle a bale of cotton pretty easy, [if] you learn to do that. You'd manhandle it out on what we called the platform. You had scales out there, and you'd raise that bale of cotton and weigh it.

Then you could swing that bale around and put that bale of cotton in their wagon. Or, if they sold it, they'd stack it at the back of that gin out there.

They had what they called a fireman, they'd have what they called two press operators, and they'd have a hand that would suck the cotton off the wagon. The water for the steam boiler came from Bee House Creek. There was a steam pump down there that could pump water from Bee House Creek to the gin.

I remember the ginner and the fireman. They'd come, and during the ginning season they would stay there at the gin. There were places around there they could stay with their cots. Bill McCurry was a ginner. He was a big, heavy, strong fellow, always wore overalls, and his first year, the first thing he wanted to know was if there was anyway he could buy sweet milk. Late in the evening, after the gin shut down and they'd caught up, he'd come up to the store and take that quart of milk from the cooler and he'd sit out there in that cool breeze and he'd drink that milk. And some night we'd be caught up, late in the season, they'd kill a bunch of chickens and carry them down there, and they'd roast those chickens in the coals from that boiler.

The fire was the main thing they had to worry about, the fire could get in the gins. I guess a spark or something would light that cotton. Cotton would be easily ignited, and if they got any fire in there, it was hard to put out. They had a power [water] pump there that could really get a lot of pressure, and they'd use that water pressure. They had a lot of fire hoses around there, and that's the way they put it out.

The cotton was graded after it was baled. At that time, it was the people that was managing the gin would buy the cotton—if they wanted to sell it, if they didn't want to take it home. I believe Akard would buy the cotton that was left there. He'd listen to the radio, somehow or another, and get the market for that day. I guess that gave him the prices he could pay for certain grades of cotton. My older brother always did that, I was just a hand. He'd just treat me like the other hands at the place.

### JEROME KEENER BLACKWELL

We made about five hundred gallons [of syrup at Brown's Creek] of which we sold most of it to the cotton pickers during cotton harvest. It proved to be one of our best money crops. Cotton and oats were also money crops but wasn't as sure as syrup. People could do without cotton in times of depression but had to eat.

The cane season brought joys and woes, as it was hard work stripping, cutting, loading, and then hauling it to Uncle Ted Brookshire's syrup mill. He wasn't really my uncle, everyone just called him uncle. At the mill we squeezed the juice and then ran the mill all night by light of kerosene lantern, and then by daytime he took over with his group of pretty girls and made the syrup all day. This was a joy to me, especially cutting out a spoon made of a cane joint and sipping the hot sweet syrup as it ran from the vat. There was an art in making molasses, and Uncle Ted had the art.

### ROBERT E. GAULT

Broomcorn is what you make brooms out of. It grows up there like cane or something, and that head is up there high, and when you pull it down you've got straw about this long on it with seeds on it. You pull that down [and head it], and you bundle and dry it, and then you take it and thrash the seeds off of it. My brother had thirty-five acres of that stuff one year. He had a Model T car, and he took the tube tire off the back wheel and put a tire with nails on there, and that's what he thrashed that broomcorn on—hold it up to that and that'd thrash the [seeds off]. And then he took it to market at Keene, Texas—that was the broomcorn capital of Texas.

I didn't help my brother then, I was too young. But I had a friend that come over one day and wanted me to help him pull broomcorn. I went over there and pulled broomcorn that day, and you pull that down and that old black soot was all over you, and it'd sting you. I went home and took a bath, and I really started stinging. I called him, I said, "You're a good friend of mine, but I haven't got a friend in the world I'd pull broomcorn for again."

### ANDY GORDON WOLF

Everybody raised cotton, that was all the money crop we had. But back in the thirties, wasn't too long into the thirties, until we started to raising broomcorn, because broomcorn was a better money crop. Then, you know, everybody had to have a broom.

We dealt in it, my dad dealt in it for years and years. I pulled many a head of broomcorn. It growed up like cane or something, it had a big head up there, and you'd grab a-hold of a shuck with one hand and the head in another and put it off. You'd put it in a pile and let it dry out, and then you'd bundle it, then you'd haul it to the thrasher, and you'd thrash it and bail it. The first thrashers we had, you'd take an old Model T wheel and put a tire on it and punch nails in there and start that old Model T engine and that thing running and knock all the seeds off the broomcorn.

We had a blind fellow, lived with us for years, that had a hand-operated broom factory. He made brooms all the time. He was a strong man, it was a shame he was blind. He stayed with us for years. He's staying with a sister-in-law, and my dad went by there and sold him some broomcorn—two or three bales or whatever he wanted. Bale'd weigh about 400 pounds, average. He told him one day, said, "Mr. Wolf, you ain't got no place I could go, would you?" Pa said, "I don't know, what's wrong?" He said, "Well, my sister-in-law's told me I was gonna have to get out." His brother was dead. And he lived with us for years, my dad brought him home and set his little old shop up in a shed, and he made brooms. That old blind man, you just couldn't think a fellow could do that, but he'd get up in the middle of the night and go out there and make brooms.

We never did make them [ourselves], but we bought and sold broomcorn, and we could haul it to Keene or wherever. Some of our neighbors down there would raise some, too, and my dad bought it from them and taken it off and sold it.

### JOHN DANIEL WOLF

My dad was a trader. My early years were my dad making a living off of my grandfather's place. He paid rent, but he didn't pay very much. We lived on what we had mostly, and got by all right. He got a few goats, he got a few sheep, and he had a few cattle. We had a payday coming in more than just one time a year, where you would if you were raising cotton.

He managed to purchase one of the Wolf farms in Wolf Valley from my grandfather, then he started raising broomcorn. Broomcorn is a sorghum, and the sorghum is kind of adapted to our part of the country, to an arid country. At that time no broomcorn was raised in this part of the country at all, it was raised south of San Antonio, in New Mexico, and in Oklahoma. Brooms were in use by everyone, they were an essential commodity. They made crude warehouse brooms that were pretty big to little delicate brooms for the woman to clean the house with, and there was a different quality of broomcorn used in each one of those brooms. My dad got pretty well versed on that, and he got pretty well involved with the industry.

My dad started raising broomcorn, and he promoted broomcorn with the other farmers. Cotton was going out: it was a poor crop, so hard to raise, and the weevils took it over. He started when he bought the first place from my grandfather. It was difficult, he had to talk the banker into financing it, and the banker [said], "Well, what are you talking about? I never heard of it."

You want the long straw, so you come along and take the top leaf on the stalk, grab the head, and jerk it down, and when you do, it breaks off at the first stem. Then you lay it on the stalks [in the field] to dry for four or five days, then you come along and bundle it, then you put it under a shed, and then you seeded it. The first time we started seeding that stuff, we took an old car and jacked up the back wheel and drove nails through a tire. Stuck [the seed heads] down there under that wheel while it was running and it'd knock the seeds off. Then we bundled it, and my dad would take his little old truck full of bundled broomcorn and would sell it to the factory in the bundles, just like oats or something bundled. There was a man in Sealy, a little factory in Evant, and a little factory in Abilene. The one he sold more to than anywhere was the Seventh Day Adventist school at Keene, Texas.

Some family members [raised broomcorn], and a few others in the community started raising it also. My dad was able to take a small truckload and make twice as much as you could on a bale of cotton. Dad lived and breathed trading, he was a trader. He just finished the third grade, but he was just about as astute a mathematician as I ever knew. When you gave him a group of figures, he listed them in his head. He couldn't give you the exact answer, but he'd tell you whether you were wrong or not. I don't know exactly how that works. A guy had a calculator when he sold three

carloads of broomcorn and took them down to Mexico. That guy was sitting there with a calculator doing all these figures, and when he got through,
my dad said, "You're wrong." It took them till nine o'clock the next morning to find his mistake. He had a mistake all the time, and it was in his
favor.

## Cash-Crop Livestock

*Many area farmers owned properties large enough to range some beef cattle,
selling off a few cows and calves every year. Families on the brushy uplands might try to grow cotton in improbable places, but by about 1915
many also ran sheep for their wool and goats for their mohair, linking
themselves to the sheep and goat economy of the Edwards Plateau to the
west rather than the cotton economy of the eastern blacklands. Little of
the nineteenth-century romance tradition of cattle ranching extended to
the sheep and goat business, but money was money.*

### T. A. WILHITE

[Around Sparta], mostly they had all the farming land fenced. They didn't
have the pastures fenced, 'cause they just turned their stuff out together.
Back in those days, we didn't mark and brand them. Everybody knowed his
own cattle, and he didn't fool with yours.

### WILLIAM AKE POWELL

Most people had their land fenced because when you raise cotton and corn,
you can't afford to put livestock in it. But there used to be several hundred
acres [near Friendship] that I really think at that time belonged to the state
or somebody—open land. It didn't have any fences, and there's several people
that let their cows and stuff run on it. It was a big place. I don't know how
many acres it was, but it was a bunch. I used to have to walk and hunt our
milk cows after I got out of school, sometimes, and they might be three
miles from the house. Just have to go get them and drive them home.

### ROBERT E. GAULT

Dad started out with Red Poll cattle, and we still had enough Red Poll in
them to still milk good. We had some that were pure Hereford. We kept a
Hereford bull, registered bull, for the last fifteen years we were [on Cowhouse
Creek]. We had good, big-boned stock, we didn't have no scrub stuff at all.
He wouldn't have a Jersey on the place, 'cause he said they ruined your

stock line, and you just can't use that kind of stock when you're raising for beef, and that's what he sold his for. He sold yearlings every year.

### JAMES W. YANCY

When my grandfather, J. R. Yancy, was first there [six miles out from Killeen], they had to put in a lot of the farmland, and they used these moldboard plows that you walked behind. They used mules to pull all the farming equipment. Horses were used for working livestock and pulling buggies. They would never be used for plowing because it would make them stiff, and they used them to round up the cattle. They wanted agile horses that wouldn't fall with them and would carry them from sunup to sundown.

At one time I think they grew some cotton. During my lifetime they grew oats for grazing for their sheep and cattle in the winter and hay for feeding their livestock. When [my grandfather] purchased some of the land, some of the sheep came with it, and his sons had to shear those sheep by hand. They used the hand shearers, it was a backbreaking situation. When the sheep got to be very valuable at one time in history, the sons talked Grandpa into selling all of his sheep. I think they concentrated more on cattle after that. They were very happy when he got out of the sheep and cotton business. They didn't like to pick cotton, either.

When they'd get ready to sell their cattle, they would usually let the buyers know. They rounded up the cattle, they put the cattle in different corrals, then the buyers would come out and bid on them. However, on occasion, we'd have to drive them to the nearest railhead, and I can remember as a very young boy I went on one cattle drive to Copperas Cove. It was a shorter distance form the western part of the ranch to Copperas Cove than to Killeen. I was very very small, they didn't want me to go because it was an all-day affair. They said I was too young and I couldn't handle it. I had my little horse! So, anyway, after crying and carrying on, Dad said, "Okay, come on." I made it to Copperas Cove, but coming home that night in the dark, I pooped out, and Daddy put me on the front of his saddle and led my horse home. I got a silver dollar for that trip.

### ROBERT E. GAULT

[Pulling broomcorn] and sheep shearing was the worst thing I ever got in. I had a neighbor that had sheep, and he wanted me to sack wool for him at shearing. And I sacked wool, boy, I mean I sacked it. Them old sacks they have them on a rack, great big old sacks, you put that wool in there and stomp it down. And I sacked there and went in to eat dinner, and everything in there tasted like them sheep smelled! That job, one day is all I did that, too. I never saw anything like that stuff.

### JOE D. INSALL

I've seen people moving sheep. They would come down the road, just be full of sheep from fence to fence, and there'd be a driver between so many sheep. And if we heard that they lost one, and you found it, they'd give you some money for it. We was hoping one would get loose. Another way we made money, when a sheep would die, you could go pick up the wool and sell it. They called it "dead wool."

### NORRIS SIDNEY GRAVES

This dog was sleeping with me in the bunkhouse, his name was Boots. He was a sheep dog. I took him to this uncle, Uncle Lillard, and he poisoned Central Texas, this dog sired so many pups. We had pups all over, I never seen so many dogs that looked like Boots. And until Uncle Lillard died, he had one of the pups. Uncle Lillard's place was outside of Gatesville about six miles on the Levita road. We'd go out there, and Uncle Lillard [would] say, "Well, I guess I better get the sheep in today." I'd say, "I'll go with you," but he'd say, "Just a minute." He'd stand on the porch and get Boots to get them—bring them right in the pen. I said, "Uncle Lillard, we've got to go shut the gate." He said, "No, Boots can handle them." He'd stand right in the middle of the gate and keep the sheep in the pen.

### ERNEST ALLEN COLE

My Uncle Charlie had quite a few cows [at Okay]. He rented part of Grandpa's mountain up there and had cattle and goats. And these doggoned old buzzards, when the kids was born, buzzards would come down and peck their eyes out and the kids would die. So my Uncle Charlie, he made a deal down at Morgan Bell's store that I could buy .22 shells, and he'd charge it to his account. I'd go up in the cove of this mountain, and I'd set there at the spring, and these buzzards would come over real slow and go down to get a drink of water, and I was supposed to shoot them. I pretty much wiped the buzzards out. It stopped them from eating the kids, but it was fun.

People came around to shear goats every ear. They were usually Spanish, Mexicans, and they had an old truck. There was usually four to six of them, and they had a shaft run by an old gasoline engine, and they'd shear six goats at a time. Uncle Charlie had 500 or 600 goats, so it took a little while. It was quite an occasion, because you carried food up there, and when one of these Mexicans [finished shearing a goat], you gave him a token, and at the end of the day they got so much for each token. Seems like it was a dime, if I'm not mistaken. They had a frame with a towsack, and they rolled the mohair in a ball and stuffed it in there.

Took it to Lampasas, sold it. Uncle Charlie had an old truck with a flatbed on it and put stakes on it and everything. We'd load all this mohair up there and take it to Lampasas. I never did like Lampasas much, because they had a sulfur spring up there and it stunk like heck.

### ANDY GORDON WOLF

We had 1,200 head of goats one time [at Silver City]. I mean, there was goats everywhere, and goats were worth fifty cents—wasn't worth nothing, hardly. That's the reason we had the barbecues. We had an old black dog, called him Old Tade, and Old Tade would catch one of them goats and never pull a hide on him or anything, just hold him until you could get a-hold of him. My dad bought 1,200 goats because somebody just couldn't afford to keep them anymore. They'd keep goats until they cleared off the land, that's what they bought them for. And they'd shear them for mohair. You never did hear of anybody having slick goats back then.

They run on a mountain pasture, that's the reason we never did get them all out of there. We had to shear them a little early one year, 'cause you had to start early and we had people to shear them, charge so much a head for shearing. They sheared them a little bit early, and it come a cold rain, and it killed three hundred of them. They piled up in caves back in the mountain.

Well, we lived up there, and 'course we didn't have no fences or nothing and had all these goats. There was a peddler come through one time, and he come up to our house. Well, it didn't make no difference if he was a peddler or what you was, everybody's glad to see you, 'cause they might go two, three months without seeing anybody. So he come up, and he had a brand new Model A automobile, a roadster or coupe, had a rumble seat in it. He was setting there trying to sell whatever he's selling, and these goats was a-jumping on his new car. It had a cloth top on it, and they'd jump up on the top and slide down that thing where his rumble seat was. And, man, I'm telling you, in a minute that fellow seen that, and he got up and left. He didn't sell anything or try to sell anything. They take all the paint off, I'll bet they's fifty goats, and they was a-running and a-jumping on that thing. Goats like high places.

### CLEMENTS W. "SPEEDY" DUNCAN

My old uncle up there, I guess he got pretty well wealthy for just a common fellow. He was the first individual that ever bought an Angora goat in a wide area around there. People would come hundreds of miles to see them damn Angora goats. They was pretty, and ringlets, their hair white, dragged the ground. At that time that hill was brush, it was just brush. You couldn't farm nothing on that hill. There was lots of money in the mohair of goats way back yonder. I forget what mohair was bringing, but he had a herd of goats. It seems like he averaged about three dollars a head off of them, which was a lot of money.

They was lots of trouble. They'd go by an old green briar, which is plentiful in this area, hang that wool in there and try to get loose. It'll go around and around and around, and if you don't go there on horseback, and looking, they killed many a goat. You've got to get down and cut that briar loose.

I didn't mind doctoring goats, because a goat wants to live. But a damn sheep, they're born trying to die and they don't ever quit. Like that little slope out there, don't look very steep, that old sheep will lay down out there and get his feet uphill, even a young one, a healthy one, they'll die. They get their feet uphill, they don't have sense to roll over or get up. It don't take much of a hill, a little slope and a sheep will lay down there and he'll die.

Sheep had wool worms in their back. Their bowels would move, and they'd get wool worms in their kidneys, the old ewes. A wool worm is a nasty doctoring. It's a different worm to a [screwfly] maggot. Instead of a screwworm, it's a wool worm. Whew!

And then you have the grubs. Them heel flies create a grub. They get them in the heels but the grub comes out from the middle of their backs. And when the grub pops out, the blowflies would get in it and then you'd have screwworms. They'd get in every little thing in the world.

Then, in the hair goats, my old uncle that lived up the road had hundreds and hundreds of them Angora goats. They shear them, and they had to be careful. If it come a cold spell, they could freeze to death. You'd have to put them in the shed and build a fire and keep them from piling up and smothering themselves to death. After you turn them out and let them go back up on that mountain up there, all around that mountain there was caves and crevices. Them goats will go in a dark place, and you can ride up there on a horse on top and walk down and catch them in under there and doctor them. They nick them shearing them. Nick their hide, just a little nick, and then they'll get full of worms.

[In a cold snap, after shearing], if you have a big old wood stove with a pen around it where they can't get to it, build a big fire, and put what heat you can in that old barn. But you'd have to be at least three men stay in there all night and keep [the goats] stirred, just walking around through them, because they'll normally get in a corner, and they'll just keep jumping on each other, jumping up and piling up in a corner. If you ain't got three men there to jerk them back off, they'll kill a bunch of them.

They'll just pile up anywhere. They will pile up not in a corner, just anywhere, just start piling up. It takes three men to run grab them by the horns and jerk them off. And you grab an old goat by the horn and jerk him back out there, and the damn scamp will jump right back on there if you don't watch him. You have to work fast and hard, you have to circulate all the time to keep them from piling.

I worked for my old uncle for several years when he needed me. You came by his house up there, there's an old tin building, a big old barn, where we put them goats when we sheared them and it turned cold. We'd put the wool rack [where] one side touched the roof and the other side was tight to get in. Three people shearing, I'd tie the wool and throw it up on this rack and run up those steps and throw it down on that sack. The sun shining on that sheet on that wool sack, that was some hot job. I had one small cousin, and I'd have to catch the sheep, we're shearing the sheep that day, I'd have to catch them big old sheep, when we got down to big ones, and tie them for him. Then I'd tie the wool for the other two shearers and throw them up there and get up there and tromp it. You tie it up with twine string, then throw it up in the wool sack, and then you have to run up there and tromp it every half-dozen fleeces you'd throw in the big sack. You'd have to tromp it pretty hard. My sweet old uncle, bless him, he'd come down there and poke it with his thumb, said, "Clements, you've got to stomp them a little tighter." Trying to save wool sacks, and those old sacks cost eighteen cents or something!

Some of them had eight drops, they called them "eight-drop rigs," where you have eight shearers. A lot of boys made a living. They had an eight-drop machine, and they'd get done with a local area, everybody's sheep, they'd load up their clothes and head west. There's more sheep west in them days. They'd go out here to San Saba on west, large sheep ranches. They pulled in one place and sheared sheep for two weeks, same damn lot. They'd just shear and shear, eight drops running. An excellent sheep shearer, very few of them, could knock out a hundred of head [a day]. That was the only big money there was, being a sheep shearer.

I sheared one sheep on my own. I had a few sheep when I was a boy, and this one was a special sheep, a fine ewe, I'd raised her. I didn't want her nicked. My cousin was running a rig, and I asked if he minded if I sheared that sheep. I said that I'd rather not have it cut. "Yeah," he said, "you can shear it," and he handed me the clippers. I thought those clippers had hung on a little burr or something, and I pushed a little harder, and it went up about that far in that sheep's belly! He reached over and jerked my hand back. He says, "I'll finish shearing her for you, you've killed that sheep." I killed the best sheep I ever owned. I sheared goats a few times, but I never did shear another sheep. I stayed clear of those.

Goddam, I never have forgotten it! Some shearers were worse than others, but I never did know a shearer that didn't nick them. You couldn't help it. Well, that thing is almost like a razor, and if it hits the hide, it just cuts it the same as it does wool. It cuts anything you stick it up against. This is gasoline motor, this is before electricity. Belts, belts run it—it ran off of belts and gears.

And dogs, I killed so many. I love dogs and I hate to kill them, but when you see a little old kid goat running around and their mama is dead, it don't bother you much then to kill dogs. When I started out, I'd see dogs and go find the owners and tell them. Later on, I'd kill a dog and go tell the owners. And then I got a little smarter—I just killed the dogs.

I ran goat here for years, Spanish goats, and they put me out of business. People would say, "Wolves! Wolves! Wolves!" Wolves don't bother you at all. I'll admit the wolf is going to kill a few, the wolf will kill to eat. But a dog will kill for pleasure and never quit. They catch them off over here in the back of my pasture, and the dog will finally give out, but they'll lay down and rest fifteen minutes, and then they'll get up and start killing them again. They're just killing them for killing them, that's the difference. They bite the hind leg, the flank first, and then they just chew them all over, they cut their throats, they kill them dead.

My uncle up here had a big old red dog, and he'd work for me just like me and him were buddies. I could use him to put goats in the lot, I could take him in the pasture roundup and wave at him, and he'd just work his heinie off for me.

Any kind of animals—cows or sheep or goats—you could work him all day, maybe you're rounding up worming sheep or going to shear them and mark the lambs, and whatever. That dog, he'd been at it all his life, and he's getting some age on him.

I was working for my uncle, and I'd get there and milk his cows before sunup. I was carrying milk to the house, and there wasn't much traffic, and come a car on the public road. I carried the milk to my aunt and went out to see. Something was going on for a man to stop there in a car. He was talking to my uncle, says, "Mr. Duncan, your dog was over there killing sheep— my sheep." Uncle Dave had on his pants, but that's all he had on. He was barefooted. "Well," he says, "surely it's one that looks like him. It ain't my dog. This old dog is probably ten years old, and he lays right here on the front porch. We use him every few days working sheep or goats, cows, or something. He's a good old dog." Says, "He won't bother the sheep. I've got hundreds of them down here! Surely you've got the wrong dog."

"Well," the fellow says, "I've just to tell you, Mr. Duncan, if he comes back I'm going to kill him." My old uncle says, "Sure, sure, kill him. But it ain't gonna be my dog."

He thought a lot of that old dog, it was a valuable old dog. That man lived south of Killeen, I guess about ten miles, and ever place between here and there had sheep on it.

I guess it had been a few days, and early one morning the sun was just coming up and I'd done milked their cows for them. I was going to the house with the milk and here he come, and Old Red was laying up across the hood of his car, big old red dog. He said, "Well, Mr. Duncan, I thought I'd bring your dog home to you. You want to call your dog?"

Uncle Dave still didn't have on his boots, still just in his pants. I remember that because he got real rolicky. Uncle Dave walked out and looked at him, and he said, "Yeah, that sure looks like my old dog." He asked the man again where he lived, and it was south of Killeen. Uncle Dave said, "Surely my dog wouldn't go that far to kill your sheep, when every pasture he's across had sheep in it."

But there was Old Red. My old uncle reached in his pocket, "How many sheep did they kill?" The fellow says, "Well, they killed so many, but there's a half a dozen dogs in the bunch." Uncle Dave says, "That don't matter, one of them was my dog! I'll pay you."

He went to counting out some money, and the fellow backed up and said, "No, no, no!" But my Uncle Dave was barefooted but he moved pretty quick, pointed his finger at him, said, "I want to know how many goddam sheep this dog killed! You're going to take the money or I'll whip hell out of you!"

He made the man take the money. He was going to fight him if he didn't take it. I guess he was mad because he had lost his dog, and he had lost sheep for years and knew how it was.

## Minor Money Crops

*More so than on the fertile blacklands farther east, local farmers hedged their bets on sheep, goats, cattle, and cotton with minor field crops and farm products. They were "diversified" out of necessity, because of poor soils and insufficient rainfall rather than the admonitions of county agents. They raised alternative crops on the side. They cut mountain juniper for posts on the uplands, picked up pecans in the creek bottoms, and gingerly hunted for rattlesnake bounty money on the rocky hillsides. Some people made whiskey—probably rather more frequently than is suggested in these accounts.*

### WILLIAM AKE POWELL

Both of my grandpas used to keep a few turkeys, that was kind of a money crop. The old turkeys, you didn't have to feed them a lot. They eat grasshoppers, acorns, grass feed, and stuff that fell in the field where you harvested. They kind of hustled for theirself. You had to follow them and find the nests and gather the eggs and do all this sort of stuff, but when you sold them you didn't have anything much but labor in the turkey raising, and they brought pretty good money. Used to sell them along about Thanksgiving, and a lot of people would get their Christmas money that way.

### ANDY GORDON WOLF

We had turkeys, everybody raised turkeys. That was another of our money crops. They run off grasshoppers and stuff they could catch in the summertime, and I've herded them many times. Ain't nothing as crazy as a damn turkey, I imagine I killed one or two chunking rocks at them. But you just take a flock of turkeys, might be 200 or more, and graze over an area. When I was a kid, I'd have to stay with them, grasshoppers or whatever they can find, just keep them moving. If you didn't [stay with them], they're liable to go plumb out of the country. And you had to go bring them in at night, so they'd roost in the same place all time and you'd stay up with them.

Ike Bay was a couple of miles across the valley from where we lived, and his turkeys roosted on our cow lot. Didn't think nothing about it, but it'd make you mad sometimes when you set down up there on the rail fence in a pile of that turkey dookey.

Fed them corn—not regular, but sometimes you'd feed them when they's a-growing to fatten them out. Fattened everything out. In the fall you'd gather them up and [sell them]. They had a turkey buyer that'd come around and buy them. Sometimes they didn't bring very much, but you take a couple of hundred of them, and if you got a dollar apiece, that two hundred dollars was a hell of a lot of money back then. They always had a market in town for them, too, but it wasn't hardly worthwhile to load a bunch of turkeys on a wagon and haul them to town. Had buyers that'd go around.

### ROBERT E. GAULT

We raised turkeys all the time [at Cowhouse Creek]. We used to keep thirty, forty turkeys, and they brought good money. They'd go out and eat grasshoppers and everything out in the pasture. They'd eat anything just about, and they were good survivors. Turkeys were easy that way, but you had to watch them to keep from losing them. Fox and things prey on them real bad. I'd have to get out and follow an old hen. You'd know they're laying somewhere, but they'd hide out. You really had to be on your toes to check those things. If you didn't get those eggs, foxes and things would eat them, you see. And we'd bring them in and set them. But they would really give you fits, they were smart old things. You'd follow an old hen, and she'd go in an old pile or brush or something. You go around there directly, and she's gone, she went out the other side. When I got big enough, they let me ride a horse and watch them. But I used to have to follow them around by foot, and there're lots of rattlesnakes in that country. I never did get snakebit. I had an old dog that stayed with me, and he'd circle all the time. He killed several rattlesnakes.

### ERNEST ALLEN COLE

My mother always had this bunch of turkeys [at Okay], that was one of her cash crops. Somehow or another, she got hold of an old turkey hen, half wild turkey, she was a little different than these great big old bronze-breasted turkeys raised. Mother says, "That old hen's got a nest. You catch her and put her in a pen." So I caught her, put her in a pen up on top of the hill, and about ten o'clock Mother said, "Let's turn her loose and watch her." So she took off the edge of the hill and flew plum across there on the road, and I saw her go into a grove of oak trees. So we took off down there, it was probably half a mile, and even before I got into this bunch of trees I could hear this old turkey hen raising Cain. I got up there, and there was a chicken snake in the nest, and that chicken snake had swallowed about six or seven eggs, and you could see lumps, lumps, lumps, like that. I shot the snake, shot his head off, took my knife, cut the snake open, got these eggs out, took them home, Mother set them, and they hatched. See, when a snake swallowed eggs, they had to wrap themselves around a tree to crush them before they could digest them. He hadn't had a chance to do that yet. Now, a lot of people won't believe that, but that's the truth.

### JEROME KEENER BLACKWELL

Turkeys were one of our money crops. We children were assigned certain ones to watch in order to locate their nest in the wild. Turkeys weren't raised cooped up in lots as today but were allowed to roam the countryside to choose their own liking for a nest. We would then mark it and go daily to gather their eggs, for if we failed to do so, the snakes, armadillos, skunks, and other varmints would get them. Turkeys always stay in the herd until ready to nest, then they single off on their own and "find a nest," as it was referred to. This sort of a chore was time consuming but a must if you expected to raise turkeys for harvest. This often led us to cross neighboring fences, and this was understood and expected by all our neighbors.

Once the laying season ended, the hens would begin to set, and you put her on a nest of eggs in a shelter near the house, and she would hatch the little ones. After their baby stage of eating curds and hard-boiled eggs, it became necessary to have someone to watch them all day long so as not to meet with harm from predators and stray dogs. As they got larger, the mother hens and old gobbler would range them miles away, and all you had to do was keep them in sight. They fed mostly on grasshoppers, lizards, small snakes, and snails, but of course you continued to reward them at the end of a day's range with shelled corn, maize, and clabber milk in a trough.

Come November 1, the turkey season would open with a market of published prices, and all the countryside would bring their turkeys in for grading and weighing. There was stiff competition between buyers, and they would court your business each year prior to the market opening, asking the privilege of buying your flock or "herd," as we referred to them. They would bring from fifteen cents a pound to an occasional thirty cents a pound, and this was cash money, which was a welcomed reward for many long, weary hours work.

### MARGARET HUNT CARROLL

When you had your crop in the ground for the season, then you went off [and chopped cedar]. This was a cash crop, cedar posts was, 'cause you'd take them right to the grocery store and swap them for whatever you needed. And if you had some left over, you got a little money to come home, or you just bought candy for the kids. You had to [chop cedar] every day or two to keep groceries going that you had to buy, like sugar and flour, that you couldn't raise in the garden. That's what you had to do.

When [Daddy] was a young guy, he would chop the cedar and the wood, he'd hire out to clear places. He could clear the land and chop a cord of wood in a day. My grandpa, that was just a little fellow, he could chop a cord of wood when he was an old man. He didn't know how old he was, he didn't know when his birthday was.

Daddy chopped cedar posts, and I short-hauled, taking the wagon and team in and getting it out of the brush, and bringing it out to the road where the buyers could get it. He'd chop them and I'd haul them. See, there's "twos"—six-and-a-half-foot straight post, trimmed, and at the top you can put your hand around it and do this, that's the way you'd measure. Everybody had probably a different measure, but that was his. He'd slap his hand up there, seeing what it was, and each one was a different price. "Twos," "threes," "fours," they were a different price. Then you went into "blocking," it was big stuff—corner posts and brace posts. They were lots more money, but there weren't so many of them, most of it was heart cedar. See, some big trees, you'd get that [corner] post out of that [central trunk], and the limbs that had grown out would make other sizes. So out of one tree you might get a lot of posts, and then some trees would just be one post. It depends on what you're finding.

And nobody touched [Daddy's] ax! He could shave his arm, that's how sharp it was. Somebody said, "You know how to chop cedar posts?" "No sir!" None of us kids touched that ax, we didn't touch that ax, that was as valuable as his razor. If they'd drop it on a foot, it would cut it off, because as sharp as it was, it was dangerous. And if you chip that ax, because it was so sheer, just exactly right, if you knocked a hunk out of it, it might take you hours to get it back down again. I didn't sharpen the ax, I turned [grind] stone while he held it at the right angles to get it down, and it took hours. No, you bet I didn't bother that ax.

#### WILLIAM AKE POWELL

I've cut a lot of them cedar posts. You had to get them out to the road, and they had a guy that'd come by and pick them up and buy them from you. I cut them old posts, I cut them big ones—four-inch tops and six-foot long, big posts. Man, they was heavy! Have to carry and drag them out to the road, it might be a pretty good ways before you found that kind. You had to trim all the limbs off of them, it had to be just right. But this guy would come along, he'd give you a nickel apiece for them. That's what you used to get for them, nickel apiece.

We'd do a little side work. Used to cut wood, sometimes, and sell it. My daddy was real tickled with his ax, he didn't want nobody else using his ax. He's gone one time, and somebody [offered] me a dollar or two a cord for wood of a certain kind. So I took his ax, and I went to cut wood. I think I got about two dollars for it and took about two days to cut it, and I ruined his ax. I hit a couple of rocks with it. The ax cost four or five dollars, so I didn't make no money on that deal. He didn't want nobody messing with his razor and his ax, the two things.

### T. A. WILHITE

Some fellow would have a big place, you know, and he'd let somebody come in and cut cedar on the halves. It's just like a bank, a cedar brake was.

There was one fellow, he went up on the Sparta mountains up there. I think he got the posts from a fellow that had a lot of them. Him and his little boy went up there, and they come back, and they's going down this mountain, and it's a long way down and real steep, and the brake broke on the wagon, and oh, he went on down. The mules couldn't even start to hold it. And it throwed him off down there, made a turn, and most of this big load of posts fell on that little boy. It just mashed him flat. Boy, it liked to killed everybody in that country.

### JOHN DANIEL WOLF

How did we get the staples [at Silver City]? I think we were lucky to the extent that the whole country down there is covered in cedars. I remember very well my dad would take two or three days and cut a wagonload of cedar posts, and he would take those to the store down there, and he'd sell them. He'd do enough for a forty-eight-pound sack of flour and for some sugar, salt, and other things my mother needed to cook with—the very, very bare essentials. If he didn't, he'd go back to get a second load. The best posts maybe would bring two, two and a half cents. You could get up to five cents sometimes for a good corner post, one of those six to eight inch at the top. Cedar posts were used by everybody. That's how we got some of the essentials during the worst time of the Depression.

### CLEMENTS W. "SPEEDY" DUNCAN

Me and my pa chopped wood several winters—Spanish oak wood and hauled it in poles, long poles, on a wagon to the house and piled it off. And in a pretty day we'd stay out in the open, not too much wind, and chop that off in stovewood lengths.

Pa was a hell of an ax man. He'd chop it off with a big old ax and pitch it over there to me. And I'd take my ax, and that stuff splits like glass. When it's cold, you can just lightly hit and split it. You'd split it and split twice more and make little sticks and throw it in a pile. I wish that somebody had made a picture of that woodpile. It was as big as my whole house. That was the awfullest pile of wood I've ever saw! We worked on it all winter.

We cut wood every winter for five winters. My daddy seldom went to town, but he went over to town, and a lot of farmers over on the prairie heated with wood, but they didn't have no timber. So he talked to them, said, "Y'all need some stovewood, I've got a pile. Bring your trailer."

My mother was crippled, but she walked on a walking stick, and Dad and I could be plowing or cutting more wood or whatever, somebody would come after wood. Well, Mother would hobble out to the gate, "It's five dollars a pile, take any pile you want." They'd back up to a pile—it was a cord—and load it up and leave. And we made money that year.

Pa was so stout, he'd just do it, just do it with brute strength. He taught me a little. We was chopping wood, and lots of timber and groves or thickets. And Pa would walk up there and look one over. He was going to cut them all right, but he wanted to see which one he wanted to cut down first. He would eyeball them for a little bit, and usually smoke him a cigarette, walk around and look at them. Next thing he'd rare back with that ax, and an old tree that big around, normally three licks. He'd hit one lick at an angle, and he'd hit one under, and the chips would fly off out there, whistling like a bullet. And he'd whop it over on the other side and that tree usually fell.

He'd cut that tree down in three licks, a pretty good-size tree, and he'd cut down twenty or thirty trees, whatever was in a little old clump of trees, cut them all down. They'd be just a circle of trees there, the tops still on them. He'd usually stop and roll him another cigarette by hand, smoke his cigarette, and look it over, walk around, and directly he'd walk in there with his ax. He'd cut off maybe two pretty good-size limbs and then cut the tree in two at the lower end with one stroke. He could slay that thing! He could cut it.

I learned a little, because one time he told me, "Whoa!" And I stopped, and he said, "Son, there ain't no use in killing yourself. Take your time, look at that, where you want to get. Look at it! Think about it." Says, "When you draw the ax back, hit there. Hit where you want to! Look where you want to hit and hit there!" He got a little perturbed with me for chopping around too much. He didn't want me wasting those strokes. I didn't pick it all up, but I guess probably today I'm better with an ax than anybody I know, because don't nobody know anything about an ax anymore. I can still hit with an ax, I know how. He taught me, "waste no effort."

Oakalla was a thriving community in 1900. This gentleman rode in there on a fine horse and some shiny shoes and nice dress clothes and stepped off his horse and inquired for anybody wanting wood cut. Everybody kind of snickered and laughed because he had on them damn shiny slippers and dress clothes and just horseback and had a roll behind the saddle, going through the country. "What does he want a job cutting wood for? He can't cut wood!"

But somebody hired him between there and Briggs, somewhere out on one of them hills. He found out the way to his house, saddled his horse, and rode out there. He cut him ten cords of wood, or a large amount of wood for one individual. The next day Pa got word about that man chopping wood. So he got on his horse and rode several miles over there and stopped and walked up, asked the fellow if he minded him watching him for a little while. He said, "No, it don't bother me, watch me as long as you want to." He still had on them shiny shoes and dress clothes. My daddy was telling me about it, said, "I sat, I watched him for hours, just watched that man." Says, "He was so careful not to skin them damn shoes. He'd step here and step there and move a twig he didn't want, but when he got set, it was amazing to watch him. He was a great hand with an ax." Pa says he was the best he ever seen, so he must have been damn good, because everybody used axes back in 1900.

Pa always told me about that old boy, says, "I learned a little from him, watching him. Said, "He didn't make no miss-licks." He could chop three cords in a day, an ungodly amount of wood that he could chop and cord just by hisself. Then he got his money and saddled his horse and rode on off. Nobody never knew where he came from or where he went to. He made his living cutting wood.

### ROBERT E. GAULT

We sold lots of pecans, we had 400 grafted trees. Sold them in stores by the pound, and we had some native trees that you'd get 500 or 600 pounds off of a tree. Great big old trees down at the edge of the field, and they were about halfway between the size of a normal native pecan and a papershell. They were pretty hard-shelled, but everybody wanted those things because they had the better flavor. My brother Frank was a tree climber, and he did pecans for everybody in the country down there—thrashed them for a percentage. He did that every year, and he sold them his percentage, and that was his wages. Frank would take an old cane pole and thrash them, get up in that tree and thrash them, he's the only one that had the nerve to do it. I've picked up for him lots of times.

### T. A. WILHITE

Oh yeah, gosh dang, they made whiskey behind every bush. Web Doss made a barrel of wine every year, and he had his bed sitting right across here, and his barrel over in a corner. And he had a tube that come over and come into his bed, and he'd wake up in the night and want him a drink of wine, he'd just undo the clothespin and suck him up a drink of wine.

He had a water washtub, and he always, it come a black cloud, there's a cement bridge right there in front of his house, he'd take this washtub and go get in under that bridge. And it come a bigger rain than it'd ever come and washed him out, washed him into a big hole of water right below and liked to drowned him. So, next day, he was digging back in the bank up there back of his house and made a hole dug in there to get in. He's afraid of them clouds.

I never did go around them a-making the whiskey, about all I know about it is they'd bring the whiskey out and sell it—there at my place, a big old rock right above the road down there. They'd always bring that whiskey out from over on Bear Creek and put it behind that rock. And then sell it and go back there and get it, you know. I was watching them when they put it there, and sometimes I'd go down there and take it all out, and there wouldn't be none there when they come back.

That was over in the Cowhouse valley, and they made it over on Bear Creek. There's a mountain between them. Bear Creek was rough. The sheriff couldn't hardly get over there to look. They could bring it out if they want to sell it. They always did kind of get by with a lot of stuff nobody else could. Marlis Drake made it up there, and I know old Joe Drake, he made some, he drank through so much of it. Up there on this bluff, you'd walk around that bluff on a narrow place and get around there, and there's bees had their nest down there. He was gonna go down there and rob that bee gum, and he got started around, and he's too drunk to get there, and he fell off and fell in an old thick tree, and it saved him.

That's what they made over there. Bear Creek was over the hill and down in a rough canyon, and they'd make that whiskey down there and bring it out and put it over behind that big rock and sell it. It wasn't no trouble. If there's a dance up in Sparta, why, hell, they'd run back down there and get that whiskey out of there right quick. I found out what they's doing. They knew if they got it there that the law would never fool with it because they didn't think I'd be a-making it.

I never did like whiskey. I know old Ben Owens got to where they made it, and he come along there one evening, and he sold my brother that's dead, he sold him a quart of whiskey. He bought it, and he carried it out to the seed bin and buried it in cottonseed. And so, that night, old Ira he got out there and got it and got a pretty drop. And he, I don't know, he was around on his hands and knees.

He'd been out plowing all day, and he didn't eat no dinner, and, boy, that knocked him for a loop. That night, Ira, he come in, and he's pretty well full of it. There was one of these rooms had a dropoff, 'bout that much, and he'd just go off that dropoff on his hands and knees. And she's just hollering, "Ira, Ira, Ira! What's the matter with you?" But I knew what was the matter with him. I laid in the bed with him, Frank Humphrey brought him in and put him in bed with me.

### ANDY GORDON WOLF

We killed rattlesnakes in the wintertime sometimes. You'd go in there and take a long stick and put a hook on the end of it, and you find a cave with rattlesnakes in it, and you pull them out and kill them with a rock. I remember one time I killed eighteen out of one hole and piled them all up, and it's a stack of rattlesnakes that high. They started to paying a bounty on them in Coryell County and Bell County, both. In Coryell County they paid a dime apiece, and Bell County paid fifteen cents. So if you killed twenty rattlesnakes in a day, you made two dollars. And two dollars was a whole lot of money then.

### CLARENCE "SPEEDY" DUNCAN

Aw hell, I still know every snake den on that hill, son! In the 1930s they paid two bits for rattlesnake rattles and a quarter inch of meat, a little meat on it. And you'd get four bits a day, if you could find a job, from daylight to dark, and it was usually hauling hay or sacking wool—strenuous work, needless to say, or they wouldn't hire you. I'd start out in the fall hunting snakes on that hill up there. Radar Hill zigzags around this way and that, and I know every cotton-picking snake den up there.

You wouldn't catch them every time you went. Maybe you'd go and get six or eight, or maybe you'd find a diggable den, one that you could work out with crowbars and jacks or something, and you might get a bunch out of that. Make good one day, and the next day you might not make a quarter. They might not be out. Them snakes, in the fall they bed up, but then come a warm day in February, they'll crawl out of them dens and get in the sun. They don't leave them, they just crawl out for that day, lay in the sun. If you know where the den is, you can get up there. The problem is that once you shoot one, they're gone. They go in the hole before you can bat your eyeball.

## Part-Time Cash Labor for Others

*An array of part-time farmer-specialists made extra money on the side. They included well diggers, chimney builders, blacksmiths, horse and mule "breakers," midwives, and syrup-mill and grist-mill operators, among others. Farmers with threshing or hay-baling rigs and the owners of the first generation of tractors often did "custom" work for their neighbors. But anyone big enough to hold a chopping hoe or drag a pick sack could find employment during the two crisis periods of the yearly round of cotton cultivation. Weeds in the rows had to be chopped out in the spring or they would "take the crop." Cotton open in the field had to be picked before late summer thunderstorms blew it to the ground.*

### WILLIAM AKE POWELL

My Grandaddy Powell, he was a well digger, he dug wells. He had a well machine. My daddy used to help him a lot when he was growing up. It had a big old heavy bit. It's run by a gasoline engine, and this engine had a deal on it that it'd go over this way and raise that thing up. Then it'd let it off, let it fall. They had some kind of a pipe or a hose down in there that run water in there, and they could pick that up and pump it out, the old white clay and stuff. He dug a-many a well. Sometimes people had to have one right away, and they'd just go dig. Sometimes you'd quit work on the farm in the middle of the day and then go late in the evening and work till after dark digging on a well. And if the weather wasn't permissible to work in the field, they could still dig them a well. I don't have any idea what he charged. I doubt that any money changed hands, sometimes. They'd trade work.

### ERNEST ALLEN COLE

My dad had his own blacksmith shop. He had a forge, they pumped air with a bellows like on a fireplace bellows, except that it was as large as this table. Had a pole you pulled up and down to keep it going. And his furnace was an old reaper wheel about four feet in diameter. He'd filled it with clay and the air came out the bottom. He was a pretty good blacksmith. He could always sharpen his plows, fix his wagons. The old wheels would get dry in the summertime, and the rims would come off. Every time you passed the creek, you drove through it, and it'd swell up and it wouldn't fall off. But he could straighten a rim and put it back on the wheel, and he could weld—not with a welding torch but heating it up and using a welding flux and bang on it and weld it. He'd go to town and get a sack of coal for the fuel. He didn't know it was anthracite, they just called it "hard coal."

### ANDY GORDON WOLF

We never did have a blacksmith, but Pa was a cowboy and he could buck-shoe a horse or a mule, and we had some old people around. My Uncle Jack, he would shoe a horse pretty good. Hell, when you think about putting the grease in a [wagon] hub or something like that, time you got somebody to do it, you'd have to ride a horse to get somebody to come back up there. You just nearly had to do it yourself. If you've hauled your stuff up there and a wheel got dry, you either had to soak it in water or pull it off and soak it overnight and then put it back on there. Everybody carried a can of axle grease, and you'd take the hub off and throw axle grease in there and grease them up. They had a way to handle everything.

And we had old man Bill Colvin over there. Old man Bill was as good a blacksmith as I ever seen. Up till he got too old, he was a dandy. He used to make these cowhorns. When you was hunting with fox hounds, you'd take a cowhorn, hollow it out, and make a blowing horn out of it. He used to come around from over the country, and he'd shoe horses or whatever there was to do to make a little money.

Finally, his people kicked him out 'cause he was so old and nasty. He lived by himself in a little old shack that he'd just throwed up down there. He's always telling these big windies. We was down there fooling with him one time, he said he was skating on the ice of the creek and the ice broke through. The reason he's telling that was 'cause he didn't have no shoes. He had a pair of old basketballs tied on his feet with a string. He said his feet froze and busted open and he couldn't wear shoes. But he didn't have no money to buy shoes, so he just made that story up. We was all down there, the Hubbard boys was kind of mean, they told him, "Bill, they just come up with a New Deal, they gonna kill all these old men over fifty years old." He said, he was real old, "By God, I ain't fifty, I'm just forty-nine."

### WILLIAM AKE POWELL

My Grandpa Dorsey had a blacksmith shop [at Friendship]. He had a bellows that you'd pump and blow the air to make the fire hot, and he had a big old anvil that had all kinds of tools that fit that anvil so you could heat stuff and cut it off and everything. He fixed horseshoes to fit, he had to make them fit the horses' and the mules' feet. He had all the things that you could bend those and make them just right. He'd heat them and put them on that anvil, and you could work them around anyway you wanted to, just about, when they's red hot. And he sharpened the plows, the sweeps for all the plows.

There's a lot of people come by there and got this stuff done. Bring those plow sweeps by and leave them to be sharpened, they'd come back and pick them up. And they'd bring their horses and mules over there to get the shoes put on. The thing there is the time that it took to take that stuff and get it done and bring it back. The transportation wasn't real good back in them days, and if you had to go to Gatesville to get it done, that was two days—a day to take it and come home and a day to go get it and come home. So you lost a lot of time that-away.

You had a wood handle come out where you could pump air, and it'd go up through the bottom and come up through the coals. Yeah, it's a big one, and I've pumped that thing a-many a lick, pumping that air up through there, blowing that coal where it'd get real hot and heat the plow points and horseshoes and all that stuff. If you was around, well, you got put to work.

### DORIS LEE WHITE THOMAS

My Uncle Burr White, Daddy's brother, after he got married he broke horses for a fee. He broke them to be a saddle horse, a plow horse, or to pull a wagon. His daughter has this little black book with the names. He has fifty-nine listed, whosever horse they belonged to, and had their name and how many they got from him. He kept a little black book with it all in there. That gives you the names of the people that lived in the [Spring Hill] area at that time.

### MARGARET BERT WILHITE BOUNDS

Daddy bought and sold cattle. After I got a little bit older and [Daddy] had a pickup and trailer, I would go with him. He'd want to get up at four o'clock in the morning, he was kind of early up and early to bed. I'd think, Oh Daddy, why can't we just sleep an hour or so longer? He would see people with maybe eight or ten cows, and he'd stop and see if they wanted to sell them. Lots of times he'd offer a price, and they wouldn't take it, but they'd pay him to haul it to the auction barn. He would offer so much for this cow and calf, or so much for this pair.

He'd buy mules—young mules when he'd buy them at a mule barn in Temple. He'd bring them home, he'd break them, and people would come there and want to see the mules. Sometimes he'd get the wagon and show them how they would work to the wagon. I remember him having several pair of red mules with white noses. He'd bring them home and they'd run away, scare me to death, him in the wagon and two of them running away with him. I'd just know that he's gonna fall out and they're gonna drag him to death. He would break them to work the wagon or to plow.

#### WILLIAM AKE POWELL

There used to be an old man down here on Henson Creek, he had a thresher, and he worked for everybody in the community. He lived out a little bit towards Ewing. He threshed this grain for anybody that wanted it. He'd plan his route. He'd go this a-way as far as he could and get it, then maybe he'd cut back and get all up this a-way. He'd go all the way around and get it all. He might stay two or three days at one farm, at one place.

We had an old team of mules, and he'd hire me, several of us, to run these bundle wagons to haul this stuff to the thresher. They used to give you two or three dollars a day for you and the team. They'd feed you at the cook shack. He had a couple of women that cooked, and they'd feed you a little breakfast and a big dinner and supper. This wagon, the sides raised up on it, and a deal made a table around it. And you'd sleep out on some kind of bunk deal that you hauled with you. You slept on the ground, bedroll of some sort. And if we was close to the creek somewhere, about dark we'd all gang up and walk to the creek and take a bath, go in swimming. I could make quite a little bit of money. That thing run two or three weeks, and at two or three dollars a day, that's a whole lot of money then. You could buy all your school clothes.

He had this big threshing machine, and it'd be set up in a field. And it's got a conveyor belt on it, and it'd take this stuff where it needs to go. And it goes through there and it gets all the grain off, and it goes through those shakers and it gets all the dirt and stuff out, and it blows the straw out somewhere in a pile.

This thing was stationary. We had a wagon with what they called a "pig-pen" on it, a built thing on the wagon that got bigger at the top. The oats was shocked, there was shocks in the field, and you go down through there, and you load it all, get your wagon full of it, and then you go up there and pull alongside this thresher. And you took your pitchfork and you took it off a bundle at a time and put it in there ever how often as that thing could take it, and unload it. When you'd be unloading that stuff, sometimes you'd reach down and get one of them bundles of oats and go to put it up there, and here comes a snake down that pitchfork handle, right on top of you. Then you had a guy that sacked the grain all up, sewed the tops [of the bags] over here where it come out, and it blowed the hay way up over here out through the pipe.

So that'd last maybe three, four weeks. He'd go all over the country and thresh everybody's grain. He took part of it, just like the grinding of the corn. He took part of the grain for it, and he paid us cash money.

**WILLIAM AKE POWELL**
My Grandpa Dorsey had a syrup mill. He was the one with the blacksmith shop and everything. People used to plant this syrup-type cane, and it'd get up pretty tall, like six, seven, eight foot tall. And they'd go into the field, and they'd take some kind of a stick or something, and they'd knock the leaves off of it. Then they'd cut the top off, and then cut the bottom, and they'd bring it stacked in a wagon by the syrup mill. They'd put it out by the syrup mill, they had a place, and everybody would take a place and put his cane there. And you would haul these people's cane over and run it through this syrup mill pulled by a mule that went around and around. The mill itself would squeeze the juice out of it and catch the juice—had a place it come out to catch the juice.

After the juice was out of it, they used to call that "pummins," and one of my jobs was to drag that off and pile it up away from the syrup mill. I used to feed the cane through there, sometimes. They had to fill that [cooking] pan with the juice—they'd carry it and put it in the pan where they'd cook the syrup. The pan had dividers in it where you could push it through with a paddle-like thing. It had to go through a long process going through that pan, cooking it. And while it was going through there, it'd be a-cooking. They'd be "skimmings"—some kind of green-like stuff that'd cook out of it—and they'd skim that out and dispose of it. Usually, my mother and daddy just about run all of it, and sometimes they'd be somebody else there. Me and my brother used to help. They made real good syrup there. Most of the time they took syrup for it, I don't remember [the cut they took]. I just remember eating lots of it. They used to use it for almost everything. I used to like them syrup pies. I don't know what was added to it, probably sugar and eggs.

### ANDY GORDON WOLF

We had a molasses mill [at Silver City], and everybody used the molasses mill. Everybody made their own molasses. Wasn't nothing to it, you just had to work together to get it done. We'd tie a mule on [the mill], and it just runs around and run. And you run a wagon up there, and then you got a fellow sits up there and pokes that cane through [that mill], and the juice runs out. Then you got a big pit over here like a big barbecue deal or something, and you put that juice in there and cook it off, and it turns out molasses.

Everybody in the country used it. My uncle and them, they had all them kids, one time they had fifty-five gallons of it, and they eat that molasses and butter and biscuits all winter. When I was a kid I'd get me a biscuit and punch a hole in it with my finger and pour some of that molasses in there. Taste pretty good. My mother would make molasses cake and molasses cookies and things.

### WILLIAM AKE POWELL

My Grandpa Dorsey, he had the hay baler, and he'd get some of his sons-in-law, and he'd just bale for whoever wanted it baled. His baler baled them small, square bales. Take this baler out there and set it up out in the middle of the field. They had a hay rake with the mules to it, and the person with the hay rake would go all over that field and rake that hay and drag it to that baler and dump it right there in front. And a guy would take a pitchfork and put it on the table there, and then another guy would take a fork and push it down in that hay baler. And a mule was going around and around, and this plunger would come back, and they'd put a block in front of it, and it'd push that hay out through that baler.

When it'd get to a certain place, they had somebody to put wires around it to where you could tie it. See, they put a block ever so often, and it had a couple of little channels through there that was left open where you could push the wires through. And when you'd get to a certain place, one guy would push the wires through there, and the other guy would go around the bale of hay and push them back, and then this guy on the other side would tie it. You know, pull it real tight. They'd use wire, baling wire.

He did that for son-in-laws and all of his kinfolks and anybody else that needed baling. A lot of times they'd swap labor, you know. And he also had a reaper to reap grain with. That was mostly for him, but he used to help anybody that needed it done.

### JEROME KEENER BLACKWELL

We somehow managed to purchase an Oliver Hart Parr four-row tractor. My father drove a very hard bargain with a Mr. Wilmouth of Waco on this trade or horses and mules, two-row and one-row cultivators, planters, and the like. I hated to see the plow teams go, but I reasoned that progress was not to be impeded, and the giant of tractor would save us many long hard days of plowing time, come fall. We purchased an eight-disc one-way plow, and it would cut a six-foot cut at a time and turn under all vegetation in sight. The cut was easily six inches deep, and all the neighbors came to see it perform. We could easily break twenty to thirty acres a day that used to take thirty days.

Needless to say, the neighbors were impressed and contracted the breaking of their land to us for a dollar an acre, an unheard-of fortune. On one day we could make as much as thirty dollars. We got all the land to break for that price we could possibly get to. We were to go for thirty miles around breaking for those who wanted it done right and in a hurry.

We also baled hay for the public with an old bailer. We had to dig a long trench to half-bury [the bailer] in the ground and pulled by two horses that went round and round, opening and closing the press. The charge for our baling, if paid in cash and not by hay, was seven cents a bale, and this was some of the hardest, dirtiest, hottest, and most boring work I have ever done. I usually tied out and drug off the bales, which meant bending over the bailer to punch the wires through the slots in the blocks. Then, when tied, you had the block to put back up for the feeder to reuse and then drag off and stack the bales of hay. I often got behind and was ridiculed hotly if I allowed a bale to slip past without its wires. It meant seven cents lost.

### ROBERT E. GAULT

After we got our cotton chopped, we could help the neighbors. They'd pay us for it, and we'd get to keep the money, and that's about the only money to get a-hold of. We was chopping cotton for Fleming, which is the next place above us, and his rows were nearly a mile long. I was eleven years old, and we was chopping cotton there one time. One of my older brothers and a sister was chopping [and] me and two of their boys. Dad went up there and told Mr. Fleming, "Well, you owe me so many days at full wages and a half pay for R. E." [Fleming] says, "Half pay, hell. He hoed a row ever time they did. He's gonna get a man's pay." Oh, I was tickled to death I got that! Dollar and a quarter a day.

My dad was a good cotton picker, he was a 400- or 500-pound man. And my sister and my next-to-oldest brother was real good pickers. They got in West Texas, my brother used to pick 1,000 pounds a day. They way they picked, 'course, it's rough picking. Four-fifty, I think, is the best I ever did, and I thought I was working real hard to do that.

### KYLE HILLIARD

My brother and I, as we got into our teens, were always very short on cash during the thirties, so we worked chopping or picking cotton for our neighbors. I remember one particular day we were chopping cotton for Mr. Dick Overton, whose farm was between our farm and town. He had a good place, good land and no rocks. It was well drained, it didn't have a whole lot of washes in it, and it didn't need terracing like some of the other land did. We didn't have a watch, we were supposed to work ten hours, so we just went by the sun. We looked at the sun, and we kept working and kept working. We were afraid that we might be quitting too quick. He didn't exactly come out there and stop us, so we worked an hour extra just for having that job, making twelve and a half cents an hour. But we enjoyed it because it was good land and it wasn't real hard work. We got to walk a good little bit between strokes with our hoes.

Another time, I was probably in school or practicing football, my brother worked for another neighbor who had a tractor, and they were pulling corn. The neighbor tied the steering wheel of the tractor to where it would go straight down the row and put the tractor in low gear and just let it run. He got off on one side and my brother on the other side, and they kept up with that tractor. It was pulling just about as fast as they could pull that corn.

Of course, you pull the corn after it has completely matured and it's no longer green. It's dead looking, it's very dusty and very musty, and sometimes those ears are tough to get off, and the shucks are very sharp and hard on your hands. I don't think my brother had a pair of gloves. We just did it by hand, and our hands got very tough. But anyway, at sixteen years he stayed with a grown man all day long behind that tractor, keeping up with his row. That was hard work.

Another time that I remember was in 1937. I was twelve years old, and we were a little hungry and needed money more. So we just picked cotton as long that fall as anybody was hiring people to pick it. We stayed out of school after school started and picked cotton all day long until we finished up. We were making pretty good money, because we had good cotton to pick at about sixty cents per hundred pounds. The kids were taking six-weeks exams, so we had stayed out six weeks picking cotton.

## **Peddlers and Country Stores**

*Daily chores, necessary field labors, bad roads, and a lack of ready cash kept families on their farms, thus setting up a situation for others to profitably come to them. A variety of peddlers plied the roads by wagon or automobile, including the ubiquitous Rawleigh and Watkins men, and farm families usually were glad to see them. It was so common to barter chickens or eggs for their minor luxuries of sewing supplies, condiments, and medicines that some country dwellers termed such people "chicken peddlers." Peddlers might occasionally come by selling pots and pans, eyeglasses, used clothing, rustic porch furniture, pump organs, carbide lighting systems, lightning rods, or who knows what. Dealing in staples rather than luxuries, small country stores in some communities sold flour, sugar, coffee, tobacco, and gasoline for cash, eggs, or cedar posts.*

### ERNEST ALLEN COLE

In this part of the country, you never made any money. You just lived on what you made, if you know what I mean. You went to the store, you bought flour, sugar, and coffee, and maybe some spices. Mother, to get her spare money, she raised turkeys, chickens, and I know she sold butter. The Rawleigh man and the Watkins man came by in his truck or his covered wagon. I remember when I was a little kid, this old boy come up here in this covered wagon. Had chicken coops hanging on both sides of it, and he'd swap Mother some vanilla flavoring for two chicken hens.

### ANDY GORDON WOLF

The Rawleigh man come around once or twice a year. We never had any money, so you'd trade him an old hen or a pig or something for whatever you wanted. We used all that Rawleigh stuff for medicine, cough syrup and everything like that. He was horse-drawn for a long time. One of the worst whippings I ever got, I was going down the road from my grandmother's, and a peddler come along in a wagon. He had candy and stuff like that, I liked it pretty good. And I rode a mile or two down the road with him, and when I got off I got off at Bill Hopson's place, and I spent the night with them. Nobody knew where I's at, and [when] my dad found out where I was at, he beat the hell out of me with a lariat rope.

### WILLIAM AKE POWELL

Mule traders and horse traders come through the country all the time. Most of them had something with them when they come through. They'd have three or four with them, just leading them behind. They stopped at every place. They had animals, they had some to sell, they'd buy some or trade.

The Rawleigh people, they used to come around, and the Watkins men. Occasionally Gypsies would come through. They'd be selling, I think, hand-made furniture and stuff made out of willow limbs. They'd have one a-selling you something and three or four looking for something to get. I've seen them come through, they'd have whatever they'd be a-driving with stuff stacked all over it. You couldn't even see it, had it piled up with their furniture and whatever they're selling. I think they just camped out and lived off the fat of the land.

And every once in a while they'd have a wild person coming through selling something it might not be too good. He wouldn't be there when you get more time to use it, he's already gone. I remember my Grandma Powell told me one time that a peddler come through selling stuff to kill bedbugs. He told her, "Don't open it, now, until you get ready to use it. So he's gone, and in two or three days the weather is just right, and she's gonna dope all the mattresses for the bedbugs. And she unwrapped the package, and when she got down to the center of it, it said, "Catch them and hit them with a hammer."

### FLORENCE JOYCE HAEDGE

We had Watkins [men], they come through all the time, and he always managed to come around twelve o'clock. Dinner! They'd have to stop at the road, they'd have to open the gate and then come. We had a little distance between us and the road, so the dogs would bark, and we'd know somebody was coming. We'd be prepared for them. We had a big porch in the back, and that was the door to the dining room and to the other part of the house. Mama would always tell me, "Shut the doors!" Close the doors, she'd tell me in German. I'd close all the doors so the smell of the food wouldn't hit him.

Yeah, we had lots of peddlers—horse liniment and salve of all kinds and vanilla extract and all kind of kitchen stuff. Oh, we'd buy stuff from them, and 'course that made them come back.

### KYLE HILLIARD

Peddling, having people call on you and you calling on people. Well, we had it going both ways during the thirties. [At Palo Alto] we had a pretty large peach orchard, but we'd have so many peaches getting ripe at one time that we couldn't use them all, we couldn't give them away. So when we had a bunch of peaches that was ready, we took the back seat out of the car and loaded up two-gallon zinc buckets with peaches, and we would head for town and sell them door to door. We even went to Temple and Belton. My brother and I both worked, as well as my dad, at peddling those peaches.

And then the other way, coming toward us from town, was the Rawleigh man. Back during the Depression when we were growing up, we were lonely. When a car would come down the road, we all looked and wondered, well, who is that? Wondered if it was coming to see us. We always noticed when the mailman came, usually about ten-twenty in the morning. But the Rawleigh man was a regular. He didn't come real often, but he came on just about the same schedule all the time. He covered 360 degrees around Killeen, in town and out in the country; his name was J. E. Thornton. He was a fine, friendly man, and everybody liked him. He gave the kids chewing gum every time he came, and he would have his basket of all these various products that the Rawleigh Company sold—shampoo and soap and various and sundry things that you might buy if you went to a drugstore. The Rawleigh man was a welcome guest in everybody's home. He had something good that you would want, and nearly every time, even though we had hardly any money, we'd buy something from the Rawleigh man.

### JOHN DANIEL WOLF

I don't know if we averaged coming to town once a month, because we had a little country store, and you could buy flour, sugar, salt, vanilla flavoring, and a few things like that at that little store. You could put the whole supply in a little room. They had a little bit of canned stuff, but nobody had the money to buy canned stuff. It sold tobacco, my dad used Prince Albert and Country Gentleman tobacco. Most of the time they had cold drinks. Sold gasoline with a hand pump. Across the road, in the early thirties, they had a grinding mill for grinding cornmeal. Had a horse to pull that, or a mule, and it'd turn these stones around and around and crush that corn. I don't know of a community store that didn't buy [cedar] posts, that was one of the things that was just absolutely essential. And a lot of them, they bought eggs, most of them by the crate.

### WILLIAM AKE POWELL

They had some stores, but it wasn't in the Friendship community. They had one down at Tama Valley, and they had one in the Ruth community, and they had had one at Straw's Mill. There wasn't any there close to where we lived, but they had a little old store, it'd be a little ten-by-ten building with cheap "taters" and kerosene outside, that sort of thing. You had to have kerosene, we used it for everything. If you cut your foot or stuck a nail in it, you put kerosene on it. Used it for kerosene lamps, kerosene stoves, used it for a lot of things.

### JOE D. INSALL

I remember when the iceman come around [at Antelope], I'd run and get the biggest watermelon I could and sell it to him for a nickel. And if my mother would let me, I'd walk a mile to the store to spend that nickel. You'd be surprised how much caramel candy you got for a nickel back in them days. One of them big old suckers on a stick, they called them "BB Bat," made out of caramel candy, you'd get it hung in your teeth, and you'd just about pull your teeth out. You'd get them for a penny apiece, and I'd be gnawing on them after I got home and had some left over.

[The Antelope store] had a gas pump in front that you worked this lever back and forth. Had a little gauge up there to tell how much gas was on it, and then you run it into your car. Go inside, and if you bought something like bacon or anything like that, they'd wrap it. They had this big roll of paper, and they'd tear off a chunk, put it over there and wrap it up. Then they had a ball of string up yonder [that] come through a couple of loops. They'd pull some down and tie it on there, and that was your fishing line.

### NORRIS SIDNEY GRAVES

This store in Pidcoke decided they wanted to sell out. So Dad said, "That might beat the telephone business." He bought them out, and for a while we had both places. We ran the telephone system and lived in the back of the store. [Our store] was on this side of the gin as you turn down the road to go to the cemetery. We lived there about three years, and I enjoyed that. People [were] in and out, and I got to pump the gas—them old hand pumps.

I had a salesman come through one time, he sold peanuts. They used to sell little boxes of peanuts, and they put coins in them—not all of them, but just every now and then. He come through one time, and he said, "Son, come over here and I'll tell how you can make some money. All you gotta do is shake those just right, and if you know what you're shaking, you can find them." I got where I could hear that nickel, that quarter, that dime, and I used to go over to Gatesville and visit every place that had [those peanuts]. I used to get enough money to go to the show.

### ANDY GORDON WOLF

Arlee and Randall Paul's daddy used to run the Maple grocery store—Silver City grocery store. They ground corn up for meal and such as that—little country store done all that. Also had a cedar yard, used to go there to sell cedar posts. Usually, you'd sell cedar posts and trade them for groceries, same way with eggs. We had eggs and cream and stuff like that. When you went to town you taken a jug of cream and several dozen eggs, ever what you had, and traded them for coffee, lard, flour.

They had a price for it. You'd maybe get ten cents a dozen for eggs, but for a quarter you could get six sacks of tobacco, and everybody smoked. We didn't have ready-rolls or nothing like that. You could take fifty pounds of corn down there, and he'd take five pounds of it, or whatever, and he'd grind it for you. He bought a lot of cedar posts, they'd pay so much for cedar posts. If you could cut a hundred cedar posts a day you might get eight dollars—a four-inch-top eight-foot post brought eight cents. That's a whole lot of money then.

You know the first picture show I ever seen? They had a tent come in, I don't think I was six years old, and this fellow showed this picture show in the cedar yard. He got up there and cranked it by hand, and it showed pictures and some writing. Hey, big crowd there, too!

### ERNEST ALLEN COLE

Okay community was almost directly south of my grandaddy's house, about half a mile from the house. The church was up on the edge of the mountain, and then the blacksmith's shop, and then this little country store where they sold staples, Morgan Bell's store. He finally sold gasoline there, too. Had an old pump with a glass ball about this big around. It held five gallons, I think, and he pumped it up by hand and then it ran in the car.

Bell ran the store, kind of a slow-talking old boy. We'd steal two or three eggs and get a nickel for them—borrowed them from your mother. Sometimes on Saturday night, [if] we was going up hunting with our dogs, we'd each one come with two or three eggs and we'd buy a can of pork and beans and one of these little square boxes of crackers and a slice of cheese. And then one of us would buy a box of .22 shorts that cost a dime. It took about six eggs for that. That's where we usually got our money.

Once, in the fall, a bunch of us boys played hooky, and Mr. Bell owned the farm down on the creek around the schoolhouse, and his trees had pecans on them. So we kids went down there and thrashed his pecan trees and came up and sold him his pecans.

### T. A. WILHITE

They're three stores over there at Sparta. You know, everybody had a bank, and it's a cedar brake. Every Friday, they'd go to the cedar brake and cut a little post, take them to Sparta, and trade them for groceries. I'd haul about 200 cedar posts over there, and I'd get a wagon bed full of groceries. Sparta had a doctor and three stores, and there's quite a few houses up and down the street there. Frances Beck had a blacksmith shop. He's a good smith, he could make anything out of iron that you'd make. At about the middle there's a grocery store, and it's a pretty big one. And on down, there's Doc Walton, and he didn't buy much cedar, 'cause it was too much work for him. Cedar posts graded out, you know, he didn't want to fool with that. But old man Jordan, he put somebody there that would fool with it, and he got all the business.

Old man Jordan, he bought that there dance hall out, and he had him a hole over behind the counter to chew tobacco. He'd go over there and spit that tobacco out that hole. He'd stick his head out, and old Les Hallmark hit him right there with a rock. And, boy, he come out of there trying to find who done that! 'Course, nobody didn't know nothing about it. Wasn't nobody going to tell on him.

## Visits to Town

*How often a family visited Gatesville, Belton, Copperas Cove, or Killeen depended upon the distance from their farm to town, the peculiarities of that particular stretch of road, and whether they owned an automobile. Model T Fords traveled at ten miles an hour or so, but wagons went much slower than that. Many families came to town only a few times a year, often on visits associated with the cash-crop side of things—trips to gin off cotton, buy school clothes, or pay taxes. In any case, excursions to the "electric light town," as one person termed it, were memorable events. Belton, for example, had electricity, flushing toilets (complete with toilet paper), bananas, and five-cent hamburgers sold on the courthouse square.*

### NORMAN RICKETTS HALL

Dad told me the story. From where we lived, we were sixteen miles from Belton. When they used to go to Belton, it was a day's trip in a wagon. You carried a mattress and some springs, usually, and you put that out on the ground, and you built a little fire, and then you did your shopping the next day. The third day you took the sixteen-mile trip back home.

### Joe D. Insall

It was seven miles to Copperas Cove, I never did go to Killeen. We hardly ever went to town—maybe at Christmastime. If you didn't have a vehicle, you went in a horse and wagon, and it took two or three hours. My dad'd be going to get groceries or something, and me and my brother'd dig us some worms, and he'd let us off over at House Creek or Clear Creek, and we'd fish until he come back by. We'd rather do that than went to town.

### Robert E. Gault

We were eleven miles from Killeen. That's where we traded, mostly. We did our ginning there and everything. Killeen had five gins and 1,100 population in 1940—a pretty nice little town. The streets weren't paved then. They used to bring the old hose out and water them down every day.

### William Ake Powell

We hauled our cotton to a gin between here and the Flat. Henson Creek crosses there, and right above there the gin used to be right on that creek. A guy name of Evans owned that gin. We'd get 1,200 or 1,400 pounds, ever what it took for a bale, and we'd go to the gin. I liked to go to the gin and get to ride in a wagon full of cotton. After they got it all in the gin, they put your seed back in there, and you'd get to ride home with the cottonseed. Took the seed home and fed it to the cows in the wintertime. When we'd get through, usually my daddy would buy some summer sausage or bologna and some crackers and maybe three or four bananas and all that sort of stuff. And I'd lie in that cottonseed and eat all the way home. I liked to do that, I liked to go to the gin.

They had that big old sucker that pulled the cotton into the gin, had a vacuum on it. Sometimes they'd let you run it around in the wagon bed. I had a brand new straw hat on, I imagine it cost fifty cents. My hat come off, and it went through there, and it was gone.

### Kyle Hilliard

Going to the gin was a big event for a kid in the 1930s. Since it was the cash crop, we were usually very, very strapped for cash by the time we got our cotton picked. Even though it was very hard work picking cotton, I was always very eager to start picking cotton, because it meant money. It meant apples and oranges and bananas and ice cream and things like that. And getting to go to town with Daddy on that bale of cotton was a real memorable event.

We went to Killeen, there were five gins in Killeen during the 1930s. Killeen was a town of about 1,200 then. All around Killeen a lot of cotton was grown, although they mixed in more stock farming and ranching out south. And so going into town on a bale of cotton and seeing the gin work, you were fascinated by that big pipe thing that sucked the cotton up out of the wagon. You drive your wagon under a big suction pipe. I used to think the best job in the world would be operating that pipe that sucked that cotton out of the wagon.

The engine that ran it was powered by steam, and the boiler was heated with coal or wood. It was steam engine, like a train engine. When electricity became more available and cheaper, some gins converted to it. When the operator sucked that cotton out of the wagon and through some ducts like air conditioning ducts, it would go into this place where there were cylinders that turned and separated the cotton from the seed. Don't get your hand caught. In fact, one of the gin owners had two or three fingers missing from his hand that he had gotten caught in one of those cylinders.

I don't remember that the gin ever broke down while we were there. They must have had to work hard to keep it in good repair so it wouldn't, because there would be wagons, farmers—and maybe some of them had driven five miles or further from somewhere with a load of cotton—with mules. Hardly anyone had a tractor back then. There would be a line of four or five wagons waiting to get ginned, and the ginner needed to avoid any delay.

We usually brought the seed back from the ginner, or sometimes we might trade him the seed or some of the seed for doing the job of ginning. And we sold the cotton to him, we didn't have any place we could store it and wait for the price to go up, so we just took what they gave us. Farmers have always been at a disadvantage in the marketplace, and they always take what anybody will pay them for their products. They people who [buy] from farmers tell them how much they're going to pay. They set the price.

Most of the time we would bring the cottonseed home, because it was real good feed for the milk cows. That cottonseed, incidentally, was one of the best insulators for a block of ice. A bale of cotton usually would weigh around 1,500 pounds before it was ginned. After it was ginned, the lint weighed about 500, so there was about 1,000 pounds of cottonseed. We would go by and get a fifty-pound block of ice from the icehouse and make a hole in there and put that fifty-pound block of ice in and cover it up. It was completely buried in cottonseed, and it would not melt at all on the long trip home.

We didn't even have an icebox, so we would keep that wrapped in various kinds of towsacks to keep it from melting. Keep it in the shade. But, anyway, coming home with that ice, the day that we took a load of cotton to the gin and got some cash, we went and got groceries. We got lots of candy and fruit, and it was almost Christmastime, going to the gin. That night we would usually have a freezer of homemade ice cream. The five of us would eat just about a gallon and a half of ice cream. That would be our supper on that day.

### CLEMENTS W. "SPEEDY" DUNCAN

I went with Pa to Killeen. We raised cotton then and hauled it to town on a wagon. We had one old mule that was real scared of cars. He'd nearly tear the wagon up when a car came by, which wasn't often. Pa would take me with him and lean [me] up against his back to watch behind us, tell him when there was a car coming. If I heard a car coming, "Whoa!" He'd have to get off and get a-hold of this old mule to hold him until this car went by, which probably wouldn't happen over once or twice until we got to Killeen.

They had electric lights in Killeen. I know they did, but I can't remember [that]. My daddy took his four daughters and went down [to South Texas] to pick cotton in 1929. He'd been raised up in this area, he'd plowed these old rocky hills all his life, and he'd never seen rows that you couldn't see to the other end of, and no rocks, and he couldn't wait until he could get down there and plow it. So that's why the whole family moved. It was two married boys and three daughters and my brother Claude and myself. I was six years old on the road when we moved. We left Killeen the eleventh day of November in Model T's, several Model T's helped move us.

We got all the way to Round Rock that same day! There's a lot of one-way bridges, and you'd have to wait at every bridge if there was a car coming, or a wagon or buggy. I'll never forget it, I'd never seen an electric light up close, and Pa rented a cabin in Round Rock, and it had one pull-chain electric light in it. I was trying to figure out what made it burn, and after a short while Pa told me, "That'll do," and that did it. But he always got up early in the morning to get on the road, and I pulled that light until we left. On and off.

### ERNEST ALLEN COLE

Usually, on a cotton farm, if rained in the fall, the cotton would bloom again and you had what they called a "top crop." That's why they call kids born after the mother was forty-five years old "top-crop kids." We'd pick it, and we'd usually get one or two bales of cotton off a top crop. Daddy would make it a point to get there on Saturday. This would be after school started, so I'd go with him. I sat on the top of this wagon with those two mules pulling it, with my slingshot, with a bucket of rocks, so I could shoot birds and rabbits on the way. This old gravel road all the way to Killeen was about seven miles. And always the thing he did, when he got to the cotton gin, he'd take me to a restaurant there in Killeen, and he'd order a dozen fried oysters, and I'd get a half a dozen. They shipped them in to the Santa Fe Railroad in a barrel with ice on them. That's the first restaurant I ever ate in.

### T. A. WILHITE

People played tricks on you. I'd be going down the road into town a lot of times and see a purse laying in the road. I'd jump out and go back to get it, and it wasn't there. I don't know who done it.

Generally, I ginned my cotton at Tom Bowles's gin in Belton. He was a good fellow, and we nearly all dealt with him. And old man Lou Chaffin, he come around and brought a bale. Everybody's getting a good deal, and he heard about it, and he come around there with a bale of cotton. And Tom Bowles told him, says, "Go up to the store and get you a free pair of britches [on me]." Says, "Them damned old britches you wearing ain't fittin' to wear to town." And the old man, he's just right in for that. I believe old man Chaffin ginned the rest of the year with him, after he bought him them britches.

Ever first Monday of the month, everybody'd take whatever they wanted to get rid of and go down there to the square at Belton. You could go down there and buy just about anything you wanted, somebody'd have it. They was trading on everything. Some of them would bring milk cows in there and maybe a baby calf on her, right there on the square. They'd bring everything, horses and mules. It's mostly men, women don't want nothing to do with that trade day.

I was always down there selling something. I'd trade mules, I'd go there and take them mules in and trade them off. I've had mules from the time I was a little kid till I was grown. I guess from a little kid I learnt the good ones and the bad ones. I could just look at them and tell whether I wanted them or not. His right ear tells you a lot of it. You wanted them to have muscle, and you wanted them to have the right kind of disposition. I didn't want to trade none that I considered was doped. You could see it from the look of their eyes. You look at them eyes and could see if they's glass-eyed. You might get scalped many times till you learn what to look for.

I went to trade mules when I was a real young boy. I guess I might have been eight or ten years old. I had a pair of little old mules. My brother had a pair of little two-year-olds, and he sold them to me on credit. Well, come time to pay for them, I had my money to pay him, and him and me come to town. They got a hundred and twenty-five dollars and put it with them little mules to get me a pair of good mules. I got down there, and old man Bill Magen from up at Moffett, he had a pair of real good mules, and he wanted a hundred and a half between my mules and his. I told him, I said, "Now, I can't give you no hundred and a half. I've got a hundred and twenty-five, and it's everything I've got. I ain't gonna eat no dinner."

So I got on a wagon with another man and rode down the avenue and come back, and when I got back he's standing there waiting for me. He thought I was gonna trade with this other man. And when I got back there, he told me, says, "Well, I want to trade you my mules." I never told that fellow [driving the wagon] nothing, just crawled out and away we went. I didn't like them mules. But any mules I'm getting from Bill Magen, now, they was real mules—heavy, young mules, six years old.

I know every mule trader on the square was follering me around and watching me trying to make these trades. The old man from Waco, he's a mule trader, he followed me, and after he saw I had the mule trade done made, he walked up there, and he said, "Kid, you made the best mule trade of anybody in town."

### NORMAN RICKETTS HALL

They had one picture show in Killeen. Just had shows on Friday and Saturday afternoon and Saturday night, and then Sunday afternoon and Sunday night. Two different shows, and you talk about a place that drew the crowds! They didn't care what was showing, it was just a movie, that was big entertainment. Killeen was a dry town. Belton sold beer, and we thought that was sin city, because they had beer joints. My folks told me, "Ever see you in a beer joint, we're gonna disinherit you." That is how I grew up. I did find out later that some of the cousins would bring Dad up a pint of whiskey, and he kept it out in the barn.

Of course, Saturday, people were in town late. I had cousins, they were all ladies, that had a big pastime. Killeen was really only two blocks long, really, the business section. They would try to get a parking spot along the street and watch the people go by. They used to say something like, "I've not seen that hat before." Or, "She wore that dress last week." And this was big entertainment.

### MARGARET BERT WILHITE BOUNDS

I remember Daddy would go to town a lot of times, and he would get extra ice for us to have ice cream. We'd usually go buy groceries. Every Saturday, nearly, you went to town. Billie and I would get up—we'd be pulling corn or picking cotton, either—we'd get up early Saturday morning, wash our hair, roll it, put it in a bandana, go to the field and work one-half day, and then we'd come home and we'd comb that curly hair! I'm sure it was dirty again because we'd been down there in that field, but we thought we looked as nice as all get-out, I reckon.

At the courthouse in Belton, they had an indoor toilet. That was different. I don't remember red wasps getting in our outdoor toilet. Maybe they couldn't stand it! My mama took ashes up there—it stunk, I guess. Me and Billie'd go to the courthouse to use the bathroom every Saturday when we's in town. Oh, that was wonderful, just flush it down and get those toilet tissues! And the bus station had a bathroom, too, but you had to use a dime to go in it. We didn't have no dime, so we just crawled under the two doors.

And they'd have bananas on a stalk [at Belton]. Had a banana knife that was sort of like a cane knife, only it was smaller, and you'd cut the banana off. James Grocery had them, and there was a little guy that come around, had a little truck and had stalks of bananas hanging up in it. And I remember going to town and getting a snowcone. That old guy had the motor of the ice crusher hooked up to his car, and he'd crush that ice. And there was a place there on the corner across from the courthouse [called] the Hamburger King, and I remember my daddy used to buy six hamburgers for a quarter, and that would be our Saturday night supper.

Farmer and sheep rancher Amos Blackwell of the Eliga community poses near a gate counterweighted with worn-out horseshoes sometime around World War I. Some pioneers like Blackwell, who died in 1926, wore their nineteenth-century-style chin whiskers to the end. *Courtesy of Nelda Blackwell Teakell.*

A ranching economy dominated the area before railroads and cotton agriculture arrived around 1880. Here the sons of Jimmie and Jane Powell pose for the town photographer in full stockman regalia in the 1880s. *Courtesy of William Ake Powell.*

In 1906 young Frank "Noog" Black had himself photographed in cow-man tack on a good horse. *Courtesy of Frank A. Black.*

Joel and Sara Blackwell's original home at Blackwell Mountain in 1906. Only the lightning rod on the roof suggests the arrival of twentieth-century technologies. *Courtesy of Nelda Blackwell Teakell.*

John and Carrie Bell Brashear's well-built farmhouse at the Tama community, probably around 1900. Although such homes might end up in the hands of rent farmers over time and the passage of generations, landowners normally built them for their own use. *Courtesy of Wilma Earl Colvin Edwards.*

Milton Graham and second wife Clara stand outside their first home, a roughly constructed, board-and-batten farmhouse. Houses like this often served for cotton-farming tenants "on the thirds and fourths." *Courtesy of Doris Nichols.*

Taylor family women pose outside a combined post office and home.
Teacher Tinie Taylor Kinsey stands on the left. *Courtesy of Zell
Kinsey Copeland.*

The Hotel Simpson, Copperas Cove, on the back of a postcard sent to Mrs. W. P. Gray in 1908. Rural people regarded market towns like Copperas Cove as fascinating centers of twentieth-century innovations and amusements, despite their dirt streets. *Courtesy of Mark Gray Philliber.*

An early family portrait from the Fort Hood area, names and date unknown. The elderly woman probably holds the family Bible. *Courtesy of Tommie L. Shults Haferkamp.*

Christy "Cris" and Katherine Brashear, their seven children, and Katherine's mother-in-law pose for a visiting town photographer in 1884. As was the custom, the empty chair to the right memorializes a dead child, and the family's most prized possession, a parlor pump organ, has been laboriously moved outside for the formal photograph. *Courtesy of Wilma Earl Colvin Edwards.*

After the usual formal family portrait standing in front of the house, the John Brashear family (with son driving) immortalizes its fine horse and covered buggy with leather seats. *Courtesy of Wilma Earl Colvin Edwards.*

Most family portraits were made at the studios of town photographers, as was this image of the William and Linda Norman Carter family, photographed at White's Studio in Killeen in 1905. *Courtesy of Jean Odom.*

Leila "Dutch" Louer reclines pensively on a wicker chair in the photographer's studio. The long exposure times required by late-nineteenth-century cameras required photographers to tell their subjects, "Relax your face." *Courtesy of Wilma Earl Colvin Edwards.*

Apprehensive young Barney Colvin poses barefooted for the studio camera. *Courtesy of Wilma Earl Colvin Edwards.*

Arrayed as a dapper townsman, Frank Smith manages a half smile and stands for the camera in his fine suit, with vest chains, pocket watch, cigar, and cigar trimmer. *Courtesy of John Gail Edwards.*

Mildly retarded because of a childhood illness and kept out of school, William Franklin Colvin lived alone in a small shack most of his life. *Courtesy of Wilma Earl Colvin Edwards.*

Women of the Chalk and Manning families pose for the photographer. Their more elegant "Sunday" sunbonnets were standard formal wear for the older generation. *Courtesy of Martha Brewer.*

Milton Graham and second wife Clara in everyday work clothes at
the Graham place on House Creek near Eliga, 1941. After about 1920,
inexpensive Brownie cameras made such informal family portraits
much more common. *Courtesy of Doris Nichols.*

Young Thomas Adolph Gray performs one of his daily chores, feeding barnyard fowl on his family's farm south of Eliga. *Courtesy of Mark Gray Philliber.*

Although everyone had his or her chores, housewives normally masterminded the subsistence side of farms, and sometimes excess domestic animals and crops were sold for cash and bartered at the store, as was often the case with chickens and eggs. The photographer has recorded the shadow of his head among the barnyard fowl. *Courtesy of Wilma Earl Colvin Edwards.*

Coleman Golden and Frank Williams harvest hay by hand along the
House Creek bottom. This was the oldest method of harvesting the
hay, harking back to medieval times. Hay was hauled in wagons and
stacked into a conical shape around tall central poles. *Courtesy of
Letha Sheldon.*

The Colvin family pauses to face the camera while picking cotton during the late summer of 1908. Family members—men, women, and children—rushed to gather exposed cotton before rain fell on it or thunderstorms blew it to the ground. *Courtesy of Wilma Earl Colvin Edwards.*

During the 1930s, near the Pidcoke community, Robert Porter and his two daughters and dog rest exhausted on a pile of seed cotton waiting for the wagon to return from the gin. *Courtesy of Grace Irene Bratton.*

Looking rather unhappy, little Nella Mae Colvin sits in a harvest field of her family's special strain of cotton, Colvin Big Boll, sold as seed at Gatesville and Killeen for $2.50 a bushel. *Courtesy of Wilma Earl Colvin Edwards.*

Members of the Strickland family stand on bags of oats at their farm in 1915, the big oat threshing machine in the background. Often small-grain threshing was an early form of custom work—the owner of the steam-powered "thrasher" struck a deal with the farmer for a cash fee or a toll of grain. *Courtesy of Billie Smith Reavis.*

A little girl supervises the feeding of her sheep. Many childhood chores involved the feeding of domestic animals. *Courtesy of Wilma Earl Colvin Edwards.*

Horseman Carl Brown and W. L. Brown survey a scene rarely photographed, a large pen of Angora goats either just before or after shearing
time. (Restless goats made poor photographic subjects.) *Courtesy of
Margaret Ann Brown Smith.*

John Brashear's large country store at Tama in 1898, with Brashear
standing second from right. Such stores also functioned as community centers—in this case providing space for the Tama post office
and the local chapter of the Woodmen of the World. *Courtesy of
Wilma Earl Colvin Edwards.*

Ruth store owner Frank "Noog" Black poses with prized Walker foxhounds in front of his place of business in 1930. Daughter Ara Mae
has slipped into the scene unobserved. *Courtesy of Frank A. Black.*

Teacher Charlie Autrey and students face the camera for the custom-
ary end-of-school photograph at Owl Creek School at Friendship
about 1900. *Courtesy of Roma Scott Bates.*

By the late 1920s, Ewing had become a fine rural school with several teachers, a Boy Scout troop (standing front and center), a basketball team (right), and a brass school bell at the top of a long pole. *Courtesy of Naoma Bell Worthington Williams.*

The Ewing girls' basketball team of 1927, with teacher and coach
Gladys Blankenship at top center. *Courtesy of Annie Lois Bond Cowan.*

The Ewing boys' basketball team of 1936. Fiddle player William Ake Powell is second from left, and R. M. Cummings, who died in World War II, is second from right. *Courtesy of Josie Kinsey Cummings.*

Francis Wolf with the homemade school bus he used to transport secondary students to Maple School in 1938. Smaller rural school districts consolidated into larger rural districts such as Maple, and later all the rural districts consolidated into town schools. *Courtesy of Mary Beth Graham Gartman.*

Part of the seventh-grade class with their teacher in front of the fine brick Maple School, 1936. *Courtesy of Lucille Hawkins Mitchell.*

As in the case of the Owl Creek School at Friendship community, some one-room schools persisted until the coming of Camp Hood in 1942 forced all rural school districts to consolidate with town schools outside the military installation. *Courtesy of Zell Kinsey Copeland.*

Students from the Owl Creek School, Friendship, wearing crepe-paper dresses used in a school program, 1926. *Courtesy of Zell Kinsey Copeland.*

The boys' snowman at Antelope School after the second big snow of January 1940. The girls had their own snowman. *Courtesy of Melba Goodwin Bennett.*

W. F. Styles, principal teacher at Stampede School, 1922. Principal
teachers taught the higher grades and took care of such daily duties as
filling out state forms and administering whippings. Before 1890
many rural school teachers were men, but by around 1910 most were
young, unmarried women. *Courtesy of Melba Goodwin Bennett.*

In this rare photo of a house interior, Maple schoolteacher Velma Brown grades papers on the arm of a chair in her rented room at the home of school trustee John Brashear. *Courtesy of Wilma Earl Colvin Edwards.*

An action shot of high-jinks near the water fountain during the end-of-school celebrations at Antelope School, 1941. *Courtesy of Melba Goodwin Bennett.*

Friends smile shyly for the camera at end-of-school celebrations, Antelope, 1941. *Courtesy of Melba Goodwin Bennett.*

The three-man Antelope school board at the end-of-school festivities of 1941, probably the last such event held before the coming of Camp Hood. *Courtesy of Melba Goodwin Bennett.*

A "dinner on the ground" crowd at the Eliga Church of Christ. Much important community social life took place in and around church and cemetery. *Courtesy of Hazel Graham Wilkinson.*

Well-dressed ladies pose for the camera near a fine buggy at Eliga
Church of Christ. Sunday services had major social as well as spiri-
tual value for people in remote settlements. *Courtesy of Martha
Brewer.*

Members of several generations face the camera in fine clothing probably intended for church service. *Courtesy of Wilma Earl Colvin Edwards.*

Congregants of the Eliga Church of Christ at the entrance to the
building. The site, in a scenic pecan grove on the north bank of
Cowhouse Creek, was much favored for summer revivals. *Courtesy
of Mark Gray Philliber.*

Pastor Chris Brashear pauses knee-deep in Cowhouse Creek during a baptizing service of New Hope Baptist Church, 1928. As at New Hope, summer revivals normally went on for one week, with the newly converted—the fruits of revival—baptized together at the end. *Courtesy of Wilma Earl Colvin Edwards.*

Veteran preacher Brother Shouse from Salem Church of Christ holds a bouquet of flowers during festivities at Eliga. He wears the long hair, full beard, and uncrimped Stetson of an earlier time. Preachers like Shouse usually farmed and ranched for their livelihood, with preaching an important sideline. *Courtesy of Mark Gray Philliber.*

A student minister from Baylor University who commuted in his Ford
to serve as temporary preacher at Friendship Baptist Church, 1927.
*Courtesy of Zell Kinsey Copeland.*

Doyle and Stella May Manning in Sunday church attire with their fine buggy. *Courtesy of Martha Brewer.*

Social life in communities on the Fort Hood lands revolved around church affairs, school entertainments, occasional weekend parties at private homes, and visits to scenic Cowhouse Creek. Here courting couples pose at Pidcoke Bridge over "the Cowhouse" in 1905. *Courtesy of Onella Williamson Griffin.*

Another courting party, this time at Potter's Crossing on Cowhouse Creek, around 1917. Only the fashions have changed. *Courtesy of Wilma Earl Colvin Edwards.*

Members of the Chalk family picnic along the banks of ever-popular Cowhouse Creek, which was recorded in a large number of informal snapshots. *Courtesy of Mark Gray Philliber.*

Guitarist Charles Lee Straw and friend Wayne Blanchard at Straw's Mill near Turnover about 1942. Musicians of any ability, with almost any instrument, were in demand for Saturday-night house parties at private homes. *Courtesy of Don Kenneth Blanchard.*

A lonely doll baby on the front steps of the Daugherty home in 1938.
Children had few playthings, greatly treasured the ones they had, and
used them until they virtually fell apart. A little girl's last doll of
childhood evoked strong sentiment. *Courtesy of Margaret Ann
Brown Smith.*

The Bailey family just before a wagon trip to Abilene, around 1918.
*Courtesy of Tommie L. Haferkamp.*

Children of the Truss, Shults, and Powell families in front of a 1929
Model A Ford, still the family car in 1942. Automobiles lessened rural isolation, but local roads periodically became impassable with
mud. *Courtesy of Tommie L. Haferkamp.*

Thomas and Virgie Shults and children on the family farm, 1941, before Camp Hood was even a wild rumor. *Courtesy of Lois Shults Cathey.*

With flag flying during the last months of World War I, the John Fletcher Colvin family celebrates the Fourth of July, 1918, at their home in the Boaz community. The coming of another world war led to forced land sale and destruction of the Colvins' fine farmhouse. *Courtesy of Wilma Earl Colvin Edwards.*

Della and Marvin Gray sit on their front porch near Eliga for the last photograph of this farmhouse before the Camp Hood takeover. *Courtesy of Mark Gray Philliber.*

Army First Lieutenant R. M. Cummings of Friendship,
who died in France on his birthday, August 12, 1944.
Some area families made a double sacrifice to Allied
victory in World War II, losing their farms to Camp Hood
and their sons in combat. *Courtesy of Josie Amelia
Kinsey Cummings.*

Relocated after the takeover, Dewie Cummings McGlothlin and husband Jim with their respective mothers at Gatesville during World War II. *Courtesy of Josie Kinsey Cummings.*

The Friendship reunion of 1998. Family, church, and community reunions are held annually at Belton, Copperas Cove, Gatesville, and Killeen by former residents of the lost settlements subsumed by Fort Hood. *Courtesy of Jack Rehm and Jim Cazares.*

Things at times might have been "harder than hardscrabble," but residents of the Fort Hood settlements lived their lives with grace and exuberance. As if to make just that point, cotton farmer Carl Goodwin raises daughter Alta Faye in one big hand at the family farm near Stampede, 1921. *Courtesy of Melba Goodwin Bennett.*

# Settlements

## Country Schools

*In Coryell County during the 1934–1935 school year, 59 rural schools still dotted the countryside, each playing a double role as community school and central gathering place of settlement life. Bell County had a greater population and even more rural schools—102, to be exact. Three-person elected boards of school trustees, drawn from local farmers and ranchers, directed these "common school districts," formally supervised by the county school superintendents in distant Gatesville and Belton. In truth, whole years might pass without the superintendent visiting a particular country school. Local people ran their own systems. Every morning, children walked or rode to their settlement school, usually taking "near cuts" across the countryside to get there. Trespass was an ignored concept, an affront to "neighborliness"; in fact, landowners often felled trees across creeks as footbridges for passing schoolchildren.*

### KYLE HILLIARD

Out at Palo Alto [School], it was a very close-knit group. There weren't that many kids. There were four grades in the little room, and fifth, sixth, seventh, and eighth—and for a while the ninth grade—in the big room. Then they took off the ninth grade, so four grades in each room—a two-teacher school.

### MARGARET BERT WILHITE BOUNDS

My mother made most of our [school] clothes. I remember that she made us pinafores and little white blouses, shirtwaist blouses. A pinafore is a skirt that has kind of like a bib and a ruffle over each shoulder. Mine was red and white and Billie's was blue and white, 'cause she dressed us a lot alike. There was two years' difference in our age. In fact, sometimes when Billie would outgrow her dress, then I got it again. Now, like our underwear and our slips and gowns and things, she might use feed sacks and flour sacks, lots of times, for the underwear. All the other girls were wearing them, too, so we didn't feel ashamed.

Mama and Daddy'd take us to town to get new shoes before school started. My sister, the first pair she tried on, she'd say, "They fit," and she'd take them home. They might rub blisters on her feet, and Mama would say, "Now, I told you to try on more." She'd say, "Well, I was afraid they didn't have another pair like this one."

### HOPE EDWARDS TURNER

In the wintertime, school days, we had traps on the mountain, varmint traps. That's where we got our Christmas money. We'd get up, and Gail and I would run those traps and see what we had in them. Sometimes we'd come back and have to change clothes if we'd caught a polecat. We got dressed, and Daddy had the horses saddled, and we were on horses to go to [Stampede] school at seven-thirty. Mama would pack our lunch—biscuits and sausage and fruit pies.

### JOHN GAIL EDWARDS

We rode horseback to school. We took two horses, most of the time. We had to go right by the cow pen when we went to school, the three of us. The calves were in this lot. Our mother had two umbrellas, black ones. We'd slip them out and play with them. We broke the calves out of the lot one day, scared them with the umbrellas. Daddy said, "How come the calves are out?" Of course, we didn't know.

We started at Stampede. Sometimes we delayed going to school until the cotton was in. There were several schools at Stampede that we went to that were just six months. They'd start school in the middle of September and let us go to school for two weeks, [then] turn out for two weeks until we got the cotton picked. [Stampede School] was a little frame building, two rooms. It had an inset porch on it facing the west, and it had a little cloakroom over here on each side for us to hang our coats in. Then it opened into the two doors, one on each side, a foyer, the principal's room, and then the little primary room over here on the right. Each one of them and a pot-bellied wood stove back in the back with a big curtain around it. It was a two-teacher school.

### GLADYS MERLE KEENER CHASTAIN

The teachers lived in the neighborhood with the farm families, because it was too far to drive back and forth from Killeen or Gatesville. So you lived with a farm family, and you usually drove a buggy to school. Me and my sister had to walk about a mile up this road to school, and in the cold wintertimes it seemed much colder than we have nowadays. Mother'd bundle us up, and we'd walk facing the wind until we'd be so cold—our faces, our hands—and we'd turn around and back a while. Then, when we got to school, we had a huge, big, pot-bellied stove in the school corner, and the teacher wouldn't let us get too close, 'cause he knew our hands and our faces would hurt too much warming up. He kept us back until we thawed out or warmed up.

When I was seven or eight, I lived during the week with my Grandmother Keener. We had lost our place up here at Gatesville, and they moved to what you call Manning Mountain, and we were living up on this mountain. All it had was rocks and goats and was really poor land. I had to go down to my grandparents and stay, because there wasn't any way to get to school from up there. The teacher lived with my Aunt Lucy and Uncle Willie, and the teacher would come by every morning and pick me up in a buggy, and we went to Brown's Creek School.

During the week I'd live with my grandmother, and then on the weekend Daddy would ride down the mountain on the horse and take me back up the mountain to stay with Mom and Dad on Saturday and Sunday. One weekend Dad took me there it was snowing, and when Dad was to take me back down to Grandmother Keener's the next day, [Mother] wrapped us up in so many clothes I don't know how we ever mounted a horse together, we were so stiff with clothes on us. I remember standing and holding to the porch post, crying, not wanting to go back.

Grandmother Keener and Grandfather Keener were Methodist ministers. She'd get me up on her lap, she's a little bitty short fat lady, and she'd get me up on her lap and help me with my lessons. It felt so good sitting on Grandma's lap, 'cause she was so squishy and loving. But ever night before you'd go to bed, they'd do their praying, and you'd kneel by a cane-bottomed chair. You'd be a little kid, and you were tired. Grandpa would pray first, he'd pray for everybody, everything, he'd pray and he'd pray and he'd pray. And about the time you'd think he was gonna stop and you could get up and go to bed, being a kid and tired, well, Grandma'd take over, and you'd be there for a spell. They believed in prayer.

### CHRISTINE FLEMING ESPARZA

My daddy was what they called a sharecropper. One year he moved three times, my first year of school. Oh my, and I was a scared little country girl that squalled every day, and I failed that year. I'd come in squalling [from] school, he told me one day, "Young lady, if you come in one more time a-bawling, I'm gonna whip you." Well, I'd bawl until I'd nearly get to the house, and then I'd quit. Because I knew my daddy!

Me and Charlotte had to walk a swinging footbridge over the Cowhouse Creek to get to the school bus. This was near Pidcoke. One year the river got so high it washed the footbridge away. There was big old cables at the top and the bottom, and then netting wire in between it, and then the boards were about that wide and about that far apart. And my daddy walked them cables with nothing under him and put that bridge back together so we wouldn't have to wade the river to get the school.

I went my last four years at one school, and that's the longest I went to any school. Daddy moved three times my first year, and he moved three times my third year, and I failed that grade, but I did go on and get my diploma. I was the oldest one in my class, but that didn't bother me. I wanted that diploma.

### NORMAN RICKETTS HALL

We moved over from Brookhaven. Brookhaven had a cemetery, a cedar post yard. You know what a cedar post yard is? At one time there had been a gin, but it had gone by the time I came along. And there were two stores that competed against each other for trade, also a school.

My brother rode a horse to school. That was quite a deal, too, and there were a lot of horses. You'd go to school, and they might have fifteen, twenty horses tied up to posts and fences around the school, and some of them even came in a wagon, and that is a very slow transportation. My brother would ride that horse, and I'd be waiting for him when he came home. I was really wanting to start to school—not to go to school, but I wanted to ride a horse.

One time we were in this Model T Ford. I was sitting in the front with Mother, and Bob, the brother, was sitting in back. And he'd come up with the idea, "Mother, what would you think about me driving the car to school this year? We could pick up so-and-so and so-and-so, and they could share in the gas?" Well, she didn't answer him, but she didn't say no, and sure enough he got to drive the car to school.

### NORRIS SIDNEY GRAVES

I walked to Pidcoke School. Towards summertime—April, May—it'd get hot there and the sand would get pretty warm on your bare feet. I was barefooted in the summer, and early fall I'd go barefooted. I had a pair of shoes, but I kept them [at home]. There was a little girl up the creek, Sydney Howell, and she rode. She lived on the other side of Table Rock, so she had a ways to come. She'd come by, and every now and then she'd pat the back of her saddle, and I'd jump up.

### ERNEST ALLEN COLE

You wrapped your lunch up in a newspaper, and some people carried it in half-gallon buckets. I liked mine wrapped in a newspaper because that left my hands free for my book satchel and [to] use my slingshot to shoot birds and rabbits on the way to school. Most kids come to [Okay] school bare-footed, particularly the boys. Some of them walked three or four miles, but it was fun because you knew you could gather kids as you went along, and you'd have a kind of a social gathering to school. It was more fun than staying home.

A lot of times we'd cut through [other people's pastures]. I had an old pet billy goat, had horns about a foot long, and [he] and my dog Nero would follow me to school. One time the goat followed me right in, and this teacher said, "Get that beast out of here! Get that beast out of here!"

### WILLIAM AKE POWELL

I went to school at Owl Creek through the seventh grade. We lived a mile and a half from that school, and I walked to school. The teacher used to board with us, and we walked to school, me and the schoolteacher. Had to climb through some fences, some places there wasn't no gates, went the closest way.

I graduated from there, then I went to Ewing School, which was the other way maybe six or seven miles, pretty good way. I started to riding a horse, [but] they didn't have no place to put your horse, just tie him to a tree, no sheds or nothing. And man, it used to snow a lot more than it does now here; it's cold and wet. So I finally give that up and started cutting straight through, walking. I think it's only about four or five miles, thataway. It wasn't but about a mile or so that I began to pick up some more kids. They'd start to falling in, and it'd be a bunch of us before we'd get to school.

Everybody carried their lunch in a syrup bucket. It was either a half a gallon or a gallon bucket. They'd punch holes in the lid where it would get air. Had a handle on it, carry your lunch in that. And I tell everybody, that's what's wrong with me, I've been knocked in the head too many times with one of them syrup buckets. You're always getting in something with some of them kids. That's the first thing they'd want to do, hit you in the head with that bucket.

### ROBERT E. GAULT

I grew up on the Cowhouse [Creek] about six miles from Antelope and about three and a half up from Eliga, but the only school was Antelope. My granddad gave land for a school back in ninety something, and that was the Latham Prairie School, they called it. Then, in 1920 and '21, Ross School and Latham Prairie School, and House Creek School and Table Rock School went together, and they made Antelope School, and it opened in 1921, I believe. That old [Latham] school in our pasture was where my older brothers went to school. And then after it was done away with, I started school in '31.

[Antelope] started out as a two-teacher school, and then in the thirties it went to a three-teacher school. When I was going there, we had 157 students, which is pretty good for a rural school. And we had four teachers—a principal, a part-time teacher, and then three regular teachers. It was a pretty strong little school there. Finally, Gatesville was running buses down that way, and [Antelope] got a deal with them that they'd pick up the high school kids and take them up to Gatesville, which was good for us. We got a chance for a little better education that way, and more diversified.

It was six miles from our place on the Cowhouse to Antelope. First four or five years, I rode a horse behind my sister. Had a great big old horse, I had to get it up to a gate and crawl up on it to get on him. We rode [that] old bald-faced horse that six miles in every kind of weather. We were raised down there on the creek, and about halfway to Antelope you went up on the prairie, and that cold wind hit! We were tickled like heck when we hit that brush on the way home. People who had lots of money went up there and built some stalls, but we had a hitching rail where we tied ours, and your saddle would be wet and everything, you know.

We was going to school one day when I must have been eight or nine, and my sister got in a race with an old boy on another horse. I was behind the saddle, and she jumped a ditch with that horse, and I landed right across here and knocked me out. Two lady schoolteachers come along in a buggy, and they picked me up and took me to the school. It had busted me up pretty good, I had nosebleeds from that for years. My sister didn't miss me till she got up to the school. She told me, "Now, you tell Daddy that you fell playing running base or something, or I'll whip you." I got home and told my daddy, and he took it like that. But he was on the school board, and he went to school board meeting that night and found out the truth and come home and whipped me for lying! That's the way sisters do.

Later, I had to ride the bus twenty-eight miles to high school in Gatesville. Walked a mile and a half and caught the bus. We had a road that run from Eliga clear to Antelope, then on to Gatesville. It was a pretty good gravel road most of the way, [but] they was a stretch about a mile from Antelope [that] stayed muddy most of the time. One morning, we were going to school on that, and it was real muddy, and we were having to push, so we just pushed it over in the ditch. Bus driver got out and grinned, said, "I'll get my horses and pull it out, directly, y'all go on home." He just laughed about it, he knew how kids were.

It took us half a day to get home. We got out there and got cow chips and fighting and everything—out there in the cedar brakes. We had a big time out of it.

[Antelope School] was heated with coal and wood, had them big heaters with a metal band outside of that to keep the kids from touching them. We used to get in trouble, we'd go out to the coal bin and get in a fight and get coal all over us. We'd get in a little trouble over that and get in more trouble when we got home. Then we had kerosene lights, [but] about the third grade I was there, they bought this Star Gas, bottled gas, put in gaslights in the school. They called it Star Gas, and they had tanks about the size of a water heater tank that set outside. Then they had the copper tubing running to your lights. Butane gas is what it really was, you see. But they put it in that school system, all the rooms had gaslights.

### ERNEST ALLEN COLE

The Okay School faced east. When I was a kid, it was two rooms. It had a dug well, and the outhouses were a hundred yards or so on the side of the road. I went from the first through the eighth there. When I started to school, I guess my mother wanted to get rid of me, because she sent me [when] I wasn't very old. I don't know if I was five or six, but I'd already memorized the primer, and I knew my ABC's. I could read the primer upside down, that's how well I knew it, and I could count and add a little bit. The second year I was there, there wasn't anybody in the second grade, so they put me in the third grade. I was a runt in the third grade, but it was all right, too. [When] you was sitting in this schoolroom, you was listening to them teach the second grade, the third grade, and the fourth grade. By the time you got old, you knew pretty well what was going on there. Now, it was kind of a shock when you moved to the next room [for] the fifth to the eighth grade.

### MARGARET BERT WILHITE BOUNDS

The first year I was in school [at Sparta], I was in the first, and second, third, and fourth—you got to hear all of that. Well, it wasn't long until I was learning second grade stuff and listening and catching on to some of the other kids. It was really kind of beneficial that I went to a two-teacher school. You heard things repeated and repeated, you're bound to learn something from it. When I was in the first, I could spell words like the second grade and some of the third grade was learning to spell.

My teacher had four grades, and then the other teacher would have had fifth, sixth, seventh, and eighth. Then they changed to one teacher, and she had the whole crowd in there. But a lot of times she would let the older kids hold the first grade and second grade classes. She would oversee them, but they would have them read. I know they couldn't do that now, there's too many kids, but they'd make book reports, and I would remember something about that book report—it stuck with me. The teacher would go down to the Bell County Library, and she'd bring books to school to cover all grades. Well, I'd start out at whatever grade I was in, then I read all below me, and then I'd read all the others.

### KYLE HILLIARD

Everybody back in those days was serious about school. The hard times made it easy to convince kids to get a good education. My dad quit school in the eighth grade, the same Palo Alto School, and he kept telling us, "Don't do like I did. Get an education." Even though he didn't find a way to save any money to help us go to college, he surely did plant that idea in our minds.

I can remember walking home one time from Palo Alto, and that was a day that Killeen had a holiday. Killeen had more holidays than we did at Palo Alto. We were very serious-minded—not very many ballgames and not very many holidays. We met one of the school trustees, he didn't have a car, he went to town about once a month in a wagon and got all the supplies he needed. I hollered at him, said, "Hey, Mr. So-and-so," knowing he was a trustee, "Killeen had a holiday today, how come we didn't have one?" He laughed and said, "You don't need none!" So that was our lot. We didn't need any holidays. We needed to work hard in our schooling and get our book learning.

### J. W. SHULTS

Most of the teachers at these small schools were young ladies, and they would board with some of the families in the community. That got a lot of the young men's attention. In fact, when my sister was in first and second grade, one of the teachers boarded at our house. She was from Temple, but Temple was a long way. My mother's baby brother married her. There was a lot of marriages made with the young ladies that came into those communities back then to teach, and the young men paid pretty close attention to who's going to be teaching school next year.

### NORMAN RICKETTS HALL

I taught school one year in Spanish Oak. I'd only had two years of college, and I ran out of money, and I was going to teach school. Then, if you could walk, you could teach, and I got a job at a one-room school, taught first through tenth in Burnet County, about twenty miles from Marble Falls.

Seems like the place where I taught, the first through the tenth grade, if you had enough students one row would be first grade and another row would be another grade and so on. I did my best job of teaching in the third grade. No students were in the third grade! I had first grade and second grade and fourth, and on up, and I had one tenth-grader that turned eighteen while I was teaching. He was drafted during the year, and I was glad to see him go.

He always asked these questions about geometry [that] I didn't think he had a right to ask. I had to go back home and talk to one of my former teachers and find out something about the questions. I had one little girl in the first grade. I probably should have been court-martialed for what I did, 'cause I only had two years of college, and I don't remember having a course on how to teach reading or how to teach math. I only had the philosophy of education and all that, which doesn't mean diddley to somebody in the first grade. I'd assign her something, and one of the other kids would more or less supervise her.

I recall that her parents came to me one time and said, "You know, we just don't feel like Susie is challenged. She's doing the same thing over and over." Well, I thought, I can handle that, so one Friday I assigned her to write to a hundred over the weekend. You know, now, they only have kids write to twenty in the first grade after a whole year. So they came back Monday morning and said, "It took the whole family all weekend to get Susie to write to a hundred."

I didn't have the knowledge to teach properly. Then, you could teach with just a high school diploma. I had two years of college, but it wasn't helping a whole lot. Ironically enough, I still keep up with some of those kids, and we visit and correspond a lot. I had one student that became a lieutenant-general in the army. I had another one that was on death row down at Huntsville. So you've got the whole spectrum, and I'm sure that'll be true of any country school.

I recall once there was a little fourth-grader, and there was an aggressive kid, must have been in the eighth grade. Every time they'd have recess, he would try to beat up on the fourth-grader, and finally I said, "What is the problem here?" As you know, [in a one-room classroom] everybody could hear everything. Like, a kid in the first grade would have eighth-grade history eight years. This fourth-grader was pretty sharp, and I would be asking questions about United States history or something. If this eighth-grade boy hesitated, this fourth-grader would answer. He didn't like that. When he'd get that kid outside, he'd try to beat him up, say, "You keep your mouth shut and quit answering my questions."

A lot times, back then, the parents would keep them out for an ungodly amount of time. School started in September, but here's cotton [to pick] and corn and all that, and you'd stay out for that. You just kind of came to school when there's nothing else to do on the farm.

I got eighty dollars a month for teaching, I got ten dollars a month for being principal. I liked that—one teacher and I'm the principal. And seven-fifty for being the custodian, I was cleaning up. Had a three-member school board, and you taught until the tax money ran out, then the school closed. I recall the county judge was the [county school] superintendent. Really, the secretary was the superintendent. She told me once, "Unless we get some more tax money, we'll have to close school the last day of April." I said, "What?" You know, that's cutting a month's salary out. She said, "There's just not any money, and we've got to close." So that's what they did.

There was very little state aid, if any, but there was tax money. If some of the big ranchers paid their taxes, you could go on. If they didn't, and sometimes they'd be in dispute, then you closed school. It went on as long as you could pay the teacher. Whenever school ended, the last day was a big deal. They usually had what we'd call a barbecue. Everybody in the area came, and I'm telling you, if you didn't have it, something was the matter. Probably the teacher got fired the next year.

The school board where I taught, honest to goodness, there were two of the school board members who were cedar choppers. They worked where the cedar grew. If they chopped all of the available cedars, they'd move their camp somewhere else. Well, there were times I'd have to get all three of them to sign my check each month. Sometimes I'd spend half a day looking. Where did they go? Really, it was kind of a loosey-goosey operation back then.

Even in your two-teacher schools, one person was designated as principal and taught full time, and the principal was just to handle to some of the paperwork and the discipline. A lot of times they tried to get husband and wife. I had a cousin that taught in Brookhaven, man-and-wife operation. There were very few places to stay, and they wanted you to stay in that community.

Sparta was a school district out on the reservation. I was only nineteen, but I went to Sparta and asked about school, they were gonna have a vacancy. They told me, said, "There's a lady on the school board lives right down the street." I'd never heard of a lady school board member before. I went down to the house and introduced myself and told her I was interested in the job. She was nice, she says, "Come on, come in and sit down." The first questions she asked just floored me. She said, "Can you cook?" I was applying for a teaching job! I said, "Well, I've always fixed soup for my dad and I." She said, "We serve the children soup every morning."

That's the first time I'd ever heard of that, eating soup in school, but I didn't get the job. I don't know whether my soup recipe didn't work, but she never asked me anything about curriculum. She did ask me how old I was and had I been to college.

### WILLIAM AKE POWELL

The Kinseys and the Warrens all had boys about the same age, and at school every once in a while the little ones would get in a fight, and it'd always kind of snowball, they'd all be a-fighting. They'd all pair off just about the same size. There wasn't no big guy jump on somebody and beat them up, like it is today.

### MARY EDWARDS GROVES

The first year I went to Stampede, that was the last year that Stampede was a school, I really didn't like it too well. My teacher didn't allow gum chewing, and I was a gum chewer. I stayed in each recess the whole first year of my schooling. I didn't like my teacher, Miss Carpenter. I never did like her, I don't like her now. In those days, we had an inspector that came out from the county seat to inspect. Well, I was so small, and my feet wouldn't touch the floor, so I had a block to put my feet on, and he didn't like the way I held my feet. He'd come in and he'd slap them down on the block, and I could have killed him. I thought, if I was just a little bigger, I could have pinched his head off. And I didn't like to wear shoes, and my daddy made me wear shoes to school. Some days, I would stop on the way and hide them and pick them up on the way home.

### ERNEST ALLEN COLE

Particularly in this one fourth grade [at Okay School], these kids had gotten smart. Our desks had an inkwell in them, and this inkwell had a cork stopper in it. Of course, we had chalk at the blackboard, and you could take a little piece of chalk, and as you got in line to go into school, you went by somebody's desk, you real quick took the cork out and dropped the chalk in. Now, this ink was an acid ink, and pretty soon it'd create enough pressure and gas. The cork would pop out and the ink would go plumb to the ceiling. I [never did do that], and I never did dip pretty little girls' hair in the inkwell, either. The little girls learned to cut their hair short so that didn't happen to them.

I can remember one of my teachers real well, a lady named Miss Rambo. She was a nice big lady—go bear hunting with a switch, that kind. It was right after Christmas, and we got a few firecrackers and things, Christmastime, and I took a box of sparklers to school with me for some reason. I was setting there bored to death one time at my desk, and I had some kitchen matches, all the kids carried them, then, and I got under my desk and lit it. Them things, you can't put them out, and I waved it in the air! When it finally went out, she come and got her foot ruler and blistered the palm of my hand.

We played basketball. That's where I broke my nose the first time, playing basketball. The goal posts were right at the edge of the court. I was dribbling and some kid hit me, and I threw the ball up and ran slam-dab into that post. And we played baseball. We had a ball that was usually a bunch of string wound up, and the bats were a board that we whittled. We played that at lunch. We usually fought during the recesses, just for fun, clawing each other, fighting with our shoes. I was usually barefooted, so I had to scratch them with my toenails.

### MARGARET BERT WILHITE BOUNDS

We had outside toilets [at Sparta School]. It was just a one-teacher school at that time, and it had rained, it was muddy. Well, Mrs. Hamilton would ring one bell, and that would mean the girls would go the bathroom and the boys would go the water fountain. She'd wait a while, and she'd ring another bell, and vice versa. This particular day, she rang the bell and the girls went to the bathroom and the boys went to get a drink of water. But they come back and started chunking mudballs at that outdoor toilet, and we couldn't come out. They're throwing big mudballs! She set there and ring that bell, but they'd just keep on chunking. The next day, I think there was twenty-one boys in school that year, she whupped about half of them one day and half of them the other.

### ANDY GORDON WOLF

Everybody'd get together once a year and saw enough wood to last the school all winter. And the boys, me and whoever else that had to, hauled wood to put by the stove.

Never had no complaints that I know of, but then we had a pretty rough bunch of boys. You know, snuff dippers. And it's pretty hard to get along with that old Ralph Bundon, he's a great big old tall boy. I don't know what grade he's in, I've forgotten, but we had a teacher name of Huckabee, and he told old Huckabee, "You ain't big enough to whip me," and old Huckabee grabbed him by the back of the neck and throwed him down on the bench and taken an old wide army belt and whipped him with it.

We had that kind of people, that's just the way it was. It's a rough bunch. We didn't have playgrounds and things, we had a schoolyard and rocks, just like this damn yard out here. Our basketball court, that's what you had, and if you fell you'd skin all the hide off of you. The water come out of a pump. We had a well down there, and you'd go down and pump you some water if you wanted a drink. You had outdoor crappers, girls one way and boys the other, and that's where you had a fight. Get mad at somebody and say, "Come on with me out yonder and we'll fight!" I've been there several times.

### JOHN DANIEL WOLF

One of the schoolteachers at Maple, her husband beat the devil out of her, one side of her face all black and blue. Her daddy, old man Herne, lived here in Gatesville, and he rode the school bus from Gatesville out here. I was on the bus when he came out. He stopped down there at his daughter's, and he told his son-in-law, said, "You don't beat my daughter anymore, you leave her alone." He said, "If you can't, if you have to beat, then you leave." She was a schoolteacher, and he just lived off of her, really. He beat her up again, and the old man saw him here [on the courthouse square in Gatesville] and walks over to the car. Told him, "I think you beat my daughter again," and he said, "None of your damn business," and started cursing. That old man emptied a gun in him, just shot him full of holes. Then he walked back toward the courthouse to the sheriff, and somebody got the sheriff, and he was arrested. Never put the old man in jail. They had the old man's trial in Gatesville. He was seventy years old and had never broke a law in his life.

### JAMES W. CALHOUN

One time, just before Christmas, we was all going out to gather pretty leaves, red berries, cedar boughs, and all that stuff to decorate the [Maple] schoolrooms for Christmas. The whole school went, every kid, and we were traipsing around the mountain. Well, we decided—me and my brother and Andy and William Doyle Wolf—we decided that's too tame for us, so we just took off from the bunch and went to explore some caves that was back in there.

We showed up before school was out, and Miss Molly Montgomery and the other teachers already had their peeled cedar switches. They got our attention pretty good, but that wasn't near as bad as it was when we got home. We didn't get a whipping, but it was dark and the old barn had rats in it, and Daddy made me and my brother go to the corn crib and shell a number three washtub full of corn as punishment for running off. The dark was bad enough, but them rats crawling around was something else.

### ROBERT E. GAULT

Oh, every once in a while you'd have a whipping. Somebody would steal something, they'd get a busting, right there. Then they'd call their daddy, and when they got home they'd get another one. I never got a whipping at school because I knew what would happen if I got one there. I wasn't afraid of them, I was afraid of my dad.

We had a good bit of trouble one year, and they hired a teacher from over at Maple–Silver City [School], just over from us. They hired this old boy, and his reputation went ahead of him. He'd had forty-nine whippings in a year over there, and he had a Sam Brown belt that had ever name on it. He stayed at our school three years and never whipped a person! That's what a reputation does for anybody. I never could understand. He was a nice teacher and a fine man, but evidently he [had] walked into a hotbed of discipline over there. But he straightened them out.

### ARCHIE SPIVY WRIGHT

The first school I went to was a little school called Salem, just a one-room school was all it was. Twenty-five or thirty kids went there, maybe not that many. We'd just play there until they'd take up books in the morning at nine o'clock. Then we'd turn out for recess just like they do now and for dinner. We'd play at recess and dinner all the time. When I started school I was just a little old boy—six, seven years old. This teacher beat me up, me and another boy. Me and another boy was spelling, he got us scared. He kept us in a lot, and he got us scared, and we couldn't spell three words. He went outside and cut himself some live oak bushes with knots on them and brought it in there, and kept us in, and gave us a beating. Stretched out over a chair like this one here, got us by the collars and give us a beating, beat the blood out of both of us. The other boy messed in his britches.

My oldest brother, Dewey, and Melvin Cox, another friend-boy there of my brother's, they went up the next morning, they were going to get him. But he'd done left out, he left that evening. We saw him going down the lane toward the Cowhouse [Creek] going to Gatesville. We didn't see him no more.

### LOUIS J. TOMASTIK

At Halloween, we always tried to do something—not too bad, not outrageous, but some mischief. We'd think it up, and I thought this up. I thought, hey, let's see if we can catch an armadillo, put it in a box a day or two before Halloween, somehow work it into [Antelope School], and turn it into that auditorium when the lights are out. I'd say probably that auditorium was about ninety feet long by about thirty feet wide, and that's where we'd have all these Halloween plays.

We figured we'd wait out until the intermission, then we'd get it in there. We went in another door, we went into our seats. Nothing happened for a little bit, 'cause the armadillo was probably on the side corner, but then after a while it started moving. Then it gets to where these people were, and they couldn't see it, it's dark, and they would hit it or something, it would try to run. And then, man, it would make the awfullest noise, them feet against that hardwood floor! Pretty soon, people, kids, especially girls, started screaming, and they stopped the play and turned the lights on. Finally, somebody caught it and took it out.

G. G. Northcutt, he's the principal there. He was kind of mean to us kids, at least we thought he was mean, a little bit hard. He was a little bit overactive. We got back at him a little bit. Tacks, he started having flats, and his car was missing. I think somebody put dirt in his gas tank.

## School Entertainments

*Starved for entertainment, rural communities looked to their schools for amusement, and woe to the teacher who failed to put on a good Christmas program or end-of-school celebration. Every school in the Fort Hood settlements had major school-closing festivities in May, sometimes lasting two or three days. These featured three-act plays, barbecues, picnics, races, and competitions of every sort, including baseball, the countryside's game of games.*

### MARGARET BERT WILHITE BOUNDS

My mother told me never to play pop-the-whip at recess. 'Course, I was little bitty for my age anyhow. These big old boys would be up there popping the whip, and they talked me into playing pop-the-whip one day. They put me on the end, and when they popped me loose, I went sailing through there about like Superman. But, oh, when I landed, my knees were full of gravel, and I couldn't go to school for two days.

### KYLE HILLIARD

[At recess at Palo Alto School] we made up our games and played annie over and running base. In annie over, one side throws the ball over the school building, and the other side tries to catch it before it hits the ground. If they succeed, they come around and touch a member of the throwing team who tries to escape around to the other side of the building. Anyone who gets touched with the ball is lost to his team. If the receiving side fails to catch the ball in the air, they throw it back, and the process is repeated. The big deal was to get your strongest boy on your team to get up fairly close and throw it just as hard as he could to keep the other side from catching it in the air. Mostly, we played softball. Someone had given the school a corner of his pasture, so we had plenty of room to play.

### MARGARET BERT WILHITE BOUNDS

We'd play baseball. We'd get up a team and then we'd play other schools like Brookhaven or Union Hill or Tennessee Valley. Even in the summer the men would get up a ball team and play other communities. Sometimes they would play on the ball field there by the schoolhouse [in Sparta], sometimes they would be at another school playing. Usually the school would have a ball field.

I played in some of them. In fact, one year I was the only girl on the team, and I got a broke finger. I reached up with [the bare hand], and that ball hit the top of my finger. Oh, that hurt!

One time, the men chose up sides one Sunday afternoon. They had to dress as women, had to have heels and a purse, and you had to carry that purse with you. You could set it down while you were batting, but you had to pick it up and carry it with you when you run, or you was automatically out. People from other communities even come to see that. They sold cold drinks and made a little money to buy other gloves and balls and things like that. [The batter] would set his purse down and hit the ball, then reach down and grab that purse. Had to go to all the bases with it.

### LOUIS J. TOMASTIK

I was twelve when I bought the bicycle. How I got it, I went around selling Cloverine Salve to all them neighbors around there, and I sold everybody as far as I could. That bike was twenty-eight dollars, the deluxe model with the brake, the best one they put out at Sears and Roebuck. You step on the brake, the back light would come on, and it had a little horn and a headlight.

Had to go to Copperas Cove to get it because the mailman didn't deliver things that big. Boy, was I proud. It was a pretty thing, whitewall tires on it. It was kind of blue, aqua-blue-type tinge, a little white trim on it.

Howard and Joe Insall had one. Lot of the time, school picnics, they'd be four or five miles off, Maple or somewhere, we'd get together and go. Of course, they'd come to our picnic and we'd go to theirs. Get on them and ride to the picnic. Those country roads are just right for bicycles. You take off fast, you see dust behind you.

### ROBERT E. GAULT

They had a picnic every year at the end of school [at Antelope], and we had a big barbecue, played baseball, and I got sick at eating. They sold cold drinks and stuff like that, and I'd always eat enough [that] I was sick for a day or two after it. You know how a kid is. They'd take a big steer and barbecue that thing out there in an open pit, and lots of people from Killeen would come out there, and some from Copperas Cove, some from Gatesville. We'd have that old grounds, that three or four acres, just full of people.

They had a ring on a post, and used a lance on a horse and running to take the ring off. [It was] put on there with a clip, and they had this pole with a prod on the end of it, and you ride full speed on a horse and catch that ring. Some of them could do it, and some wouldn't.

And then they played baseball up there. Gatesville used to have a big boy's reformatory school, and usually their baseball team would come down and play the "Antelope Outsiders." And at noon we'd have dinner. If it was a political year, we'd have politicians, of course. And then we'd have plays at night, the last three nights of school. Something else we had at Antelope School I enjoyed, [on] Easter Friday the kids would come to school, and they might have a few classes in the morning, but about ten o'clock they'd go down to Leslie Thompson's place. He had a spring and a beautiful valley there, where we'd have an Easter egg hunt and play baseball. After I got to going to school at Gatesville, I'd get off [the school bus] there on that morning, I'd always get off there at Antelope and stay. I never did get in trouble over it, don't know why I didn't.

### JOHN DANIEL WOLF

There wasn't a whole lot of entertainment. When it came time for school to be over, about the first to fifteenth of May, it was a routine at all the rural schools that they would have a three-act play. That was to be performed the night of this weekend that was set aside for the school ending. At the same time, they had a big barbecue, and somebody would donate a half a beef, somebody would donate a half a hog, and they would put that all in the deal. There was some tremendous eating, a tremendous barbecue. We had what everybody considered the expert in the community that did the cooking and the seasoning of that barbecue. A half a dozen men would gather the day before. They cleaned the pit, they got the meat ready and chopped it up. Have you ever seen a syrup pan that they cook syrup off in? They used that to cook barbecue in [at Maple School]. And ooooooh was it good! You'd smell it all over the place cooking.

We tried to make all of those weekends. After I was twelve or fourteen years old, we tried to go to every school ending that we could. Ewing had theirs, and then the Antelope School and the Brown's Creek School, they had their end-of-school deals. That was one of the big highlights of the year for entertainment.

To be perfectly frank with you, we had fights all the time. At those end-of-school deals I remember some bad, bad fights. As far as I know, there wasn't anybody thought of taking a gun and shooting somebody or cutting them with a knife. Two old boys eighteen or twenty years old would get cross-ways with a girl or something, and they'd just fight until they got bloody. A lot of times they were about evenly matched. Two brothers get into it, and then their brothers get into it. I remember that happening two or three times. The whole family, sometimes.

### DORIS LEE WHITE THOMAS

I think they got the name Spring Hill because the school was up on a hill. And there was a spring across the road from the schoolhouse, and it never went dry. Every year, the last day of school, parents and students came. They had a play day, a picnic-like thing, parents and all. Genieva White Thomas tells me that when they got old enough, they would have partners, a boy they wanted to walk with, so when she thought she was old enough to do that, she went walking across the road over there to the spring to get them a drink and come back to the schoolhouse. They's walking along there talking, and she said, "I kept hearing some footsteps behind me, I wondered who was following us." She turned around and looked, and it was her daddy follering her and listening to what they were saying. Said, "He never did ever say a word, he just followed, just followed."

### WILLIAM AKE POWELL

They'd have a last-day-of-school picnic, and they'd get a bunch of [musicians] to play, and my daddy would play his fiddle. They'd have a picnic and a play that night. Adults would get a play-type thing, and everybody would pick whoever they wanted for the parts, and they'd practice a few times, and then they'd put that play on the last night. I remember they used to build a stage that fit in front of the Friendship church house, and that's where they used to put the play on.

Back then, people come from all over to see that. All adjoining communities would come to one of those last days of schools. They used to always have a big barbecue for the dinner that day. My daddy used to help barbecue, he's pretty good at that, and all the women would bring dishes. And they'd have that spread at dinnertime, and you talking about eating, now, there's plenty to eat. Didn't cost anybody, it's all free.

When I was going to Ewing over there, they used to have a baseball game in the afternoon. And they had a black team here in Gatesville, and they put on some kind of show when they'd play ball. Everybody loved to watch them. Local people would get up a ball team, or they might have one that played sometimes, and they'd play this black team. This black team could cut all kind of capers, throwing the ball or doing this, and people would come from all over to see it. They didn't pay them anything, but they'd feed them and maybe have a big watermelon feast when they got through.

I went this year at Gatesville, then I played six-man football at Flat. I'd never been around football, I'd lived out in the country, and we'd played a little basketball with other schools, but I went out for football. They had

212 |  HARDER THAN HARDSCRABBLE

two coaches, and the defensive coach put me to playing defensive end. I weighed about 125 pounds, I guess. He told me, "Now, I'm going to let you in on a secret that nobody else may know." He said, "So-and-so is gonna get the ball, and he's coming right around this a-way. I want you to get him."

I said, "I'll do my best," but he didn't tell me about that 200-pound guard that was coming around there ahead of him! Whooh, that guy knocked me about twenty feet. That was my introduction to playing football, right there.

I played at Gatesville that year, then they wanted to organize six-man football at Flat. They come and got me. I was about the same distance from the Flat, I transferred to the Flat, and come to play six-man football with them. They didn't have enough people, and we didn't have a very good team, but we played all of them anyway. I played six-man football with them two years at Flat and graduated from down there in 1940.

You just had three men in the line and three men in the backfield, and that was the size of it. Flat has a lot of rocks, and we didn't have a football field. Man, it was tough, there's a lot of skinning up going on. We played Jarrell one time, and they played in a cotton patch. The cotton had been cleared off, but it was an old cotton field, and you'd hit the ground in that old red dirt, and, man, talk about skinning you up! We didn't have too many pads then. That was a Bohemian settlement, and those boys called them signals in Bohemian, I never will forget that. I'll tell you, I didn't have a bit of hide on me when I got home.

It was rough. We played somebody one time, and they knocked me plumb out. They drug me off to the side. We had an old coach, his name was Harry Morman, and he come over there and shook me, got me up. Says, "Where we at?" I told him. He says, "Well, who we playing?" I told him. He says, "What the hell you doing out here? Get back in there!"

I've picked cotton with broke ribs and everything else. I've been all skinned up and could hardly walk, but I always showed up to work. My daddy used to tell me, said, "You can play football all you want to, but when it comes Saturday morning I want you to able to pick cotton or do whatever we got to do."

### FRANKIE JUANITA WRIGHT TRANTHAM

I hated school [at Antelope], except for the basketball. Oh, I loved basketball better than anything! I could play all the time. We had a boys' court and a girls' court. We usually ended up playing on the boys' court as much as they did. It was dirt, just clean dirt, just cleaned-off white-looking dirt.

We never did play inside until we went to Gatesville to the tournament to play. We always played out on the dirt.

I was on the team, and we had three guards and forwards back then when I was playing. We usually went to Pidcoke and played them, and we'd always beat them! We always enjoyed that. The last year that I played, we was having to play all the other schools that was out around. Like Pidcoke, or Levita, Ewing, and those different places. Ewing had great old big tall girls, and they could beat anybody, I think. We just couldn't beat them, but we did beat Levita, and we won second place in the basketball tournament.

We had a principal named Mr. Barton, Charlie Barton, and he was a good guy and a good basketball coach, too. His sister-in-law Joy taught there. She was just as cute as a pie, and she got out there in them high heels and would play basketball with us—practice, you know. For a while, it seemed like we couldn't win very many games. Joy Cousins, our schoolteacher, had been coaching us, but Mr. Barton took us over and started coaching us hisself. He told us one day, he said, "I want every one of you to eat, however you want it, a raw egg every morning. Every morning, a completely raw egg!" He said it would help us to have longer wind, and we wouldn't run out of wind so easy. I would have done it or died, because I loved that game so much.

We had little white blouses, and then we had green shorts, shorts that come just a little above your knee. And we were so proud of them! We had to take care of them ourselves, wash them and keep them clean. We had played basketball with Pidcoke one day. Mother knew I was playing, and she didn't mind me playing, but she was so strict with everything. I come in that evening after we'd gone and played, and I had that suit to wash. And ah-ha! She found out what it was! She said, "Well, you're not playing basketball anymore! If that's what your going to wear, you're not playing anymore!" So I said, "Well, okay, I'll just play with my dress on." I always played, I wouldn't have given it up for anything. I loved it too much.

## Family Visits

*The most common social event in the Fort Hood settlements was the family visit—announced or unannounced. Isolated on their farms, families hungered for new faces and news of what had happened a few miles down the road. Reciprocal visits by blood relatives and neighbors made up much of community social life, and the visitors might stay a day or a week. Other amusing visitors also were welcomed—known or unknown, blood-*

*related or not. Every stranger coming down the road had amusement value and might receive the standard country invitation to "Tie your horse and come on in!" even if he traveled by Model T.*

### NORMAN RICKETTS HALL

Those communities back in those different places were lost to the rest of the world, because that was their own neighborhood, everything was pretty much there. And, gosh, the families met, they'd have a big meet at a house, and they'd play dominoes, and the ladies would quilt or gossip or whatever they do. You'd have one of those most ever week.

### ANDY GORDON WOLF

Dick Hill, he had a big family, and they lived back up on Manning Mountain. That was my mother's first cousin, see. And they'd bring all their family down and stay two or three days or whatever, and everybody would put them a quilt on the floor, whatever, and sleep. Have a big domino game, and we'd chase down a chicken and have chicken and dumplings and have a real fine time. They went five or six miles in a wagon like that, take them all day to come down there.

We had a game we called high five, and everybody'd get excited at that high five game. It was a card game, it wasn't gambling or anything, choose up partners and play. Nobody plays it anymore. One of my brothers died, and we don't even have anybody knows how to play it.

### DORIS LEE WHITE THOMAS

People back then didn't talk in front of their children. They did not tell them anything. Be quiet and get out of the way and don't bother [us] and don't listen. They didn't say that, but you got the idea you're not supposed to learn anything about what your grown folks are saying.

One of my cousins said they was at Grandma Wittie's [in the Spring Hill community], and their house was up high a little bit. She and another cousin decided they'd crawl under the house and listen to the women and visiting and maybe learn something that they wasn't supposed to know. But she says, "They never talked about a thing that we wanted them to talk about!"

### WILLIAM AKE POWELL

The grandkids all used to come visit my grandpa in the summertime. One of my aunts had nine kids, and there's several of them had four or five, and you put all that bunch together—! For two or three days a week in the summertime, we'd go to Grandpa's house and spend that time after school is out. My Grandpa Powell had what he called a "gallery." It ran all the way down the south side and the west side of his house at Friendship. And he had a bunch of grandkids, and they'd put pallets out there on that, and it'd look just like cordwood. That whole porch would be full of kids sleeping out there at night. We had one of them was a sleepwalker, he used to keep all of us awake. He'd get up, walk all over everybody, go out the gate. Somebody would have to go get him.

### GLADYS MERLE KEENER CHASTAIN

Grandmother Hopson ran the post office at Maple. She had a wood-burning fireplace, and I remember when I was a kid, and I used to go spend the night with here, I loved sitting there and watching that fire crackle in the old fireplace. Your legs would get red-splochity, you'd be setting up so close to get warm, that was all the heat in the house, yet you'd be cold on the back and everything. I remember that post office desk, the letter-sortment thing. There was a postcard there, and a devil with a pitchfork on that postcard. Where it came from I don't know, but I can remember it to this day, and I'm seventy-five and a half years old. I thought, I don't want that sucker to get after me!

My Grandmother Hopson always wore a long black checkered apron over her dress. Mother's dad and mother had had twelve children, and I thought their house was really rich, but now I know that it wasn't. They did have a cistern at the end of their porch, and all of us grandkids would take turns pumping that cistern. All the kids and grandkids would come to Grandmother Hopson's on a Sunday and visit. We had wonderful time, the kids going up to the mountain. Granddad Hopson loved flowers, even back then as poor as we were. He had a beautiful flower garden at one end of the house that he was proud of, all kind of flowers. And he was for making birdhouses on tall long poles.

In later years, my grandfather's mind got bad, and so he'd gone off hunting something in the pasture and got turned around, got lost. To this day I can still hear them hunting him in the corn field—hitting the corn stalks, calling his name, trying to find him. Thought maybe he's laying down in the corn stalks. They put all us kids on a pallet to sleep. I remember all us kids laying on the floor on pallets, because all the other family members were out hunting my grandfather, and they finally found him.

My other grandparents, when it come cotton-picking time, all the families gathered in to Grandma and Grandpa Keener's—all the brothers and sisters, sisters-in-law and brothers-in-law—to help get the crops in. All of us kids was out in the cotton patch playing. We wasn't big enough [to help pick], we were all under seven years old, and there were about five or six of us. We got in a fight, and we tore each other's clothes. And so Grandma Keener come got us and took us back to the house and made blue and white checkety dresses for us, and even made the boys shirts out of blue and white checkety. And we all grabbed hands and went back to the cotton field [to show] our parents, just as happy as we can be, holding hands.

### DORIS LEE WHITE THOMAS

Farmers didn't go visiting until it rained. I was just three years old, we had to cross Owl Creek to go to Grandpa Dunlap's house, and we went in a buggy. We got to that Owl Creek, I'll never forget it, and I'll never cross it again. We got down there, and the creek was up so high and a-rolling and tumbling, all this muddy water going everywhere. They stopped the buggy, Mother and Daddy was sitting there talking. Should they cross it or not cross it? I thought, Let's go home!

Two young men came up on their riding horses, and Daddy went out, and they talked and talked a long time. Then, first thing I know, Daddy was reaching in that buggy, and he set me up in the front of one of those saddles of those men. He says, "Grab that saddlehorn and do not turn it loose for anything."

He didn't say I was going across the creek, or I might have fell off the horse right there. The man started across the creek, and I thought, Well, Daddy said to hold on to this horn, I am going to hold on to it no matter what happens. I guess men back then knew the strength of their horses. Why [else] would anyone have done such a thing? It washed us down a little piece. The fellow never said a word to me the whole crossing; he was watching his business, I guess. We got across, and he turned around, and we watched Mother and Daddy and the other young man that was across the creek watching us. They started to cross that creek, and that buggy washed around even with the horse, and they drifted way down. I never was so scared in my life. And no way would I ever do anything like that. Nothing's worth that. I still see that water, just rolling and a-tumbling.

### ROBERT E. GAULT

I didn't go [to town] until fall, when we went to get school clothes. We'd go fishing on Saturday evening usually, and Sunday we'd go to church. And somebody would come to our house to eat Sunday dinner, [or] we'd go with somebody else nearly every time. My mother had a German lady, a Mrs. Albert Kindler, she was a Lutheran, lived up there close to Antelope, and we ate dinner with them one Sunday a month, and they ate with us one Sunday a month. They had a half-time church, and we had a half-time church, and they'd go to our church when theirs wasn't going on. They were the finest people I ever knew. We'd go to their house, and some Germans come in and go to talking German, and Mr. Kindler would get on them, say, "No, I've got friends here that don't understand that, you just hush that. You're insulting them." My mother was closer to her than just about anybody.

### JOE D. INSALL

We'd go to church at Antelope when we had to, we'd get out of it when we could, and we'd go to neighbors listening to the radio. We'd go listen to Gene Autry on Sunday evenings. He'd sing songs and sell that Doublemint chewing gum. The people that lived next to us were Czechs, the Tomastiks. They talked Czech; in fact, their mother never did learn to talk English. They made kolaches, and they grew poppyseeds to put on them. Them girls was a whole lot older than me, and they was always teasing me. They said them [poppyseeds] was fleas they'd picked off chickens. The old man grew his own tobacco that he smoked in a pipe, had one of these old crooked pipes. We'd steal a little bit of it and get us some brown paper and hide in the bushes and roll a cigarette and light it and get sick.

### ANDY GORDON WOLF

Uncle Bob Dorsey was an old fellow, I think he lived with his daughter, but he come through the country about once a year, and he'd stay with us for about a week. He'd talk, he'd been to town and he'd tell things; it's interesting to hear him talk. We'd have to make a crop, so we'd just finally have to go off and leave him talking. But he was a fine old man, you know what I mean? And that's what he done, he'd visit people that he knew.

People come around every once in a while, that's the only people you would see. It didn't make any difference, who he was, somebody'd come along and it might of been a month or two months or three months since you'd seen anybody, so [you were] glad to see them. There's an old saying, fellow'd come up there on his horse, and they'd say, "Tie your horse and come on in!" If it's time to eat, said, "We're fixing to eat, just pull up a chair there." That's the way everybody was. That's the way it was. That's from a different world.

### KYLE HILLIARD

My parents were Joe and Edith Hilliard. We lived on a small tenant farm [at Palo Alto] about three and a half miles northeast of Killeen. My grandparents were R. M. and Clara Hilliard, who lived across the Post Oak Mountain from us. We called it "Grandpa's Mountain." My grandparents had nine children, my dad was number eight, and we were real close to the whole family. There were two married uncles who lived over there near Grandpa, so we had a lot of cousins to play with, and we visited back and forth. They lived on the north side of Post Oak Mountain, and we lived on the south side.

I can remember one trip to Grandpa's with my dad in a wagon where we went straight across the mountain. It was about three and a half or four miles if we went around the road, but we went right across the Halls' pasture and through their side of Post Oak Mountain and then crossed it and went on down to Grandpa's, and it was very rough going. Some of the time you just barely did make it down some of those rocky slopes.

Another memory that stands out in my mind was from when I was about four. We had been over to Grandpa's in our buggy, and we came home, and it was a winter night, but there was no wind. It was clear, lots of stars in the sky. My brother and I were lying on the floor of that buggy where they made us a little pallet. The main parts of our bodies were under the seat that Mom and Dad and Sister were sitting on, but we were looking right straight up into the sky. And boy, was that ever a big sky.

That was just family, just a quiet silent ride, looking at the stars above, and feeling cozy and warm lying in the bed of that buggy, covered up real good, Mama and Daddy there in the front seat taking care of this world. That was a cozy introduction to the many, many stars in the sky.

I have a fond memory of a friend, a neighbor, whose whole family were close friends. We had ice cream together a number of times and even tried to play a little bit of music. I played the harmonica, poorly, and Mr. Everett played the guitar, so we had some good get-togethers. Here's what farm boys would do back in those days. On a Sunday afternoon or a Saturday, you were liable to look up and there would be a boy that lived five or six miles away, walking up the road towards your house. Back in those days we didn't call anybody, even if they had a phone and we had a phone. We didn't call them to say we wanted to come over for a visit, we'd just go. People went to other people's houses unannounced. If they weren't there, they didn't stay, of course. If they were there, they stayed, usually.

So one Sunday afternoon Burl Everett walked the two miles over to our house. He and my brother and I hung around there for a little while on the place, and then we just started walking. We just walked along, we got on the road to Killeen. We walked past the Ramms, past the Cantwells, past Oscar Harris's, past Dick Overton's—just walking along there, talking. Every once in a while we'd pick up a rock and throw it and see if we could hit a fencepost or a telephone post, just walking and being together on a beautiful Sunday afternoon. That was as good a time as I ever had, really. And that boy died in 1940, he was sixteen years old.

During the Depression, the real depth of the Depression, which was about 1932, '33, '34, and '35, don't be surprised if some relative, some distant cousin even showed up at your house. They would maybe hitchhike to Killeen or come in on a boxcar or maybe in a bus. Anyway, people would walk out to your house, and here they would be—some uncle of my mother's or a brother of my dad's—and they'd stay three or four days, sometimes two or three weeks.

One such face was Cousin Tom McHenry. He told us some very interesting stories, so we enjoyed him very much. He sold patent medicine. He looked at me and said, "You have floating objects in front of your eyes, don't you?" I said, "How can you tell?" I didn't know what to call them, but I knew I had these things, these designs. He said, "Well, I can tell by looking at you that you do." And so he sold his patent medicine, and he told stories. He had known some Indians chiefs in their later years, when they stopped being chiefs and stopped fighting and there's no more Indian wars. We heard stories from the old-timers when they came by, all of us sitting around the fireplace and telling stories.

Speaking of the fireplace, one cold, rainy winter night, with no radio, no television, and bad weather outside, a marathon domino game took place in our fireplace room. Bob Smith and Weldon Hall came to our house that cold winter night, and Daddy and Herman and Weldon and Bob played dominoes—four-handed, playing partners. They played a long time, and Daddy, who liked chocolate fudge, said, "Edith, how about getting up and making us a batch of chocolate candy? So Mama went in there and built a fire in the wood stove and made a batch of chocolate fudge, and set it out there.

They played dominoes and played dominoes and ate candy, the hours ticked away, and finally it was all gone, and they kept on playing. After a little while, Daddy again asked Mama to make another batch of that chocolate fudge candy. It's the Depression, everything is so dreary and so hard. Why not just live a little bit and do what you enjoy? You know, live for today, let tomorrow take care of itself. So Mama got up and made another batch of chocolate fudge candy. And they played fifty-six games of dominoes that Saturday night, and each side won twenty-eight games.

### NORRIS SIDNEY GRAVES

Every Christmas, all of us kids [would] come to get the cedar tree and put on candle lights. Oh, I tell you, that was amazing, it was beautiful. We'd sit there, and then we'd go upstairs, and they'd sing a little bit. My mother played the guitar, and I had an aunt that played the piano. One of the men, Uncle Clay, he played the banjo. And when he got to cutting up, he'd take his shoes and socks off and strum it with his toes.

### MARGARET BERT WILHITE BOUNDS

My first remembrance is we didn't get a lot of gifts. We got an apple, an orange, and maybe a candy cane in a sack and some pecans and nuts and stuff like that. As I got a little older, I remember getting a doll for Christmas, and then one year I got a silver brush and mirror and comb set. We'd go up above the house on the hill there and get a tree. We'd put popcorn on it and red berries, and sometimes we'd make those chains out of construction paper and put on there. It'd be pretty decorated up, we thought. And we'd take chewing gum wrapper, and we'd cut stars out of pasteboard, and put that on it and make silver trees on the tree.

We made a lot of our own toys. When Mama would get our new Sears and Roebuck catalogue, we got the old one to carry to the toilet, but me and my sister would go through and cut out paper dolls. Take Oxydol boxes after Mama started using Oxydol and soda boxes for cars, and we'd make our own furniture out of pasteboard things. We had a playhouse, too, and we would use old cracked dishes, broke dishes. We'd take the bigger part, and that was our butter dish. In back of us was a clay hill, and we'd go and make our clay shaped like butter and put on there. And we'd make bowls. We'd take and roll the clay and wind those rolls around and make the bowls.

### ERNEST ALLEN COLE

We had a Christmas tree, one of the mountain junipers. We owned half of a mountain, just south of us. For Christmas dinner, we might have two or three families get together. On Christmas night we hung up our stockings. We got an apple, English walnuts, a stick or two of candy, and about two packages of fireworks—little old firecrackers and a box of sparklers and maybe a Roman candle about this long, shot about ten times. Out in the country, you got all your fireworks at Christmastime. So that was Christmas. The girls usually got a doll. I remember, one of the best presents I ever got, I got a bicycle tire. Usually, one present was all you got. As I told you, you didn't make a living in this country; in this country, you lived on what you made.

### DORIS LEE WHITE THOMAS

There was a store at Straw's Mill. Yes, because Ruby Wittie was telling me her last doll she got at Christmastime, the last doll she ever got, she was expecting a great big beautiful doll because it would be her last one. And it rained so her daddy couldn't even come to Gatesville in the wagon and get anything—rained and rained and rained and rained. So he got on his horse and went to Straw's Mill. She said, "I was so hurt, [but] Papa was trying." She got three little celluloid dolls in a box.

### JOE D. INSALL

We never did get much for Christmas. They didn't have any plastic back in them days, but I got a little rubber car. I wore the wheels off it, and I just kept on playing with it. [My aunts] came over for Christmas. We always hung our stockings up. Didn't have no fireplace, but we hung them up somewheres, and we'd get them full of pecans and a apple, maybe one of them little red and white sticks of candy. We were upstairs. They had it floored and had a couple of beds up there, we were looking down through them cracks. And they were down there by that kerosene lamp a-putting presents out. And they had this little black baby doll, when you wind it up it'd crawl on the floor. We were watching that. One of them twins was going to get it, my mother's youngest sister.

### KYLE HILLIARD

My mother and my dad tried to make Christmas really something. They went all out, even if it was on borrowed money. So we had good Christmases; we got lots of gifts every Christmas, some way or another. Just to make conversation, I can remember asking one of the boys at school what he got for Christmas, and he pulled out a little coin purse thing and said, "That and an apple and an orange." I felt very sorry that I had asked him the question. He didn't get hardly anything. They had several children in the family, and they were very, very poor. That's not the way to make a conversation.

But our Christmases were outstanding. We would get out in the front yard where we had a nice smooth pasture, a softball field that was ready-made, we'd get out there and shoot fireworks. One Christmas, I believe it was 1930, Uncle Ray and Aunt Dona Hilliard and their two daughters came over to our house Christmas Eve. We had a roaring fire in the fireplace and the kerosene lamps all lit up bright. It just seemed like the brightest place in the world.

## The Sporting Life

*Every community had a fox hunter or two, ready to stay up late into the night around a campfire listening to his dogs and those of other men run the gray or red fox. The communal hunt or group fishing trip to Cowhouse Creek or the Leon River also punctuated the yearly round of community social life. These might be family affairs, or—as in the case of most of the fox hunts—they might not. Teenagers or adult males might get together at times for rowdyish entertainments, discreetly hinted at in the interviews below. In his memoir of the Brown's Creek settlement (which had a serious "sporting life" reputation), Jerome Keener Blackwell wrote: "Our community was a typical back-woodsy one with all the extras that went with such a small Texas community. We had a church, school, ten whiskey stills, chicken fights within a ten-mile radius, and on Saturday night the young entertained themselves with a dance (stomp)."*

### CLEMENTS W. "SPEEDY" DUNCAN

We used to pitch dollars, real dollars, silver dollars. All those little old communities would dig a hole in the ground and pitch dollars at that hole for pastime. It wasn't all pastime, they'd bet some on it.

It was twenty-five feet, I believe. There was a regulation on it to learn, it would be to the inch. They'd dig out a hole, a very small hole, with a pocket knife. They'd wear out fairly soon, and they'd have to move over and dig a new hole. They'd be sometimes five games going on in that little old town, Oakalla over there, of dollar-pitching.

It counted three points if your dollar went in the hole. But the opponent over there, he had three dollars in his hand, if he pitched one in the hole, yours didn't count. It killed yours. And the closest dollar to the hole would count one, and twenty-one was the game.

Then, after a while, times got hard, and we pitched washers! My dad and I pitched ever day for all year. So often we didn't have anything to do but pitch washers, and you take a kid and you let him do something long enough, he'll get fair at it. My daddy, he could pitch a washer in a hole, he just could pitch it in there.

We're there one day, me and him pitching washers, and two fellows come by with money in their pocket. My dad and them talked a while and got up a washer game, and Pa said, "Well, ain't nobody around, I guess that kid will do—I can use him until somebody shows up." We was pitching and I wasn't putting them in the hole. I wasn't bearing down enough, wasn't putting in enough effort, I was just playing. Directly, my pa walked around there and got up close and said, "Son, pitch them washers in the hole! I'm telling you, pitch them washers in the hole!" I didn't know he was betting the egg money on it. But we soon relieved them people of all the money they had on them. I guess that's the first gambling I done in my life.

### ROBERT E. GAULT

We had family, especially in the summer months, that'd come stay a week or two. We were on that creek there, it was good fishing down there, and in the summertime they loved to come there and stay. People in those days, they took longer to get anywhere, so they'd come and stay longer. I've seen people there, to where we had four or five bedrooms and three big porches, and there'd be people sleeping out on those porches on pallets. We never thought anything about that.

People really enjoyed what they had then. We didn't have much, but we enjoyed every bit of it. We made our own entertainment in those days.

Then, just above our place on Cowhouse [Creek], there was a crossing, what we called a gravel bar. We had a Fourth of July picnic there every year, and you'd have 100, 150 people come in there. The day before, we'd go in and seine fish, and we'd have a big fish fry out of it, you see. We had a good swimming hole right there close, and that was always a big thing.

### ANDY GORDON WOLF

We'd ride horses every once in a while and go down to Cowhouse—just boys, four or five boys, and you had to go five, six, seven miles over to Eliga. Eliga was another community.

Everybody let you in, and we went down there and tied our horses up, set lines out. And we'd catfish, stay a day or two. There was a swimming hole there, and we all knew where it was. They had a swing tied up in a big elm tree, and we'd swing out across that, and the water's fifteen or twenty feet deep. We went up there one time, I believe the Manning boys and us and maybe one or two of the Hubbard boys, and we set lines down there and slept in the church house. The church house was open. That's all we done, we slept in it. I can't imagine a kid now wanting to sleep in a church house, be kind of like sleeping in a graveyard.

When I was five or six years old, I'd go by Will Wilson's place to go to my grandmother's, five miles walking. They had a bunch of geese. Mrs. Wilson, she raised them geese for feather pillows and feather beds. Back then, if you was first class, you had to have a feather pillow or feather bed. But ever time I'd go by there, them damn geese'd get after me! Them things would just squawk, set their old heads out and try to get a-hold of me, and I'd outrun them. That was just the way to go to get to the main road. Brown's Creek, where you crossed it down there, was just a road across solid rock, wasn't no bridge on it. I walked it many times.

I went up to see my granddad and grandmother, and Grandpa Hill was deaf, and he had two or three old cur dogs. Anyhow, he said, "Come on, I'll take you possum hunting." There's a bunch of big persimmon trees on the creek down there, so I went with him, and we walked down there and got down there, and it was in the fall and the persimmon trees was full of persimmons. Possums, you never seen the like of possums in that persimmon tree! I clumb up there and grabbed one of them by the tail. The old persimmon tree's a hundred foot high, I guess, it's a big old tree, but I'd climb up there and grab one by the tail and throw him out, and the dogs would kill him when he hit the ground. Killed five or six of them like that. My granddad, before he died, he was setting there one day, and he said, "You remember when I taken you possum hunting?" I said, "Yeah, I do remember."

My dad was a fox hunter. He kept two or three hounds all the time, and this Noog Black, he had a bunch of hounds, and Luther Greenway, who run that store, he had a couple of hounds, and they'd all get them hounds together, and sometimes run one fox all night long. He'd get him a tree and then hold the dogs and chunk him out of that tree, and he'd run again, and then the dogs would pick up his trail and take it up again. They didn't like to kill one at all. They never killed one hardly, 'cause sometimes they had to go a long ways to find a fox.

You couldn't follow the dogs, they'd run too fast. But you get up there and build you a big fire somewhere and listen to the dogs run, and each one of them dogs had a different sound in his voice. Them old fox hunters, they could each one of them tell you which ones was barking.

They used Walkers and Redtick hounds. Old Noog Black had a dog called Old Redwing, and he sold her to Pa, and there ain't no telling what Pa paid for that animal—more than he had, I imagine. She had pups, and they went right on and run with her, they made good fox hounds.

**JOHN DANIEL WOLF**
That was [Daddy's] favorite pastime, and I went with him a-many a night—

up on the back of a horse behind him and he and some other guy chasing their doggone dogs all over the country, listening to them run. Who's out in the lead, and who's lost the trail, and all that. They knew those dogs' voices so well, they could tell you. To some degree you'd have to chase the dogs to keep them in hearing distance. Up there in Wolf Hollow and that old Brown's Creek there were canyons, and through experience they knew where some fox hung out, the kind of places that were good locations for finding a fox. And when they'd come up on the dogs the dogs would have the fox in the top of a tree, they took the dogs and went home. It was all over. They never killed a fox.

No coyotes in this country at that time. There were a few wolves. Sometimes they would get their foxhounds after a wolf, and they didn't like that. They'd get them off that wolf quick as they could. Some of the foxhounds would get in the habit of running jackrabbits, and, boy, you talk about a dog getting a beating!

### WILLIAM AKE POWELL

My daddy used to be a fox hunter. They used to all just meet at a certain place, bring their dogs. They knew where they was most likely to, they called it, "strike a fox." They'd all meet at this place and bring their dogs. They'd get out, get the dogs a-going, and then they'd build a fire and sit around the fire and listen to them run, listen to them bark at the fox. And if they treed the fox, somebody would have to go jump it out so they'd run again. But they all worked on a farm, and they'd all have to go home like two or three o'clock in the morning and get a little bit of sleep.

Sometimes them old dogs would tree that fox, and used to be my job next morning to go jump that fox out or get the dogs. One time they treed not too far from my house, and me and my brother five years younger than me, we went down there to get the dogs or jump the fox out, and this big old fox was laying up there in the fork of a tree. My daddy and them used to hold the old dogs and jump the fox out and let the young dogs run it, 'cause they wouldn't catch it so easy. This was a tree that had a briar thicket all the away around it. We got in there, and we called them dogs, and I told my brother, he had about three or four of them in his hand, I told him, "Now, you hold them dogs, I'm going to crawl up there and jump that fox out." Well, I climbed up there and got this limb, and I whipped that fox out. When he hit the ground, them old dogs run my brother through that briar thicket! He left a good bit of hide on it, he was plumb upset.

### CLEMENTS W. "SPEEDY" DUNCAN

I had a brother-in-law come to see us one Christmas and brought his hounds. My brother'd come with him too. We went up on that hill. Way in the night we'd been chasing these old hounds all [over] them old hills—you drop off of it and then you come back up there. We chased them old hounds until way in the morning, and fog rolled in, and it was thick. You couldn't see twenty feet, you couldn't see nothing.

My older brother was with me, and we sat down at a rock at the edge, wondering where the hell we was. He said we was in McCowan Cove, which is right around from Radar Hill, kind of. I said, "Well, brother, I'm turned around. Damn, I think we're way up towards Copperas Cove." He says, "Oh, no, no, no, I know where we're at, I've hunted this hill all my life. We're in McCowan Cove." I said, "Well, I'm glad, because I'm tired of walking these hills. Let me rest a bit." I had heard a train in the distance, and sure enough that train come along right down there and proved him wrong. We were right up at Copperas Cove, a long way from home. That Radar Hill is a deceiving hill.

### T. A. WILHITE

Daddy, he went with a fox hunter ever once in a while, but I never did go much with them. It makes you go too many miles. I went with old man John Wiseman, and we'd get on a high point, a mountain. You could hear them for miles ever way, and I'd get up there with him. He knowed them dogs just as well as I know his voice, could tell ever dog he has. He'd usually call his name when he barked. Say, "Old so-and-so's getting a start now." And he could tell by his dog's bark what they's after. When they went to barking, he'd say, "That's a wolf." Or a fox, he'd tell you. He taken them dogs hunting every night nearly, and he could sure tell you what them dogs a-running. I'd go with him to get to listen at him tell about the dogs.

When he died, his boy come up there and was running a fox pretty close to the house, and he died listening to that fox race. He was in a bed. They had to raise the windows, and he could hear these dogs running pretty close. He died listening to the dogs.

## House Parties and Dances

*Every young person (and most of the interviewees were teenagers during the 1930s) recalled Saturday night house parties and dances at private homes. The sponsors moved the furniture from a room, rolled up the lino-*

*leum, if they had it, spread cornmeal on the bare wooden floor, and got
ready for company. Depending on local religious policy, these might be
"ring plays" or "musicals" (with seated spectators only tapping their feet,
as at Sparta), or they might be flat-out dances and "stomps," with liquor
available outside the building (as at Brown's Creek). Jerome Keener
Blackwell recalled of the latter affairs that "the music was always loud
and the crowd rowdy. If some man's gun fell from his belt, he would simply kick it into a corner and pick it up at the end of the music." More than
one killing took place at such a Saturday night dance.*

### MURREL L. THOMPSON

All those Thompson boys danced. Yeah, they loved it! Some of them played
the fiddle, too. I think when they were growing up they ran around everywhere. They might go to Gatesville, twenty miles horseback, and come in
just in time to go to work the next day. Those boys did everything, had a
good time. See, before there were lots of fences, there were friends and
school kids that lived way down past our place, and they'd come through
our pasture or field to cut distance. Sometimes they'd be walking and sometimes riding their horse. Back in those days no one worried about trespass-
ing—nobody cared.

### ANDY GORDON WOLF

Country dances would be at somebody's house. We had lots of them. They'd
clear a room out like this here and have musicians there and everybody'd
dance. They'd take turnabout just about every dance. My dad and them
give a dance several times, and they'd have musicians, mostly guitar and
fiddle players. They'd have one or two, always. Arlee and Randall Paul,
their daddy ran the Silver City grocery store, they was both musicians and
they'd come and play some. Sometimes they all get in a fight, get drunk on
that old home brew and white lightning. Sooner or later one of them'd get
to saying how tough he was, he'd challenge somebody else, and first thing
you know you'd have everybody fighting. One time they had a big dance,
and they put us [kids] under the wagon to keep from getting hit with them
rocks. We went down there in a wagon, it was five or six miles from where
we lived.

Brown's Creek always had a bad reputation. They'd say, "The meanest
damn people in the world come from Brown's Creek." Yeah, they drank
that old white lightning and always getting in a fight or something, but
we's all cooped up. You think about living off a damn bale of cotton for a

year, that'll make you mean! If you got a chance to get out, cleaned up and everything, and rode your old horse with a bottle of that hooch on you Saturday, you liable to be pretty mean time you got here. I've seen them ride a horse seven or eight miles, girls and boys both. Any social event was just something else.

They had ten or twelve kids under Uncle Buck, and once a year he'd take cotton off to the gin. He'd always manage to get him a bottle of booze, and he'd come in, hollering just loud as you could hear him for three miles down the road. That's the only time I ever know of him drinking, that one time a year. That's the only time he had money enough to buy anything like that.

### GLADYS MERLE KEENER CHASTAIN

Mother was sixteen and Dad was nineteen when they married. He came all the way from the Brown's Creek community to court Mother. Well, there wasn't any place to take her unless she went to church or revival. She stayed at my grandparents Hopson's house on the front porch in summer. Mother said she never kissed Dad all the time until they were married. She said one time he came from Brown's Creek, which was eight miles, riding a horse, and it was raining and really cold. Said when she went to tell him 'bye one evening, I'm sure he went home before dark, she said she wanted to kiss him, but she said, "I didn't." So Mother never kissed Dad until they married.

Uncle Willie introduced Daddy to Mom—back then, brothers married sisters. I don't know if Dad ever had a girlfriend before her or not, or Mom either. I don't think so. They probably had friends that they claimed in school. Just like when we were in school, you claimed a boy—you gave each other valentines and wrote notes.

At Silver City they used to have parties, they called them—dances, when we got a little older. And you'd play ring games, Spin the Bottle and different things like that. I went to spend the night with my friend Ruth Graham, and we had gone to a party at this Miss Murphy's house. She was a schoolteacher, and she'd gave a party for us young people. Ruth was a couple of years older than me, and she was dating, so her boyfriend was at the party and he wanted to take her home. So that threw me to have to walk home with her mother and her brother, Vernon Graham. He was younger than I was, it wasn't a boy-girl thing. I remember Mrs. Graham holding my hand, 'cause it was dark, we didn't have a flashlight or anything, I don't know how we seen, and this Vernon stepped on a possum. I remember that just as well.

Those were fun days, everybody just looked after each other. You never heard of any great accidents or great problems. The only thing I ever heard of is my cousin getting knifed and died. They both were claiming the same girl, and they went to a dance, and my cousin, which was a Hopson, got killed.

### MARGARET HUNT CARROLL

[On Saturdays] we come home and unhitched the team and fed them and milked the cows, and we took a bath and got dressed up and walked seven or eight miles to a party. We didn't have saddle stock, saddle stock was for the cowboys. [Our team] had worked hard all week, we'd carried stuff from the store on Saturday, and my daddy turned them out on Saturday, and they got Sunday off like everybody else.

Somebody [at the party] that had a good voice would sing these old songs, and we'd play ring games, "Swing your partner left and right, do-si-do," and all that kind of good stuff. Kids didn't have time to hunt up or pay a musician. They just went down there and had somebody that would sing their heart out until one or two o'clock, and go around and around.

### MRS. F. A. BARRINGTON BOWEN

We had community dances. Always, someone in the community knew how to play violin and guitar, and different ones would give dances and invited whoever they wanted to invite. You called on the telephone, and of course we had those telephone lines where everybody listened in. If someone got a date, the whole family knew who you had a date with.

We'd go, and the girls stood around the side of the wall, around the wall. The boys were out in the middle, and they'd come and ask you to dance. There was a fellow in our neighborhood, we called him "Sprinkle" Parker, because he sprinkled on you every time he talked to you. We'd just stand around the wall and hope he didn't ask us to dance!

We did the waltz and one-step and two-steps, and I did the Charleston. I went to a neighborhood school, Willow Springs, and we had a stage. There were some times we'd have music there, and someone would perform, different ones in the community, and sometimes I'd get up on the stage and do the Charleston. Different fellows would throw money.

### JOHN DAREL BAY

It was not long till we moved out of there that I knew of the first dance that happened in that community. Most of them were just playing little ring games at a party. They'd go around in a circle holding hands. I don't know if it was a little thing they sang. It was a type of dancing, all right, but they just held hands and went around in a circle as a group. As I say, they didn't have no dances over there in that community. This wasn't music, they'd just sing themselves, go around, whatever it was.

Maybe three or four times later they held what we did call a country dance. Dances always had a band, a two-piece band, [but they might] just have a French harp, a Jew's harp, or a harmonica. I remember that over there one time an old boy had just a harmonica and they was dancing. Well, if you've got no entertainment, you make entertainment out of a lot of things.

### JOE D. INSALL

The Tomastiks [our neighbors at Antelope] were pretty much musicians. Jerry had an accordion, and I think Johnny played the fiddle. They were real ambitious, I don't know if they played at them house dances or not, but we'd go down there and listen to music if it was close by. I've seen them put cornmeal on these old wood floors to make it slick. I bet they've knocked all the splinters out of them. They'd start playing, they'd get to stomping floor.

Usually they'd have twenty-five or thirty people, wouldn't be room for everybody. They called them house dances. Then, a lot of them religious people was way against it, but there was some of them that would do it. We had some neighbors that would have one ever once in a while. We didn't go far, 'cause we had to walk. In later years you'd get to travel a little more. I remember going to one at Sparta, but I was so bashful I wouldn't go on in. I'd just look in the window.

### MARGARET BERT WILHITE BOUNDS

[At Sparta] they played ring games. You know, "Go out one window, idey-ho, two windows, idey-ho." It was about like dancing, you just sang. Even when they had musicals, you didn't dance. You might pat your foot and clap your hand and get pretty excited about the music, but you didn't dance. That'd be maybe like this man played a guitar and that one played a fiddle, or maybe they'd have two guitars and a fiddle. They'd play breakdowns, dance music, but nobody could dance! Or nobody was brave enough to dance—maybe I would put it that way.

Now, in Tennessee Valley, they would have house dances. Maybe one family would give a house dance on Saturday night, and they'd take down the bed and even move the linoleum out, and have kerosene lights. They'd vacate one room. You didn't dare wear out [the linoleum] by dancing. Put cornmeal on the floor. Everybody had to dance in the same direction more or less in rhythm, 'cause it was so crowded.

I would tell my mother, but I didn't really tell my daddy where I's going. In Tennessee Valley they made moonshine, but they didn't bring it in at the dances, you had to go outside. Some of them would [drink it], but I don't remember seeing drunk people at the dances. I guess they kept dancing until it didn't show up on them. I remember my husband-to-be, he just danced with me all night. He didn't go outside and drink.

I went in a group. 'Course, the guy I married, I claimed him as my boyfriend while I was in school. His folks were Baptists, and they gave dances, and his uncle and cousins would play the fiddle and guitars, and they'd have their own house dance. It would be hot in that house in the summertime, and with them kerosene lights it would be even hotter.

[My sister] Ernestine wanted to go somewhere on Saturday night, and Daddy wouldn't let her. She was about thirteen years old, but she was big for her growing. She looked like she's probably eighteen. So she thought she would get back at him. Sunday morning she gets dressed up to go to church, and she tells me, "Bert, just wait here in the car with me. I'm not going in right now." She put on Maybelline, she had them eyes—it looked like coons' [eyes], nearly. She didn't set in her seat where she usually set in church, but when Daddy got up to lead the singing, he looked up and saw her, and he made her go over to the neighbor's house and wash her face and come back. That backfired on her.

We had a swing on the porch, and my sister just older than me, Billie, had a boyfriend, and he come to pick her up. She was about sixteen, I think, I's about fourteen. She wasn't quite ready, so he set on the swing and I set on the porch and put my feet on the first step. He was playing a Jew's harp, and he said, "You didn't stand up." I said, "Why was I supposed to stand up?" He said, "I was playing 'The Star-Spangled Banner.'" I started laughing, and he got plumb mad at me, and he told her I wasn't respectful.

My oldest sister was ten years older than me, and she got married at fifteen. Well, Daddy heard about it, and he went down here to the courthouse in Belton and told them not to sell her a marriage license. She and her boyfriend went down there, and they wouldn't sell one. So they and another couple went to Gatesville, and before she went there she wrote "18" on a paper and put it in her shoe. So when they asked her was she over eighteen, well, she was! Daddy wasn't happy. I remember he cried and cried after that.

### T. A. WILHITE

I used to play fiddle for the house dances [around Sparta]. The whole community would come. Now, they's a lot of them wouldn't go to dances, but all that'd dance would come. We'd have a guitar picker and a fiddle to make the music, and they'd be a-hollering what they wanted you to play. They'd clear it out and put cornmeal all over their floor. Boy, you could dance on that. My brother got in a big fight there, and I raised up and handed my fiddle over to John Birdsong at the door, told him, "Take my fiddle, somebody's gonna bust it." So he took it over and got it back in another room. There wasn't no fighting going on back there. They watched out for them fiddlers. 'Cause, if they didn't have a fiddler, they didn't have a dance.

I'll tell you, they had some rough dances up there. Two started to fight, and one said, "Any of you son-of-a-bitches want to fight, come on. I'm from Nolan [Creek], and the further up the creek the worse they are, and I live right on the head of it!" Nobody never bothered me, though; I was playing the fiddle.

### MARGARET BERT WILHITE BOUNDS

Sparta had a lot of singing conventions. On Sunday they'd have all-day singing with dinner on the ground and lots of good fellowship. My daddy enjoyed that, because he led singing at our church. The Church of Christ didn't believe in musical instruments, but when we went to Brookhaven, I remember one little lady, an older lady but she was short and fat. She'd set up there and just bounce and play that piano. Oh, she could play it! She played by ear, and she used motions with it, bounced up and down on that piano stool. I'd think, as a kid, one of these days she's gonna bounce plumb off that stool!

[Daddy] had a good voice. We had a battery radio, and we could listen to the Stamps Quartet or something like that, and we did listen to the *Grand Ole Opry.*

We had a piano, and Daddy gave the two oldest girls piano lessons. A lady came out from Belton twice a week. My oldest sister Kathleen had a beautiful alto voice, and she sang in church, but she had no idea what that piano was about. Ernestine came along, and she'd get the sound of the tune by note, and then she'd take off by ear and play it. Whenever Billie and I came along, I guess he'd got kind of disgusted. He didn't give us music lessons. I think he thought that as we grew up, we would form a family quartet, but then my oldest sister got married at fifteen.

My uncle, T. A. Wilhite, played a fiddle, and he would come [to our house] and bring his fiddle and play, and I would second on the piano to him. Then my sister older than me, her husband, Burton Thompson, played a fiddle. He was from Tennessee Valley. He would play and I would chord to his music. Then another uncle, they called him "Pud" Wilhite, he played a guitar and he'd come and he'd play. That might be on a Wednesday night or during the week sometimes. T. A. and Pud would come, and we'd be having a get-together at Grannie Wilhite's, and sometimes we'd set out in the yard in the shade of the house or a tree or something and play music.

There was twelve kids [in Daddy's family], and all of them played an instrument but Daddy, and he loved singing. He had one sister, Pauline, that could play any instrument. They went to visit some of the kinfolks, and they had an accordion, and she'd never seen one, and she picked it up and played "Home, Sweet Home." Pauline mashed a blackhead, or a spider bit her, and she had blood poisoning on her face, and she died.

### WILLIAM AKE POWELL

My grandpa was a fiddler. He's hard of hearing, and he played loud, anyway. You could hear him for two or three miles up and down the creek. People could get out on their porch and listen to him play. He'd get through with all his work, and he'd get out there about nine or ten o'clock, and he'd really bear down on it. He played all old breakdowns and all that stuff.

That's about all the playing he did, that I remember. And my daddy, he never played for dances, my daddy didn't. They would have a last day of school or a picnic or something, and they'd get a bunch of them to play, and my daddy would play.

When I was about twelve years old, my daddy had always had a fiddle, but he didn't want me to play with it none. That was his, that was something that they didn't come by too often, he didn't want kids playing with it too much. He'd never let me mess with his fiddle. But when I was twelve, my Uncle Cecil Dorsey, which was my mother's brother, decided he wanted to play a fiddle, so he bought one or traded for one or got one from somebody. It was a pretty good fiddle, but he decided it wasn't cut out for him, so he decided he'd trade it to me. I plowed cotton for him ten days and furnished the team for this fiddle, and I've still got it back yonder in a case in the closet.

My grandpa and my daddy both played, but they really didn't show me anything, and it took me a while to learn how to play. The thing of it is, you didn't have that much time to practice. We got up early, and we went to work. We worked all day. You'd come in about dark, you'd carry that water for them old cows, and you had to milk, and you fed the horses and the hogs and everything, and eat supper and everything. Well, man, it'd be nine or ten o'clock time you got to here, and you was pretty give out and you didn't have a whole lot of time to fiddle. But I used to get out on the porch, we had an old long porch in front, and I'd get out on the porch, and I know my mother and daddy got tired of that. Man, I'd saw that thing! My mother says that the first time I hit a tune, I come running in there and wanted her to listen to it. First time I played one where anybody can recognize it!

That's the way I started, and I finally got to where I played pretty good. Got some cousins, first one thing and another, we got a little band up, called it "Powell String Band." We used to play at some of the house dances up and down the creek. The old people would want to have a dance, and they'd move the beds out of a couple of rooms, and we'd go play. And, man, they had a big time, and we did that. After I learned to play, I couldn't even tune my fiddle. I'd get ready to go play for a dance, I'd take my fiddle to the field where my daddy was, and he'd tune it for me before I'd leave.

These dances would be in people's homes, they didn't have no other place for it. They'd want to have a house dance, so they'd move the furniture out. We'd just say "Hi" to everybody and get cranked up. They'd get two rooms usually, and they had somebody, we used to call them the "bookkeeper." People would pay to dance, they'd have so many sets, and they'd have enough people on a set that they'd be plenty of room in those two rooms to dance. So when they called your number, you could dance. They used to play two sets for a quarter, and you didn't dance unless you were on a set. They had a guy to see after all of that and make sure everybody danced when they're supposed to. Money was hard to come by, and sometimes we'd end up with knives and all kind of stuff they traded to get to dance. We had an old boy used to see after all of that for us, and he'd take whatever they had. We didn't make any money.

They had fights at some of them. There used to be a Wolf family and used to be a Whatley family, and they was kind of feuding. They always come to the dance, and they always had a fight or two while they was there. They always paired off to about the same age, they always got into it like that. Maybe two of them would get into it, and then the other two, they'd take it up. Just go outside and fight a little. Sometime it'd pick up a little bit, and they'd be three or four of them going. But they never did all jump on the same one; "fair fistfight" is what they called it.

I remember one guy, I think his name was Francis Wolf, he wore suspenders. He'd get out there and want to fight, and his wife could hold him back with those suspenders. He never did break a-loose! She'd hold him by them suspenders—he never did get in a fight, but he's always ready. He knew just how hard to pull, he wasn't going to break them. We played for a dance one time at Leon Junction, a big old two-story house, and I guess they got too much home brew or something. There was a rick of cordwood out in the front yard, and had a big old porch all the way across the front, had a tin roof on it, I think. And they go throwing that cordwood on top of that house, made a terrible racket. I remember that, I never will forget it, 'cause that scared me to death.

Later on, Mr. W. T. Hicks, used to own Western Auto here in Gatesville, he paid radio time for us and we used to play over KTEM, Temple, on Sunday evening. They'd put us all in a little old room about the size of that refrigerator there. No air conditioning, and, man, was it hot! We'd get in and play for thirty minutes. We wasn't making no money, but we'd go and have a big time and lots of people would listen at us.

## Neighbors Helping Neighbors

*Blood relatives and neighbors were a family's only support groups at the remote settlement, and virtually every person interviewed commented at length about this old-time neighborliness. Over time, people in a settlement tended to become related, either by blood or marriage, and those who were not related often acted as if they were. No wonder historians sometimes call settlements "kinship communities." Communal work events—quiltings, barn buildings, crop workings, goose pluckings, funerals, etc.—merged group labor with socializing, and in time of serious family trouble neighbors almost always were ready to help out.*

### MURREL L. THOMPSON

The women in the [Antelope] community would get together, and they'd have quilting parties. I've been to those when I was little, I can remember crawling around on the floor. I'd get so tired, but I'd about have to wait until Mama got ready to leave. They'd sit there and quilt all day, a bunch of them get around that frame with that quilt. They made quilts all the time. We had quilting parties at our house. The majority of the families had these quilting boards, or frames, where they'd sit around. They'd take all the scraps, whatever there was, and make the quilts. There might be five or six women there, sewing, working on it.

### JOHN DAREL BAY

People were good to help their neighbors. If a man was sick over here, he had hard luck with his family—of course, these were all mainly farmers out there—the neighbors would take their equipment and go over and farm his land for him. They didn't let him go without a crop or making a crop. If it had to be gathered, they'd gather it, the whole thing. Anybody down on their luck, I'd call it sickness mainly, you went and helped that person out. Or anybody was sick otherwise, somebody would go sit with them. And I mean all night and all day.

### MARGARET BERT WILHITE BOUNDS

My mother would can a lot of extra stuff [at Sparta] just to give to people whenever bad times fell on them, and she would go help nurse them back to health. All the ladies in the community, if somebody had a sickness and they had to sit up with them, they would work it around where nearly everybody in the community got involved in that. [They'd] bring cooked food in, and if it was a woman that was sick, they would do her washing and just kind of help the family along, whatever needed to be done.

I remember there was a man that got sick, and he was sick for two or three months, and the men of the community just filled in and gathered his crop for him and put it up just like they would their own. And if they were building a barn, lots of times they would go help build the barn. Or if they's building a house, lots of times they'd go help. You know, I'm a carpenter, I'll help do this. The women would go and help, and then they'd cook a meal for those helping. It was a community effort.

When a person died, the men of the community went out and dug the grave, and then you would go to the funeral. I remember going to a house with my parents, and they set up all night long with that dead person. They'd take a door down. I was little, but I remember that—they took a door down, and they laid this person on that. And they bathed her, the women did, bathed her and dressed her, and then they laid her on that door and they set up all the night. Then the next day they put her in the casket and had the funeral.

I remember one time I went to a funeral, it was an older woman, they had her in a black dress and a black bonnet. I remember how that woman looked laying on the door with black bonnet or black dress on.

The preacher always preached, and usually the men and women of the church or community sang the hymns. The men would [have dug] the grave and lined it with cheesecloth, and after they had the funeral, they would put the coffin in that. Then, of course, couple of men of the community that had dug the grave would stay and cover it up. Then the ladies of the community would fix dinner to take to whoever's house that the person who died [was] a member of. For several days they'd take lots of food in. I guess it was expected, but everybody just did it. That is something that's kind of lost.

### John Gail Edwards

[At Stampede] Daddy would keep a bunch of cows, and if one of the neighbors got destitute for a milk cow, he'd loan them a cow. They'd come get the cow with a young calf, and the only thing he asked them was not to hit his calf in the head with a churn dasher. Don't starve my calf.

Daddy raised Red Polls. He finally went in with a registered Hereford bull. There were no bull clubs, we just used each other's bulls.

We had a meat club where they'd butcher a beef and you took a part. Next week, you furnished a beef and they took a part. It'd go around like that.

### William Ake Powell

It was harder than hardscrabble for the Kinsey kids, 'cause their daddy died, and their mama raised them on the farm. They lived on my Grandpa Dorsey's place, and they worked for him. He helped them some, I'm sure they ate out of his garden. There was G. W. and Troy and Seth and Vincent and Taylor—there was five boys. The two older ones was pretty far ahead of me, but I went to school with all the rest of them, went in the service with two of them. We'd come home from school, and my grandmother would have their supper fixed in an old pie safe out on the back porch. And I'd take them Kinsey boys through there, and we'd take all of the supper down to the creek and eat it, and then she got to cook again before supper. We'd gather all that stuff up, I'm feeding them boys. Hell, we's all hungry, so we'd go through there and get it. The Kinsey boys had a tough time, but they made it.

### T. A. Wilhite

Come a big tornado cross here [near Sparta], set my house back about nearly the length of this room—pushed the whole thing back. I had a clock like setting on the mantel, and that clock was still running the next day. I don't know how it ever done it, but it did. All the neighbors from out of Sparta and Union Hill, it was so many people come to help that you didn't hardly have room to work. I got a bunch of help there, and we lifted it back up and go on a-living in it.

### NORMAN RICKETTS HALL

Fire was always a real concern in rural areas. I recall the house above us, it must have been half, three-quarters of a mile away, but you could see it when it caught fire, and of course the neighbors always responded to this. When we drove up, the man came out on the porch, must have been six feet above the ground. He came out of the house, had twenty dishes, and just pitched them out. I guess he broke every one of them. But you know, he was just beside himself, he was just trying to save anything [he] could. It wiped families out when that happens, 'cause that's everything they had.

The family that lived closest to us did not have a storm cellar. I recall being in bed at night, and it was thundering and lightening, and [I] could hear the neighbor's car start and soon would be at the storm house. I recall once the man hollering, says, "Doc, aren't you all coming down to the cellar?" And Dad says, "No, I don't think so." And he said, "Doc, you're gonna get blown away sometime." They had two boys and a little girl. The girl would always be crying, every time, and they'd go down in the storm cellar. The family had a kerosene lamp. The father would usually sit on the steps looking at the clouds before they closed the door. That happened not once or twice, but five, six times a year. There were people really afraid of clouds. Dad was pretty much like, "Well, if it happens, it happens." I grew up that way.

### ROBERT E. GAULT

I never heard of embalming until about '40-something. Usually, if a man died that night, you had that funeral the next day if you could. They would lay them out one night, and people would set up with them all night. We'd take turns about sitting up that night, two of us at a time.

Used to, we dug all the graves, the people in the community dug all the graves. We went out to the Schley Cemetery, which was in Fort Hood. Went out there and we dug and we hit water—old yellow clay, and the water would rise up. And we put the casket in there, and we had to stand on it till we buried him—to get the thing held down, there's so much water. We dipped water and we'd dig, and we'd dip water, and we was just wet mud, yellow mud, all over us. And we had to stay there, 'cause we had to cover it and everything, too. It'd float till we got enough dirt on there to hold it. That's the awfullest thing I ever got into.

### JUANITA GRIFFIN DUNCAN

My grandfather died of snakebite in his fifties, and my grandmother, I think, was fifty-four. There's two or three months difference in their deaths. I was the last grandchild, and there were quite a few of the family there, and I was the last grandchild to kiss her good-bye. She was real sick, a lot of the family was at the house, and she called all of the grandkids in to kiss her good-bye. I was small enough that I had to tiptoe to reach her for me to kiss me. She kissed me, and I walked around to the foot of the bed, climbed up on the foot of the bed, a big old iron bedstead, and they put the sheet up over my grandmother's face. I said, "What in the world are you covering up my grandma for?"

Nobody told me. I walked out on the little back porch, and my mother was carrying my brother, and my brother was crying and my mom was crying. I remember pulling on my mother's dress and said, "Mom, why are you crying?" And she said, "I'll explain it later."

My grandmother was a large woman, wore her dresses completely down to the ground, and she always had beautiful flowers, always had a yard full of beautiful flowers.

### NORRIS SIDNEY GRAVES

My granddad died [at Pidcoke] in 1930 [when I was six]. We were on the ranch, and we came back, and we got there thirty minutes after he passed away. I remember his death just like yesterday. It was misty, rainy, it was a bad trip, and we came in an old Model A all the way from San Angelo, "put-put-put-put." Table Rock Creek runs right below, and we'd stop down at Table Rock Creek, and Mother would get out and get her a towel or a rag, and she'd clean my face and wash me, change my clothes.

But we got there a little late, and these two aunts took me into the dining room. They had a big long dining room, beautiful dining room table, and they fed us, they knew we'd been traveling. My dad come in and told me, said, "Do you want to go see your granddad for probably the last time?" [I said,] "Noooooh!" [But] these two aunts got to talking to me, says, "Why don't you see your granddaddy? He looks just like he's asleep." So they got me by the hand, and they took me in.

He was laid out. They'd took a door off and laid it on some sawhorses. I got to asking questions, you know how kids [are], "What's he laying on? That don't look like his bed." And they took me in to look at him, and he's just resting on this big tall door. They had a pillow under his head and the sheet over him, and they had two candles at his head and one at the foot, and they said, "Now, doesn't it look like he's sleeping?" That was the last time I saw him.

The next day, sometime in the day, they brought a casket from Gatesville, and they put him in the casket and put him in the parlor. They had a parlor there where the girls used to spoon and all. They put the casket in the parlor, and I wouldn't go in there and look. I wouldn't go. And people started bringing in food, everybody in the country, 'cause he was known everywhere. The next day, they took him directly to the cemetery and buried him.

### CLEMENTS W. "SPEEDY" DUNCAN

Good neighbors tried to stop trouble in the community. This old guy lived beside the road [at Okay], and we walked, we didn't have no car, and his damn old dog wouldn't bite you, he'd get your britches and tear them. And the old man wouldn't do much with him that owned him. Everybody walked by there. My grandpa, very seldom he walked, he usually rode something, but he'd pull up his britches.

I had a friend that had an old Model A pickup, and we met at this little country store drinking a pop, and that old dog had torn our britches for three or four years. He said, "Let me go up this hill," which was a hill there up towards Copperas Cove. He said, "I'll go up there on that hill and turn around, turn around over on the other side of you. You be out there ready, and I'll top that hill and blow my horn. Says, "I'll take off with all that old pickup's got in it. When I get down there, that old dog will run out and bite at my tires, and I'll get him." And it worked.

So I went home. You don't go to the store every day, [but] a few days I sent back and my friend said, "Where's your gun?" I said, "Hell, I ain't going hunting, I come after some kerosene oil." [Says], "Well, everybody in the community is carrying their gun." I said, "What in the hell is going on?" "Oh," he said, "old man Bell," he was the old man that owned the dog, "he got Sonny Whitehead down and just beat the hell out of him for killing his dog." Says, "Then, [Sonny Whitehead's] daddy come back up there and beat hell out of old man Bell, like to have killed him. All the Bell kinfolks has got guns, the community divided and all them had guns."

It like to got serious, it sure did. I was seventeen, I said, "Well, I'll go tell Pa." I told him, I said, "Pa, I sure started trouble." He said, "Well, son, that damned old dog needed killing. He's tore my britches before, so I don't blame the boy for that." I imagine the best thing to do is go talk to Mr. Bell right now." He left a-foot. I guess he went and neighbored with Mr. Bell, and they put up their guns. But it all blowed over. I never heard no more about it.

## Churches and Religious Life

*Religious fervor varied from settlement to settlement, as did so many other things, but it ran deep and strong at most places. Sunday church was a major social event of the week, although it might be only Sunday school, with the pastor visiting once or twice a month. Methodists and Baptists, in particular, often attended each other's services—whichever church had a pastor that particular Sunday. Summer revival weeks, followed by baptisms, were the high points of the religious year.*

### TOMMIE L. SHULTS HAFERKAMP

When I was kid, when I woke up on Sunday morning, I knew it was Sunday. No outside activity, everything was shut down. You knew it was the Lord's Day, you knew it was Sabbath, and everybody went to church. We didn't pass too many houses going to church, but there was no working in the fields. It was Sunday.

We were isolated, and seldom did anyone come by our house. But on this Monday morning Papa was doing something outside when a man named Ross Roberts and his wife Thelma came driving by. I think they had a little brown Model T. They stopped to talk to Papa, and Ross said, "Well, I guess we'd better get going on to church." Papa said, "Ross, today is Monday morning. Are you having a revival, or something?" Ross just thought Papa was teasing. I don't know exactly what he said, [but] then he noticed that Papa had on work clothes. He said, "Oh! We picked cotton all day yesterday!"

### MURREL L. THOMPSON

I don't know how many people were there, but [Antelope Baptist Church] wasn't a big church. They had a choir, had a piano, and they'd sing, and the preacher'd preach. And the preacher'd go to somebody's house for Sunday dinner, and they'd have fried chicken nearly every time he'd go. And then that night, they'd come back and have a little service and you'd go home. But that was something to do—going to church on Sunday—that's what you did. You went to Sunday school and church in the morning, and church that night, and then get up the next morning and get on your horse and go to school.

### JEROME KEENER BLACKWELL

The Brown's Creek Methodist Church was located on a cutout of our farm on a branch southeast of the house. This too consisted of a one-room building set on rock blocking, as was our house and the school. [There was] also a quite large graveyard to the west where my sisters, Sally, Daisy Dean, and myself spent many hours mourning the death of the multitudes buried of which we were not familiar. It seemed the thing to do, seeing they were not here anymore and we were. There were twin springs near the church on our branch. All who attended church felt it fitting to take their aluminum collapsible cups and drink the pure, cold spring water. One and all would always acclaim it was a rare gift of God, and I would certainly agree. For after hearing Brother W. B. Keener and Brother George Siler for about two and a half hours in the heat of summer, the water was a miraculous gift of the Almighty.

Going to church on Sunday morning was an ordeal for my mother, as she had eleven kiddos to clean and see dressed fit for church, but to me it was the high point of the week, especially the annual camp meeting held each summer under the proverbial brush arbor. The men would light the kerosene flares to light the arbor for night services, and then on Sunday morning would arrange a large makeshift table, and the women of the community would fill the table with fried chicken, peach cobbler, berry pie, potato salads, and chocolate cake, of which we youngsters managed to eat enough to make us sick.

**MELBA GOODWIN BENNETT**
We bought shoes and socks to wear [to church and school], but we were not permitted or wear our shoes around the house. We even walked to church barefooted till we got to Cowhouse Creek. When we got there, we would wash our feet, sit down, put our shoes on, and walk up to church, which was just past the creek bridge.

It was a tabernacle called Refuge, they had built it for a meeting place in the community. A tabernacle is not closed in on the sides. They did make some swing-down protection, if it was windy or what have you, but they built a framework and covered it with cedar at the top. A tabernacle has sides that can be let down or raised up, an arbor is an open framework with a cover on top only. When they were going to have a meeting, the men would go out and cut cedar limbs and cover it. We had services there, mostly with a traveling preacher, someone who would come in, but we did not have a regular pastor. I do not believe there were services every Sunday, maybe once a month. It was known as a Baptist community.

Dad taught family practice at home by reading the Bible at the table a lot. He taught the boys to read, the girls were not permitted to read [the Bible in public]. We could read the Bible when we wanted to [in private], but we were taught that it was a man's place to teach Bible.

When we had a camp meeting, a preacher would come and stay in a community. We were always fortunate in getting to have the preacher stay with us, most of the time, and he would stay an entire week. We'd go to meetings at night, then have an all-day meeting on Sunday—dinner on the ground, so to speak, and services maybe in the evening. We only had the kerosene lights or lanterns.

### DORIS LEE WHITE THOMAS

We called them camp meetings, they would stay several days. One family brought their chickens in a coop and killed one each day. They put their meals all out together.

The entertainment when [we] were growing up was neighbors getting together and singing at night, religious songs. They had parties in their homes [at Spring Hill], and they had Sunday afternoon singings. The school-house was a church house, too. They'd have the Methodist preacher one Sunday and the Baptist preacher the next Sunday, but everybody went to both of them. Singing in the afternoon.

I have to tell you the story about Grandpa when he got religious. He was out in the corn patch! I don't know if he was chopping, hoeing the corn, or pulling it, but the Witties lived nearby and one of their daughters was tell-ing me about it. He just got really happy and a-shouting and ordered some-body to go get the preacher. They had to stop work and go get the preacher and get him baptized or sprinkled.

### ROBERT E. GAULT

Down on the corner of the [Antelope] school grounds, they had what we called Missionary Baptist Church, the same thing as your regular Southern Baptist now. We had a little church down there that met every other week. We had a rural pastor, and usually those pastors in those days had a couple of churches, and they'd be in one church one Sunday and the other one the next. We had a pretty strong little church there, and usually we had a spring and fall revival. You'd always have a good attendance at those revivals, the building would be full for them. People were hungry to hear the Word preached and the singing, and there was a lot of pleasure in it. Then the last day of the revival, you'd have singing all day and dinner on the ground. It was really a big thing. They had evangelists that would come through, [and] they'd usually hire an evangelist for a week or two-week revival in the summer. And it was real good, we really enjoyed it. People were hungry for some place to go, and it was natural that church would be the center of your social activity.

My mother was the finest Christian woman I ever knew, and my dad didn't go to church. When the kids got old enough to drive, we went to church, we were six miles from Antelope. And she influenced me. You learn more at your mother's knee than just about anywhere in your early life. I don't think anybody ever influences your life like your mother does. I told them, they talked about stars in your crown, "Well, if there's anybody rewarded with stars in the crown, it'd be Christian mothers." I sure believe that myself. I was baptized in Cowhouse Creek, down at Eliga, August 14, 1940. We went down there to the Cowhouse, it was accessible by gravel bar, and you could walk right down to the water.

### KYLE HILLIARD

We did not go regularly to church all the time we were brought up. Mama would very much have liked to, Daddy didn't care that much about it. We went to school six years at Palo Alto in that two-room schoolhouse, and very little was ever said about church in that school. Never heard anybody talk about going to church. I think very little church-going happened during the '30s around Palo Alto. At Sugar Loaf, there was a church and a tabernacle, and occasionally somebody would hold a meeting over there, and it would be nondenominational—Baptist, Methodist, maybe Church of Christ.

Religion was sort of put in the background. You would think as poor as we were, we'd be praying every night, but we didn't. I didn't hear anybody praying for things to get better. That doesn't mean that people weren't feeling religious deep down inside, but it certainly wasn't on display. It was very private. They were all good people, all good people, [but] religion almost was forgotten.

### JUANITA GRIFFIN DUNCAN

We went to church [at Brookhaven] every Sunday morning. My mom played the piano, and my daddy was the Sunday school superintendent. Later, after I married and left, my dad became a deacon. The little church house belonged to the Methodist congregation, but the Methodists and Baptists went to the same church. We had Methodist preachers, Baptist preachers, and we didn't know who was who until they had a business meeting. They met on alternate Sundays.

My Grandfather Simms furnished the great big cedar logs that was in the tabernacle, and he and the three boys and then the men of the community built the tabernacle. The tabernacle was a community building, but the church belonged to the Methodist people, but they shared it.

Sometimes we had what they called revivals. There would be a visiting preacher come in, and they would stay two weeks. It was usually in the summertime, July or August. I remember one preacher and his wife. She built an ark for the kids. She took a substance that she mixed with salt and flour and made all of the animals and painted them—two of each, pairs. That was so impressive I will never forget it, and at the end of the revival she gave all the animals to the kids. I remember, I got the hippopotamus and the giraffes.

They usually came home with the people to eat meals. One time they were at our house, and there was a biscuit left over. She took this biscuit and squeezed it up, and she made an animal out of that biscuit.

### NORRIS SIDNEY GRAVES

All of my family were Baptists. My daddy's side and my mother's side, they were Baptists—strong. But when I first started there [at Pidcoke], the Baptist Church had [services] every other Sunday, and the Methodist Church had every other Sunday. They interwove to where we had four full Sundays of preachers there, every Sunday we were set. We'd go to the different church or when they had a revival, [and] you'd take your songbooks from the Baptist Church, and the song leader would announce in the Cokesbury songbook its page so-and-so and in the Baptist hymnal it's so-and-so. And when the Baptists had theirs, the Methodists would bring their [songbooks] down. It was a real harmonious deal.

But my Granddaddy Graves, he was a strong old Baptist. I remember one time his youngest child, which was my Aunt Dan, she and I was laying on the bed playing cards. My granddaddy came in, and he looked down and says, "What are y'all doing?" Says, "Well, we're just having a game of rummy." Boy, I tell you what, he snatched those up, he walked in to the fireplace, and he just threw those cards right in there. Says, "If I ever catch these in the house, any cards in the house again, I'll do this again." Then he got on my aunt.

He was strict, he didn't allow cards, he didn't allow dancing, [but] he's got the best bunch of kids that were dancers I ever saw. Dancing comes naturally, I think, from my grandmother's side, my dad's mother's side of the family, because she's Irish. I remember my great-granddaddy, his name was Dukes. One Christmas he got up on the kitchen table and did the Irish jig like you wouldn't believe.

### J. W. SHULTS

In the Owl Creek community there was a Primitive Baptist church, which was what people called the foot-washing Baptists. Like Jesus washed the disciples' feet? They did the same thing. Everybody in the church didn't participate in this foot-washing. On the months that had five Sundays, they had a Fifth Sunday meeting, and it didn't matter what denomination or if you were nothing, everybody went to Fifth Sunday meeting at Little Flock. That was the name of the little church.

Some of the men that didn't participate in the worship, they stayed outside and told stories and visited and talked about dogs and horses and whatever, but most people went in for the morning service. They turned benches back to make a long table, and they'd put out food. It was some of the greatest eating you ever tasted. Everybody would eat, and then they would go back in and have the ordinance of the foot-washing. For a little kid, seven or eight year old, you'd peep around the corner to see if you could see what was going on, and it was an experience. So everybody went and visited or participated, whatever they chose to do.

They also were of the belief of predestination. What was to be would be, regardless; you didn't change it. And they'd have a sing, and these people sang in a different manner than I'd ever heard before. They sang in a monotone, kind of "un-un-un-un-un."

### NORRIS SIDNEY GRAVES

Dad loved chickens. We had chickens coming out of the ears. He liked white leghorns 'cause they laid better, more eggs, and he sold eggs. When we moved into Pidcoke, he built a big pen and raised registered chickens, white layers. Something started getting into his chickens there, and he had a hard time. He checked that fence. He said, "I can't get over it. There's no place where a fox or anything, a varmint, can get in. I can't understand this. Where are they going?" He kept his gun with buckshot in it, and these chickens would be yelling. One night, when the noise was going on, he jumped up, and he ran out there, and he saw something white, white shirt or something, and he fired, and he hit it, and what it was, was the Baptist preacher!

The poor preachers, they didn't get any money. My dad was so sorry as he picked the shot out of him. He said, "Why in the world didn't you let me know that you were in this state, if you needed something like this to eat?" And he said, "Well, I don't really need it to eat, I trade them for some money. There's no liquidity."

That's right, no cash. Dad said, "I'll talk to the deacons and see what we can do for you," and all that. This particular guy, and it's in the history of Pidcoke Baptist Church, he didn't stay around much longer. They got up a collection of money to buy songbooks, and the preacher and the money left.

### JOE D. INSALL

The had a scandal in [Antelope] church one day. I missed that. Things had happened that wasn't supposed to, and this lady got up in front of the church house and told about it. A pretty respected citizen was involved, and she was a single lady with a couple of daughters. It wasn't too long after that one of the preachers was preaching. Had all the windows and doors open, 'cause they didn't know what air conditioning was. They had these little fans you fanned with. And you could see this guy's house, it was about a mile down the road just past Antelope Store, it was burning down. So I think they all went down there. They had two or three exciting Sundays there, and I bet it was all connected.

### NORRIS SIDNEY GRAVES

They built a brush arbor down there [at Pidcoke]. The story has it that they built a new one. All the men, Methodists, Baptists, got together and built a brush arbor. They pulled all the brush away from it, ready for the deal, then they set the brush on fire and burned the building, too. Then they went back and got busy and built another brush arbor. That's where the camp meeting was, and that's where I know they had a revival down there, and that's where I joined the church. On the left-hand side of the bridge, the Bee House and Cowhouse creeks come together, that used to be the old baptizing hole. That's where I was baptized in 1936 with my cousin Donna Fay and a whole bunch of people that we knew. At that age, it's like a bunch of sheep, one goes and they all start going. When I came up out of the water, I said, "Hey, I don't see any change." But I remember that I was a better boy after that. I really was, I was better. That was a big turning point in my life.

### MARGARET BERT WILHITE BOUNDS

[At Sparta], it was on the Cowhouse [Creek]. They called it the "baptismal hole." I was baptized there. They were having a revival under the tabernacle, it was in the summertime. You'd be back, they'd be singing the hymn, and you would go forward, and he'd ask you, "Do you truly believe in God and Jesus Christ and that He resurrected from the dead?" And you tell him "I do," and he would announce to the congregation whoever was gonna be baptized, and they would meet down there at the baptismal hole.

It was on the Denman place about half a mile away, you went down a little lane. I think Mr. Denman baled hay between there and the river. There was a gravel bar there, and I don't guess it was too deep. Everybody parked around where they could shine their lights for the preacher and whoever went in the baptismal hole. They sang two or three songs, and then he baptized everybody.

### T. A. WILHITE

Brookhaven had a brush arbor. I's a little old kid, and my brother used to carry me with him everywhere he went nearly. Got up there, and when they's all just coming out from under that brush arbor, I got right by where they come out. I caught him by the coattail, he says, "Spook"—he called me Spook—"I'll be back in a few minutes." I just thought, yeah, I'll be with you when you come back. I went out there, and he had a rubber-tire buggy with a top. Had a flap under the back, I raised that flap and went in head first down under there. He carried that gal about a mile up there and un-loaded her. Started back, and when he's going down that hill, that old mare, she's just trotting. She's a race-trotting mare. I come crawling out from where I was, and he says, "Where in the world you been?" I said, "I been under the seat." I told him, I said, "I wasn't gonna stay around there. They have to go to that arbor to have funerals. I don't know whether they was ghosts or what they was there."

They didn't have no brush arbors at Sparta, they had a tabernacle there. My oldest brother, he always led the singing at the church. And he's stand-ing up there, he's just bought him a brand-new tie. And a screech owl, he's right up over his head, and he didn't know he's up there. And he messed on him, and it hit him right there and just sprayed the whole front—that shirt, tie, and everything. Yeah, just splattered all over him. He had to go up to old man Jordan's store to wash up.

### JOHN DANIEL WOLF

One of the big highlights of the year for entertainment was revival meet-ings at churches, where all the communities around ganged up at one re-vival, whether you were Baptist, Methodist, or whatever. The biggest one in our community was at Eliga down at Cowhouse Creek, and people came from miles around to it. I don't know why, they were a small community of Church of Christ people, but they were kind of open.

I'll use Brown's Creek as an example. On Friday they would get things ready, and on Saturday they would hold a church service and a singing and a tremendous lot of music, but if you want to know, the main activity at the church revival was visiting. They did have church service, and they had conversions, and the preacher preached fire and brimstone—the more, the better they liked it. Then Sunday at noon was a time that they all spread their lunch and ate a tremendous meal, really tremendous. Then an afternoon service, and it'd all be over.

One of the reasons that Eliga was so well liked by everyone [was] because it would meet right in the bend of the river. Big live oak trees, the river came around, the kids could slip off up here and go swimming, and I did a number of times. And a big iron bridge across the river and a country store on the other side. In the summertime, when it was hot, it was real nice. Pecan trees everywhere and you could just camp under the pecan trees—come down there and just stay there two or three days, and a tremendous lot of people did.

# CHAPTER FIVE

# Modernizations and the Takeover

## Communication Breakthroughs

*Area families were almost as isolated during the 1930s as they had been during the 1890s. In some sections, any big rain raised the creeks and muddied the roads so as to thwart travel. It did not matter if you owned an automobile. But at many homeplaces telephones now provided links to the outside world even if the creeks were up, and in the still hours of the night the farm family's quartz-crystal radio might pick up distant Nashville, Tennessee, or even Paris, France. Intrepid mailmen braved the local roads in all weathers, and peddlers and the "iceman cometh."*

### JOHN DANIEL WOLF

Especially in the thirties, transportation was not developed very well, roads were not developed very well. They were buggy roads, and therefore in bad weather you were isolated pretty quickly. Each community had a little store. Brookhaven had a store, there at Maple we had a store, and the others, most of them had stores and schools earlier. A lot of the stores had closed down. There were communities all around here, some of them had little schools, but in the mid-thirties those schools started disappearing because you flat just couldn't afford to keep them up any more. Besides that, we had automobiles. The first bus we had to run from Brown's Creek community over to Maple was a kind of old van. It handled eight or nine kids, and they paid the guy ten dollars a month. Maple had already lost its high school at the time the bus was running, just elementary kids that I'm thinking of. High school kids were bussed into Gatesville.

So things were changing in the thirties fairly fast. Roads were improving all the time, they were putting a little more gravel [on them]. The rural mail carrier, he got to where he didn't get stuck so many times. He was a contract Star Route carrier, he only drove the main roads, and they accused him of going squirrel hunting before he'd get the mail there. I think he did every once in a while. [His] Model T pickup had kind of a cab up there, and he put a whole bunch of mail by him in the seat, and he had a back seat [for] packages. My mother would send me about a mile and a half or two miles to the mailbox. He's supposed to be there at one o'clock, and it would be three o'clock before this rascal would show up.

It was quite common in the spring for them to order three dozen baby chicks, and usually he'd bring it to your house. [The iceman came around] similar to the mail carrier, similar situation. Had these big old tarps over ice in the back of it, and surprisingly it didn't melt that fast. You could swap two dozen eggs for a block of ice. And many a time we had a tremendous treat, because we made homemade ice cream with that block of ice.

### WILMA EARL COLVIN EDWARDS

Grannie was a rural mail carrier for five years when her children were real small on the Star Route from Gatesville to Boaz. That was about thirty-five miles round trip a day. She did it in a horse and buggy. There were open saloons in Gatesville at the time she did the Star Route, and I have her ledger where she entered small sums for "traffic," so I know she delivered "likker" right along [with] the mail.

### WILLIAM AKE POWELL

We were on a Star Route and the mail carrier used to drive a buggy down the road. I remember, my Grandma Powell used to put a nickel for a spool of thread and tell him what color thread she wanted, and the mail carrier would bring her a spool of thread the next day. And if you had a letter you wanted to mail, and you didn't have no postage, you'd just put the letter and the money in there, and he'd put the stamp on it and mail it for you. You know, that sort of stuff, they was real accommodating.

### JOE D. INSALL

This old mail carrier, he had a Model A Ford, his name was John DeWare. We used to have a little poem we always said, "John DeWare lost his underwear." We ordered a little red wagon from Sears or Montgomery Ward. That's the only two ways we had of buying things, and we'd look at them catalogues, that's about all the literature we had. We kept waiting down there at the mailbox, and that old mailman would come by. One day one of us asked him, "When are you going to bring our little red wagon?" And he had been hauling with it for a long time, but the address had washed off of it. It got in the Cowhouse [Creek] in high water. He didn't know where to take it.

### NORMAN RICKETTS HALL

We were using an icebox, and that was quite common out in the country, because "the iceman cometh." It was just like the mail. Incidentally, the mailman was a big part of the community, because he brought the gossip. "Did you hear about so-and-so?" Sometimes it took the mailman all day to get around. We used to have a mailman [that] when he drove by a corn field, he would stop and get out and get roasting ears. And if he came by some peach crop, he'd stop and get peaches. He didn't ask, he wouldn't ask. Nobody thought anything about it. His name was Brewster. Everybody accepted it, that was part of life. Brewster had been here, he'd picked the corn on that row.

We had a mailbox. Some people's mailbox might've been half mile or two miles from the house, ours happened to be just outside the front gate. You usually kept a fruit jar lid in the mail box, and if you had something that had postage due, [the mailman] would put you a note in the box, and the next day you put three pennies, or whatever, in the fruit jar lid. And, boy, if you didn't, you didn't get your mail maybe for two weeks.

### WILMA EARL COLVIN EDWARDS

There was no electricity [at Boaz], and unless you had a crystal set, you didn't have a radio. Granddaddy had an old crystal set, but it was squawky and poppy. He could get Germany and Russia better than he could get anything in the United States! You know, just weird things like that. We didn't have a radio.

### JOHN DAREL BAY

People come over at night and visit, back and forth. I think we got our first radio in '25, that's the year *Grand Ole Opry* came on. That was the one that had all these batteries, it was long and had a lot to it, and I bet you had a dozen knobs on that thing to turn to tune in. It had an old high antenna outside. People would come there to our house on Saturday night. They made us kids get outside or be quiet so they could hear that music from the *Grand Ole Opry*. They'd come there and set around, and I can still remember the old men sitting there patting their foot. But you kept quiet, you didn't do no hollering or playing around there as kids. 'Cause you couldn't hear them old radios back then. They'd fade away so you wasn't getting that signal, it'd just fade out. You'd hear it squeal 'cause of the static, a lot of static grinding on it. We didn't listen to the radio that much. You kept that thing off because you had a battery, and you were going to run that battery down. Had to carry it to town to get it charged.

### H. P. BROOKSHIRE

The Bighams had the first radio that came into our part of the world, and we'd go over there every Saturday night and listen to the *Grand Ole Opry*. Then I remember when we got our radio—went up here at W. T. Hicks and bought that old Truetone radio. Back then, it's like when TVs first come out, we had this wire outside for our antenna. It had a wet-cell battery that it ran off of. Those Model A cars had two batteries. Put one on that radio, and then when it'd go dead, go out there and switch it off of that old Model A. Then, cars had generators on them. Your battery could be plumb dead, but that generator kicks in and it charges that battery up. In later years Aunt Bud and Uncle Ira had a wind charger, and all it was, was a generator with a propeller on it. It'd charge that wet-cell battery and that would just run the radio, was all it was good for.

Everyday at dinnertime we'd listen to W. Lee O'Daniel and the Light Crust Dough Boys. That's when W. Lee O'Daniel was running for governor. Then, they'd have several programs on in the evening, like *The Lone Ranger*, *Captain Midnight*, *Gildersleeve*, *Jack Benny*.

### NORMAN RICKETTS HALL

The radio really changed things. I can remember when the first radio came, and, boy, that was living. The radio changed things considerably, because you heard the news, you heard these advertisements. Had to have an aerial, couldn't plug it in 'cause it had a battery. And then when the batteries ran out, if you didn't have enough money to purchase a new one, you were cut off from the world.

The radio kind of brought the world to you. News was what interested my dad, and there would be plays or things like that. My dad sat in his rocking chair, and there was a straight-back chair nearby. I would sit on my knees leaning up on this table, and I could control the radio, right there. My ear was right up against the radio, and I'd sit there every night until they made me go to bed. I remember they used to have a program called *Inner Sanctum*, and it was a horror deal—you know, scary. It opened [with the sound] of a creaking door. Lord, you could hear that thing creaking, and it just ripped down your spine! The neighbor boy always listened to it, and we would exchange our views. "What'd you think of that story?"

But it really did open a new adventure. Before that, it had been the newspaper, that was the only connection with the outside world. Even when you went to town, there was not a lot of outside dealing with the world, it was just your little world in Killeen.

### ROBERT E. GAULT

We got our first radio in 1937. Battery radio and a fifty-foot aerial up in the air, about high as you could get it, and good radio pickup. It was such a novelty that the first Saturday night we had it, we had people all over our porch listening to *Grand Ole Opry* with us. You know, it used to go nearly all night in those days. Then, the Joe Lewis and Max Schmelling fight came on right after that, and we had a big crowd at that. You get addicted to that. We used to lay on the porch at noon, come in for lunch, and listen to the Beulah Chuckwagon Gang and W. Lee O'Daniel's Hillbilly Boys. That was the first change we had, right there.

### NORRIS SIDNEY GRAVES

Pidcoke did not get electricity until after the war. The army camp helped get R.E.A. in there, and they helped to get some paved roads. When I was younger, going to school there at Pidcoke, we didn't have electricity. We had coal oil lamps, and we had Aladdin lamps. We used to have domino parties, Forty-Two parties, and they'd have these Aladdin lamps setting around, and it was pretty bright. But a man came around through the country, and he talked to my dad and I was out there listening, and he said, "If you'll let me put a wind charger on this pole here, I'll wire your house for electricity, and you'll have electricity if you let me use this as a demonstrator."

My dad said, "Well, nothing to lose." [But] wiring the house in a couple of rooms is all we got, and we couldn't run two lights at one time. Well, we could run one light and a radio, that's the first time we got a radio. We could listen to *Lum and Abner*, *Amos and Andy*, *One Man's Family*, and we never did get electricity. We never had lights as long as I lived in Pidcoke—I mean, real lights, like they do in the city.

### WILLIAM AKE POWELL

There got to be a telephone system [at Friendship], I don't know just what date. We didn't have no telephone office, I don't know where it was. But I know they used to send me with a bucket of water to run pour it on the ground wire where you could hear better.

### KYLE HILLIARD

We had a telephone [at Palo Alto] when I was about five years old. That would have been in about 1930. Things got so rough just a few years later that Mom and Dad decided we could get by without a telephone, so they didn't pay the telephone fee. The Hall family that we got the water from and used their storm cellar, we also used their telephone. My dad was very close to his mother, who lived across the mountain from us, and every three or four days, if he didn't actually go over there, he would go out to the Halls and ask to borrow their phone and call Grandma. I'd go with him when I was a little boy. I'd frequently go with him anywhere he would let me go, whether it was plowing, planting, or whatever. I'd follow behind the plow lots of times.

I can still hear my dad turn the telephone ringer, pick up the receiver, and get Central. He would say, "Central?" Central would say, "Yes?" "1-W, please." Since 1934, I can still remember that my grandmother's number was 1-W. Call Central and ask for 1-W and you would get Grandma. I could hear Daddy's side of the conversation, talking with his mother.

### NORMAN RICKETTS HALL

People were real close. We used to have two ladies, two sisters, we called them "old maids," that lived down the road from us. Great ladies, but they were well up in years. And if they went to town, and there was a strange car parked at anybody's house, they'd call them and ask, "Whose is that? Who's in the car?" We had telephones, eight people on the party line. I had a brother that was in college, and of course he would call home occasionally, and you knew these ladies were listening. Every once in a while they'd come on the line and say, "Lola, what did he say?"

### ROBERT E. GAULT

[We had] five, six, or seven people on a telephone line, and there's always somebody eavesdropping on you. Usually, you could hear them when they open it up, you could hear a little "ding." They wouldn't never admit they was on there. That's Rural Telephone Company there at Killeen. But we had a storm one year when I was a kid that ice broke all the lines down, and we were nearly a year without a telephone system. And when they put it back, we had to pay our share to get the lines put back up. Had them old Kellogg phones. I had an aunt on the line, and we had another woman on there, and they was on the line half the time. I'm telling you, these women got to gossip somewhere. It got to where if you had an emergency, you'd just say, "This is an emergency, can I have the line?" When we lived at Turnersville, we had a telephone like that, too. I think it's four parties on the line, and I got to where I wouldn't call a girl to ask for a date, 'cause everybody in the country knew it as soon as I did.

**NORRIS SIDNEY GRAVES**

When I was a little boy, we lived in Pidcoke, and my dad and [mother] owned the local switchboard service. Dad would go out and work the lines and try to collect the money, and she would sit there and take those [calls]. And in a sense that served a purpose. If somebody died or was dead, they'd call the switchboard, and they'd ask you, and you'd tell, you'd put out the word. If there was not gonna be school, you'd put out the word. The switchboard was a very interesting thing and was very essential.

It was during the Depression, and [Dad] would go out, and if somebody hadn't paid for two or three months, he'd cut them off. Time he'd get back to the house, they'd already hooked it back it up. It wasn't complicated. So he finally started cutting the wire and rolling it up, and that's when he found out that they [were using] barbed wire [to patch their hookups].

## Roads and Automobiles

*Mud at times still held the upper hand over motor cars during the 1930s, but local roads were improving, and for families only a few miles out of Gatesville or Copperas Cove or Belton the Saturday trip into town had become commonplace. The last generation of horsemen had struggled with the transition to machine operation, and some of them never made it, choosing instead to designate an older son or daughter as official driver of the family's automobile. Mules and horses began to be traded in on tractors, though some farmers could afford to retire faithful work stock to peaceful pastures.*

**CLEMENTS W. "SPEEDY" DUNCAN**

I had this old 1928 Chevrolet car that didn't have no top on it, and it had a right-front-wheel brake. That was the only wheel that had any brake. This [Okay] store was in a dirt area, and it was a big area open out there. I'd come up to that old store, and I'd put my left foot on the brake and get my right foot on the footfeed, and I'd turn this wheel. It had no bed on it and nothing on the tail end, it was light and it would start to slide. I'd give it all the gas I could and hold that brake, and it was just making loops out there. And needless to say, I was stirring up lot of dirt, and if the wind was right, it was all blowing in this old man's store.

He'd hustle over to the phone and call my mother, Rosie. We had four rings, but it didn't make a damn if you just rang Central, everybody took down [their phones]. Four rings would get everybody's attention, and five rings was the party-line ring, that was emergency for everybody. But four rings was our ring, we had one long and a short and a short and a long. Everybody had a different amount of rings. Whenever it rings, you listen to it, and "That's old so-and-so." We knew everybody's ring. But he'd say, "Rosie, that boy's over here speeding again!" So that's where I got my [name] "Speedy."

We probably got a Model T in 1928. And every time when they bought Motel T's, they'd go off from the house a ways and build a shed to put them in—a house with walls on the side.

My daddy didn't drive, so my older sister learned how to drive, but she wasn't available, and it was coming up a rain, and the old car was setting out of the garage. My dad told my mama, "I'm going to put this car in that car shed." He went out there and he cranked her and headed for that car shed, and when he got to it, he said, "Whoa! Whoa! Whoa!"—and out the back of it he went! He didn't know how to stop it.

It didn't hurt nothing. It's not hard to repair an old shed, but my daddy never got under the steering wheel again. My sisters, they all drove. One sister drove all the way to Corpus Christi in an old Model T, and we went through San Antone. Lord knows why. This old Model T ain't got no tail-lights, so we lighted an old kerosene lantern. It gets dark, that when the rhubarb would start. It gets tiresome holding an old kerosene lantern out the back end of a car. Keep someone from running over your hind end, you know? And the rhubarb would start. "He held it last night." "I held it last." Directly, Pa would pick out one and tell them, "Hold that lantern," and that was all of it. Whoever it was, they got to hold the lantern outside. I don't know how many days it took us to get down there, but it was quite a few.

### J. M. CARROLL

I never even owned a car until I was twenty-seven years old. Whenever I was riding horseback, I'd ride up and down the road. Especially in the fall of the year, when they were gathering corn, they'd haul their corn in, a lot of it would fall out, fall off, fall on the road. I'd stop there and gather that corn up, and I'd have corn to feed my horse.

You might find one place maybe for two or three miles that it was good road. Then all of a sudden there'd be a bad place there—a sink place, or a creek come across it, or something or another like that. They had iron bridges across Cowhouse [Creek], and they was passable, but they was a hell of a long ways from being good.

I'll tell you how good the roads were. One of my cousins and I used to go to a bootlegging place south of Killeen. You could buy whiskey over there, and I bought half a pint. We'd already been drinking, but I still had this half-pint that never had been opened. Another one of my cousins had an old bob-tailed Ford—it was chopped off, they'd use it in the pasture. He come in and he got with us. He said, "Let me have that half-pint of whiskey. I've got a lot of catching up to do." So I handed it to him, and, man, he downed the whole cotton-picker!

We started home, and he lived over in Coryell County, and he told us, "You better drive, I'm pretty drunk." Coming back, it'd been raining and ruts were deep, I was driving along there, and I got the front wheels in one set of ruts and the hind wheels in another set of ruts. He leaned over like this to see what was happening, and he like to have fell out. Man, it sobered him up, just like that! He said, "I believe I can drive from now on."

That's the way the roads was everywhere. You might get stuck right in the middle of the cotton-picking road in bad weather.

### NORMAN RICKETTS HALL

Part of [our road] was not graveled. I recall once we had rain for several weeks. We lived a mile from the paved road, and Mother was the driver. Two neighbors and Dad had cut cedar limbs, and they walked ahead and put the cedar limbs in the ruts. She came along in the car, and sometimes she'd have to back up, and they'd have to put more cedar in the road. It must've taken a half a day to go that mile to get to the gravel road so she could go on to town. And then you had to dread coming back.

It was an all-day trip to take a load of cotton to the gin. The main person they were interested in was the road commissioner, because you needed that road graveled and maintained. I can recall any number of times the road commissioner would come and sit with Dad sometimes a half a day out by the mailbox, planning. How can we get these roads to work? The sheriff and the road commissioner, they had an influence on you.

### NORRIS SIDNEY GRAVES

My grandfather [George Augustus Strickland] set up George Junior in Pidcoke, downtown. Bought a little place there and built a shed on it, and set him up as a blacksmith. He worked on anything—plows, anything—and automobiles began to come in about that time. In 1919 or 1920, my granddaddy decided he would buy an automobile. And he went over to Gatesville, rode his horse to Gatesville and bought a Ford automobile, but he couldn't drive it. He tried, the dealer tried to show him how to drive it,

[but] he just didn't feel safe driving all the way back to Pidcoke in that. So he rode back to Pidcoke and told George Junior that he'd bought a car if [he'd] go get it, and he did.

We have a picture of [George Junior] at the threshing machine, and he looked like he was miserable. He just didn't like anything to do with that kind of work. They tried to get him to haul hay to the thresher, and he didn't like that. But they got the idea that maybe he was miscast, and they said, "How would you like to run this thresher? How would you like to lubricate it and check the belts and all that?" That was it, they got him. He was all right then. But my granddaddy was a [horseman and a] cattleman until the day he died. We have a picture of him roping on his horse.

### JOE D. INSALL

When my brother was thirteen years old, he put a Model T together. He had the frame and the steering gear and the wheels. He traded a .22-caliber rifle and three dollars for a motor. He got the .22 selling Cloverine Salve. One day I was playing in the sand, and he called me to come and help him. I was real thrilled, because he didn't have too much to do with me. I run down to help him, and I said, "What you want me to do?" He said, "Hold that spark plug." I said, "Where's it at?" He showed me, and I held it, and he started to turn that crank. When it got on mine, it gave me quite a shock. I didn't much want to help him anymore. But he got her going, and about all he had to go by was a *Popular Mechanics* magazine. But he was a natural-born mechanic. I turned out to be a carpenter.

### KYLE HILLIARD

Daddy paid twenty-five dollars for a used Model T sometime in the early thirties. Even poor people were beginning to get used Model T's.

They would be worn out, but they would run most of the time. We got a '27, one of the last of the Model T's, after it was used. Later on, we got used Model A's.

Then the buggy became obsolete. You'd see abandoned buggies in the corner of a pasture or out behind somebody's barn. The buggy became a toy for us farm boys growing up out in the country with no TV and no radio, no electricity, no running water, no nothing. We would push them out on the mail road that went past the Halls' house, push them up the gentle slope, and then ride them down.

The Model T started with this crank thing, and when we'd play cars as kids, we could play like we was cranking it. We would make the sound that it made. You had a little wire thing with a loop in it sticking out there by the radiator, and when you wanted to choke it, you'd pull on that wire while you'd turn the crank handle. Then you'd let it go, and it made a little different sound when you were choking it from when you didn't. So we learned how to sound like a car was sounding when it was it was being cranked while it was being choked and when it wasn't, and we learned to make like we were a car running.

We parked our car under a big live oak tree just outside the barbed-wire fence that was our yard. When Daddy went to town, we'd say, "Can we back out with you?" Sister was on the running board one day, and he started backing out, and she fell off. The wheels were cut so they were going to run over her, he was scared that he might, and he pushed down on the brake and pulled back on that steering wheel so hard that he broke it. The wheel part was gone, and he had two little old things that he could hold to, the spokes. The Model T didn't have a top on it, and it looked funny with him driving off to town like that holding on to these two little spokes. Fortunately his car [had] stopped before it got to Sister.

In 1931 and 1932, that black, muddy dirt was not a very passable road. Norman Hall's mother was the driver in their family, but when it came a good soaking rain, the first one that would drive out to the turnpike that took us to Killeen, Palo Alto, Brookhaven, and Sparta would be Daddy. Mrs. Hall would ask Daddy to drive her car to the main road, she figured he knew more about how to keep from getting stuck. Daddy would make deep ruts, just sink down in that mud, but these Model T wheels had a larger diameter than modern cars and they were not as low-slung. After the mud dried and got hard, there were those deep ruts, and drivers would straddle the ruts. Just for play, my dad would get down in those ruts sometimes and show us how he could drive along real slow without even doing any steering, because the wheels would not jump out of those deep ruts. You had a track you were running on.

In 1934 came the Work Projects Administration, the Roosevelt New Deal, putting people to work, which was very, very life-saving for people trying to find some kind of a job. One of the things they did was gravel all of these black dirt roads. It might have been called busy work, but it was getting bad roads made into good all-weather roads. You could drive after a five-inch rain with no trouble at all.

**NORRIS SIDNEY GRAVES**
About 1930, late one evening [at Pidcoke], an airplane came over, and he

was a-popping and a-pooting and sputtering and everything, and he landed in my granddaddy's back [pasture]. It was a man that was plotting a mail route for the air corps in an old double-wing biplane, and he said, "I need more gas, I'm gonna try to make it in." I don't know which way he was going, down towards Austin, I think. So my granddaddy said, "Well, what kind? We don't have any aviation gas or anything." And he said, "Oh, I can burn anything." So we got in my granddaddy's old car and went down to one of the stores in Pidcoke, got two five-gallon cans of gas, brought it back, and filled him up. This guy cranked it up, and it ran, he was satisfied with it. Then he came over and said, "Would you like to take a ride?" My granddaddy said, "No! You're not talking to me." Then he said, "Well, would the boy there like to take a ride?" I said, "Can I, Granddaddy?" So anyway, I got to ride in an airplane—flew over Pidcoke and over and come back around.

### JOHN DANIEL WOLF

I remember a steam-operated tractor as just an old empty, junked thing. My dad had the first one that was actually used, a Farmall F-12, bought brand-new. He swapped his teams for it and did custom work for others. I remember my grandfather, the old patriarch, [saying], "Tuck, that damn thing will pack the ground until you won't be able to raise anything by that damn thing." Well, either the first or second summer he had it, my grandpa got behind. It rained so much he got behind, and he couldn't get his land put up to plant. So he had to come for my dad to get him to take that tractor over there and plow that land to get it ready to plant. He never said anymore about that [tractor], he never said any more about it.

It was an F-12. We classified it as a two-row, because we did have two-row cultivating and planting equipment with it. My dad had to make this to pull behind it. We were at the time mainly raising small grain, such as oats. He did a good bit of custom work for the community around. I remember a dollar or a dollar and a quarter an acre for breaking land. My dad was a trader, he didn't sit still for anything. The Poston brothers here in Gatesville had a Farmall dealership, and my dad dealt with them. One of the Poston boys came out to finalize the deal and bring the tractor, and I sit there and listened and watched he and my dad talk. He had an Aggie ring on. That was pretty impressed in my mind, he had an Aggie ring. My one dream in life was to go to A&M.

## Government Programs and the Takeover

*Government interventions began with the compulsory agricultural pro-grams of the New Deal and ended with the land takeover by the U.S. Army in 1942. As elsewhere across the South, waste-not, want-not farmers had painful memories of cattle killed and burned and cotton plowed up, even if they voluntarily had taken part in these programs and accepted the government's money. With the "takeover" came government intervention of an entirely different magnitude. No matter how buoyed up people were by remembered patriotisms of "the good war," the forced land sales of 1942 and 1943 left bitter memories of lost homeplaces and abolished settle-ments. Rent farmers often shrugged these off, older landowners suffered greatly, and the sons and daughters of both left to serve in the war, most of them never to return to the farming life.*

### ROBERT E. GAULT

My dad came home in 1936, the crops all in and everything. He said, "Well, I've got a hundred dollars in the bank. That's the first time since '28 I've had any money in the bank." We raised anything you wanted there [in our garden] just profusely, and we had a peach orchard by our house, and we kept bees—we always had ten to twelve hives of bees. They were self-pre-serving people in those days. But we made it through the Depression that way, we got by. And lots of them didn't, we had people all around us that went under. When Herbert Hoover ran for reelection, Dad's neighbor had to borrow a car from him [to go vote], and he voted for Hoover. Dad said, "He's a damn fool!"

### JAMES W. YANCY

In the '30s, the Depression was on. We had plenty to eat, we didn't have a lot of money in our pocket. I can remember Daddy saying that the total income that year was about two hundred and fifty dollars. He sent a truckload of sheep to Fort Worth to market to sell, and they just barely brought enough to pay expenses. He sold sheep for twenty-five cents a head, and goats, you could hardly give them away. Calves sold for about five dollars.

Later on, the government came along and killed a bunch of the cows, hogs, and sheep. We had to skin our sheep that we killed and send the hides to the county seat in Gatesville. Those hides, lots of them, were used for [lining] the flight jackets of World War II pilots.

My grandfather was dead at that time, he died in 1930. I can't remember how much [the government] gave you for the sheep and the cows. I can remember the man from the government coming out there with an automatic .22 and standing up on the fence planks and shooting cattle in the head. Daddy felt so terrible that we had to do this. We had to take them and bury them. There was a place where they had dug out for a tank, so we dragged them there with mules and buried them. A few families did use the meat from the animals that had been killed, but you must remember the people didn't have transportation, and they didn't have refrigeration.

### WILMA EARL COLVIN EDWARDS

I heard [the cattle being killed], Mother and Daddy wouldn't let the kids watch it. They had a kill right up in the corner of my granddad's place two or three hundred yards from their house. It was at the corner of the public road and across the fence between their house and the Lindauers. They killed several there, and they burned those. We could smell that smoke terribly for several days.

### NORMAN RICKETTS HALL

When Roosevelt came in, there was a lot of overproduction, and they plowed up cotton. Another thing, they had too many animals. Everybody on the north side of Killeen brought their stock they wanted to sell to the government to our ranch. We didn't know what was going to happen, but they had a man that would come and offer you a price, and there was a man with a .22 rifle turned up there. He would say, "Okay, here's this Herford, [we'll] give you three dollars." Guy'd say, "Okay," and POW! Shot them right between the eyes.

Well, the day was over, they'd killed over a hundred head of stock, and they was laying dead on our land. The government had hired somebody, and they drug them off up to a canyon. Stacked them all together. Lord, there's a big pile. There were poor people there that were cutting the hindquarters and other parts of beef, but that was just a drop in the bucket. Then they took gasoline and just saturated them all over. Those fires burned for days, because they would come back after two or three days, put more gasoline on, burn them again. It just literally destroyed that canyon. For years after that all you could see was burnt bones and rocks, and no grass would grow there.

### JOE D. INSALL

Like I told the guys at work, "I got the edge on y'all. I know how to starve to death, and you've never had no experience at it." I remember one time when my next meal was running loose in the woods, but we had all kinds of vegetables if it rained right. We didn't have a freezer 'cause we didn't have electricity, but we canned lots of things and dried them. I remember way back in the thirties when they killed all them cows to raise the market, I don't know what year that was, but Daddy wouldn't bring that meat home 'cause he figured it was stealing it. Of course, we didn't have nothing to kill. I'll guarantee you, I'd have got me a hindquarter, or something.

This boy was working at a CCC camp, it was the last year we was at Antelope. He come up there to the house and had a little old scrawny dog with him. He said, "Old Spark Plug treed a coon down there, I think. I built a big fire, but I still couldn't see him." He said, "Do y'all have a flashlight?"

It was hard times. Way they worked that, one of these boys joined the CCC, they had to make an allotment out to somebody at home. It was more or less to keep folks from starving to death. He had to make one out to his great-aunt and uncle that lived close by, and of course they saved the money and give it back to him. He'd go visit them and get paid again, and he had to walk to get there.

We had a flashlight, about burned out, and we went back to the [coon] tree and couldn't find nothing. So we just went a-possum hunting, and that little old dog got four of them that night. He said, "Old Spark Plug was hitting on all four!"

### JAMES W. CALHOUN

When the government had the cattle reduction program on that killed a lot of cows, they'd give all of that you wanted or that you could use. We sliced beef and put it on a sheet, covered it with a sheet, on a tin roof. It actually made jerky, was what it was. Mama'd chop it up in the wintertime, soak it overnight in water, and then make gravy on it, and it was as good as anything you ever ate.

I remember right there at Maple they used to make cotton mattresses. Franklin Roosevelt had the idea that a farmer couldn't do a good day's work unless he got a good night's sleep, so they had all this government surplus cotton, and they would give them the cotton. They'd go to Gatesville, haul it out here, and then all the women would sew the ticks and make the mattresses—big fifty-pound cotton mattresses. Everybody started sleeping a lot better after that.

One time when the Work Projects Administration, WPA, was on, [Daddy] went and signed up during the winter months. They were building the Mound schoolhouse, and they was sawing the limestone out of a quarry right there close to the Mound schoolhouse. Daddy said them people were so lazy, and they kept getting on him about working too hard. He was having to get up early in the morning and walk four miles to Maple to catch that truck to go to Mound. So it just got the best of him, he didn't stay at it very long. If he was gonna work, he was gonna work. They wanted to goof off, make the job last.

### JEROME KEENER BLACKWELL

For me, the government was a huge beast I had heard about but never seen, yet it was to play a major role in my later life. The only function I could determine it performed in our little [Brown's Creek] community was the annual dipping of all the cattle in our area in the local dipping vat located near the school. It was quite a sight to see the long herds of cattle being driven down the public roads with dust clouds so huge it seemed to me like a threat of rain. But the cowboys on the sweating horses, cursing and yelling at the strays, choking on dust, they knew the difference.

Word was circulated that there was a crash on Wall Street. I didn't know what Wall Street represented, but as we traveled to town I was sure I would see some signs of the wreckage, as I imagined it to be a local thing brought on by the government that had all those poor cows to swim the stinking dip every year.

People with large families began to infiltrate the country on foot from town looking for work if not for pay (because there was no money to be had), just for something to eat. My mother and dad had a big heart, and he would give the men of the families wood-cutting jobs, which we boys normally did, and my mother fed them all until they could hold no more, and then she would fix a sack of food for them to take home. These people were actually starving.

[Later] the government figured that the killing of cattle would somehow solve all the problems of our economy, so one day three men came to our place and killed about half of our stock with a rifle. You could skin the animals and sell the hides or use the skins for home tanning. We chose to skin and sell them, as this meant fifty cents a hide, and money was scarce. The younger calves were canned, and for a little while life was very busy disposing of the carcasses. People starving in the surrounding towns came with sacks and pans like vultures to salvage the best of the meat.

We had a fine crop of corn and cotton, and an order was given to plow up a portion of our cotton that was beginning to open. We did as ordered, and I believe this, along with killing our cows, aged my father ten years. Neither he nor I could see any sense in plowing up a good crop we had worked so hard to plant, thin, hoe, and cultivate.

We were the sole owners of this land [at Brown's Creek] until Fort Hood came in 1942 and acquired it by force. We were not bargained with, simply given the order to "be out in ten days."

### WILLIAM AKE POWELL

They weren't very happy about the way [Camp Hood] took place, but they didn't have no choice. They just come there and told you how much they was going to give for you land and give you two or three weeks to get out and took a bulldozer and pushed your house down. And that's all there was to it.

Everybody wanted to do their part, and as a general rule they didn't raise too much sand about it, 'cause they wanted to be patriotic and do what was right. I don't believe either one of my grandparents bought another place, but my mother and daddy did. My grandparents just kind of quit. They was pretty old, anyway.

### JOE D. INSALL

When Fort Hood came, we had the eight acres and the house and the barn, stock tank, and just lots of fruit trees. They gave us six hundred dollars for it and moved us out. When we were moving to Copperas Cove, I think the army furnished us some trucks. I know my brother led the milk cow, and I led one horse and rode another one, and she was pretty skinny. Didn't even know what a saddle was, [and] my rear end was pretty raw by the time I got there, seven miles.

Life was pretty dull in Copperas Cove, 'cause I had to walk half a mile before I could start hunting. After a while, I had a paper route and forty customers, and that covered the whole town. Those first GI soldiers had these old World War I helmets, and when I saw the new-type helmet, I didn't know whether I'd go close to them or not. I thought they might be foreigners.

### TOMMIE L. SHULTS HAFERKAMP

The day that Pearl Harbor was bombed, I remember that day like it was yesterday. It was on a Sunday. Uncle Sam and Aunt Bessie had visited us, and you know how after you've had company, you're kind of keyed up and everybody was kind of winding down. And Papa went to the cow pen and milked and came in and turned on the radio. We did have a radio at that time. It was on a battery, so we could only use it for special occasions—the *Grand Ole Opry* and the news. And Papa turned on the news, and they were talking about Pearl Harbor.

Then, the next year, there was talk of taking our place. They went to a meeting at Ewing, and a general talked to them and told them they would be getting their letters just in the next few days. Mother and Father, when I got home from school, they'd been there, and they said, "Well, it was definite." That was the second time I saw Papa cry.

I didn't care, I didn't like it down there. In fact, I knew there was a better life somewhere else! I'm sorry it had to be like that for them, because I don't think Papa ever got over it.

We moved out in December of 1942, they actually moved us in army trucks. It was cold.

Papa never said a lot. Except, sometimes in the wintertime, if we were sitting around the fireplace, he would tell old stories about how things used to be. He kept a lot of it inside himself. They were so patriotic, they never questioned, none of them ever questioned but what it was their duty to do that, even though it was painful. My daddy grew up on that place, it had been in the family all those years. Now that I know how much I love this place that we worked for, I understand what it was like for him. But at that time I didn't. I didn't care, I really didn't.

### T. A. WILHITE

They just come in [at Sparta] and took over everything, and you didn't have no say about it. But they did pay a little for you to move. I think they gave me seven hundred dollars to move everything, but I had so much to move it took nearly all the time a-moving stuff out. Most all that moved was moved at the same time. It was eighteen loads off my place and went down to where I's moving to.

I know the year I moved off from up there. That whole area down in there, ever bit of it is under water. There's a big iron bridge crossing the Cowhouse River right in front of my house. They didn't move it, they left the old thing there, and water covered it up. It's still down there under the lake. And Sparta church. Deep, too.

Hugh Armen wasn't gonna move. They kept after him trying to get him to move, and he wouldn't do it. One morning they drove up there to his house with a bunch of trucks. Asked him, "Where you want to move to? We're gonna load you up." They loaded him up, and he moved to Killeen.

### JOHN GAIL EDWARDS

It was sometime in the spring of 1942. Our neighbors, Elder Cox and his wife, had lost a baby, stillborn. I had a car then, [and I] drove our parents to Copperas Cove for the funeral of this baby. We heard the rumor that day, that the government was going to buy our home and build an army base. My daddy laughed at the idea and said, "No, they won't ever do that." But we had an uncle, our mother's oldest brother, who had taught school all over the country, and he was a Baptist minister, out in the public a lot, and he told Daddy, "No, John, it's going to happen." That was the first time I heard about it, and then it developed real fast.

It was the spring of '42 that we left there. It was fifty-six years since we moved out—May 2, 1942. We went right up 281 here north of Lampasas about twelve miles. We didn't have any money, they didn't pay us. We left there May 2, and sometime in August that year they paid what little they paid. If we hadn't have had a little cash, what kind of shape would we have been in?

I moved us out, our daddy was bedridden. He had had a nervous breakdown, and we moved him in an ambulance. We pulled up to this old house out there, just an old shack of a house we moved in. It was summertime, it was warm and dry. I don't know how many snakes there were. We run them out pretty quick, moved in with them. We had five army trucks that came to move us, and the first trip we took most of the household furniture except Daddy's bed. Pulled up in front of the house, and there was just a line of people here, cars all around, and I said, "What in the world is going on? Who knew that we were going to move in here today?"

I don't know to this good day how the word got around, but the neighbors all around there were there, and my aunt and uncle and cousin. So, how happy I was. They had that furniture set up, that wood stove set up, and a bed made for Daddy to be put in in nothing flat.

I am going to write a piece on the takeover, but I don't want to hurt your feelings. It killed our parents young. It robbed us of our heritage and our inheritance.

### JOHN EASLEY

Ewing School had a space out behind the tabernacle, they called it. It was attached to the back of the building, a covered area, the floor was dirt. It was where people sat to watch school plays. As I remember, that's where we first learned that Fort Hood was taking our land.

I remember the moving. Daddy, in the wintertime when there wasn't stuff to do on the farm, he cut cedar posts and sold them. So [we] even had some cedar posts that he had not sold. The army came in trucks early one morning and loaded everything that was ours, and we moved away, took everything in one time. Some of the chickens we couldn't catch because they roosted in the trees. We went back one night some days later to get those chickens. And it's a strange feeling that here this house sat vacant that you'd lived in all these years, and you couldn't go in there and stay the night.

We took it in due course, not being landowners. And too, the prospect of employment, steady employment for Daddy made the move for us a whole lot different from those who owned the land. He did go to work helping build Fort Hood and was employed there until just shortly before his death in 1946. So from our perspective, it wasn't that big a deal.

When I was in the army in 1953, I was training in North Fort Hood. We had a compass course at night. You had to read a compass and walk so far, and then somebody'd be there to initial your piece of paper, and you'd made that point. And one of the compass points was two graves. It had a very very old ornamental fence around it, and I read the stones, and then I knew who they were. My grandmother said that was her grandparents, the Browns.

### MURREL L. THOMPSON

I never had heard of Pearl Harbor, didn't mean anything to me. I remember my mother and my daddy and everybody talking about it, we were going to be in a war. It was shortly after the word got out they were looking to build an army camp, and then in June of '42 everybody was out of there. Now, that's pretty quick!

Daddy and them, they had to get out to try to look and find a place they might could buy to move to, and then plus getting everything you had to load up ready to go. These people in the surrounding areas, they knew that these people in the Fort Hood area had to have a place, and they'd go up on their price. What was so unfair about the pricing of that Fort Hood land, they didn't have any real appraisers that knew anything about the land. A good river bottom, as good a land as you ever seen, might be appraised for less than the sorry caliche hill with cedar all over it. They just barely did get enough money to buy another place. People didn't borrow money back in those days. Some of them couldn't take it. It was a strange time.

[Our neighbors] the McDonalds had about eight hundred sheep, and that's the way they made their living—they farmed, too, but mostly from those sheep. Mr. McDonald just couldn't take losing his ranch. He was born and reared there, just like my daddy. When the time came that he actually did have to give it up, they found him in the sheep shed where he had shot himself.

### J. W. SHULTS

When it begin to be rumored about Fort Hood and it finally became reality, it was mass confusion. We'd get a letter from the Department of the Army and say you have thirty days to evacuate your premises. Then the next day you'd get another letter that said you had ten days to evacuate. Everybody was running just anywhere. It was a heyday for the real estate people, and land began to double in price. A lot of people bought land in places that they didn't really like, but they had to have somewhere to live. People scattered in every direction.

A neighbor of one of my uncles had told him he would not ever move. They said, "Yeah, you will have to move," and he said, "I'm not going to." They would bring out soldiers with trucks and help you haul your furniture and things, anything except livestock. You put your name on a list, and they would tell you what day they would be at your house to help you. This man had made the arrangements, and when they pulled into his driveway he was sitting on the front porch. He had been sharpening his pocket knife all morning, and he reached up and cut his throat and died in his front yard. He had told them that he'd never move.

### ANDY GORDON WOLF

Old man Jim Stevenson always had a bunch of wild horses, couldn't be worked, and he kept them just fat as they can be, feeding them corn and stuff. Uncle Jim, he cussed a whole lot. We was picking cotton up on the hill there close to Maple, and old man Jim lived just down the road. There was a steep hill come off my Grandpa Jack's, and them horses ran away with him on [that] damn rolling stalk cutter. You could hear him all over the country, "Whoaaah, you son-a-bitches!"

They throwed him off, and they run that stalk cutter over him and broke some of his ribs and things, and he never did get over it. His health was bad from then on. Then they told him he's gonna have to move out of Fort Hood, and he committed suicide.

### ZELL KINSEY COPELAND

I had a lot of relatives [that owned land]—the McBrides and the Beasleys and the Schultzes. People would say to us, "Well, I know that killed you for the army to take your land," but I don't ever remember hearing a one of them complain. I think they felt that was just a little thing for them to do, because most of them had sons that was in the war. My husband went, four of my brothers went, and my sister's husband. My mother-in-law had to move out too, and she said, "That's the only way in the world I'd of ever got away from down there!"

### FLORENCE JOYCE HAEDGE

We had lots of cattle, and the saddest thing was, whenever the time to leave [came], big old eighteen-wheeler came up there and he had to let them go on that truck. Daddy had to sell everything, that was sad. I'll never forget my horse Jim. He was old already, I had to lead him to the truck and let somebody carry him off. I don't think anybody in their right mind, or has any sense at all about farming, will ever forget leaving their home.

Our barn was the last barn there—didn't have no roof on it or nothing, somebody already tore it down, but the corn cribs was still full of corn. That's when our church people helped us again with their trailers, as they did with the other stuff. My cats and dogs set there with their tongues hanging out, 'cause they could not kill all the rats that come out of there. Everybody's rat from everywhere [had come] over there. Everybody [else] was already gone, they'd moved themselves.

[During the war years] Mama and myself would go to the church, then go out to where we used to live to eat. Well, one time we went there, the house was full of sheep. I just thought, that's a little too much. I opened the door and let them out. Then the tank destroyers just went right through the trees and just smashed them. We had beautiful cedar trees and hackberry trees planted for shade, really pretty yard, they just split them open. Towards the last we went there, the house was burned. You could tell it was burned, everybody's was burned.

We had a carbide plant for lights, and it had a pit in the ground. One Sunday, Mama and I, we's eating and nearly through, and all of a sudden a soldier jumped out of that pit. He was hiding in that hole. First thing he said was, "Ladies, have you got anything left?"

### FRANKIE JUANITA WRIGHT TRANTHAM

I just always rode a horse. We lived about two and a half miles from the old

Georgetown road, where the mail route was, and I'd get on my horse and go to the mailbox. I'd ride my horse everyday, I guess. And, oh, I felt free!

Mostly, I rode on our property. But sometime I got it in my head I was going to sell garden seed, or some kind of salve, or something. I remember one time going way down close to Eliga, horseback.

When we had to move out of the camp, my dad told us one night, "I want y'all to drive the sheep from here to the new place." It was out southeast of Gatesville. So we started out and drove them, was on the Georgetown road with them. At that time, some of the soldiers had moved in up on Georgetown Road just before the Gannaway Hill. That was the first bunch that moved in. There was quite a few pup tents out there. And we got up there, and the sheep wanted to start straying into where [the pup tents] were set, to where the soldiers were.

Oh, that just thrilled them soldiers to death! They had never witnessed anything like that, a girl riding a horse and herding sheep. They just come up [and said], "Let me ride your horse. Get down and let me ride your horse for a minute! Let us take a picture on him!" Things like that.

I told them, "We don't have time, we have to go and get those sheep up there. You know what we're doing it for? Because y'all running us off our place!"

But they just kept on, and finally I got off and let one or two of them get up on the horse, and they took some pictures. And then we got on our horses and got the sheep together and drove on.

### ROBERT E. GAULT

First thing we know, it came out in the paper that Fort Hood was a possibility. The first estimate was forty to fifty thousand acres, and it just kept on growing. We had a mile of the Cowhouse Creek and then a half-mile back the other way, that's a half section, 320 acres. Dad went there when he was six years old, his dad had bought the place then. He lived there from the time he was six till the government moved him out when he's sixty-six. And he was a just like a fish out of the water for the rest of his life. He lived till '47 and died then.

It was Granddad's old place. Dad took it over after Granddad died in 1906. He got a federal loan and bought out his sisters and kept it. He'd gotten all of his federal loan paid off about the year before, and he was ready to enjoy himself. He had about sixty head of cattle on there. We had ninety acres of good bottom-cultivating land and real good pasture. We raised half, three-quarter bale of cotton to the acre. We had real good cotton land, and on the upper land that was lightest we raised oats. We rotated oats, maize, and corn, you see, and then cotton—diversified farming.

We went to Turnersville to that rock pile up there, that's all we could buy with the money we got. Dad was offered more during the Depression than what he got for it. We had to sell all our cattle off in the spring. We had forty-nine head of Herford cattle we sold for thirty-five dollars a head, they'd just come through the winter, and they'd have brought two hundred and fifty dollars or better by the fall. We had a big loss there. We had four hundred grafted pecans, and they said that wasn't an improvement, that's just part of the place, didn't allow any pay for it. And it'd cost lots of money grafting all of those pecans, and they was bearing, we was making $1,000 to $1,500 a year on pecans.

And they'd take one on ten—if you had ten places, they would take this tenth place, here, and give him a good price. This one place down on where the House Creek runs into Cowhouse, a place water went across it every year and it's washed down nearly to bedrock, they gave him sixty-four dollars an acre. And we was up there on prime property, we got twenty dollars an acre.

That's just how it worked out. There was a few got good money and that was all, only a few. Our appraiser was from Chicago, Illinois, so you know he knew Texas land prices real well. They never do use a Texas man to do anything like that. There's no system that the government used at that time that was much sense to it. They had hearings. Old man Jim Gannaway had a place, and he wouldn't take their price. He died and never had gotten any money out of it. They just kept putting him off to where he never did get anything. You know how the federal courts and things are. I guess his son probably settled with them later.

Everybody moved out. The army was going to move us, gonna give us thirty days. And they go fifteen days, and they sent six-by-sixes with canvas on them out there to move us, we paid outside truckers one hundred and twenty-five dollars per load. And they didn't let us have our fences, and they took those things and just run right down and ground them into the ground. And they wouldn't let us have our house, and they fired into them and burned them. Yeah, that's the way they done it.

The first troops came in from Fort Meade, Maryland, and we got out of school to see those troops come in. We couldn't understand them! We'd never heard any Yankees talk, it tickled us. But we found out them old boys was mostly Pennsylvania Dutch in that outfit that came in here, and they's the best old boys you ever saw. They invited us to come back there, and they'd take us out on those half-tracks and everything, riding. It'd just be us kids. They was a nice bunch of boys—after we got to where we could talk to them.

We had a big cemetery on our place there where that school was. It's a pretty good-sized cemetery, Latham Prairie–Salem Cemetery. It was sixty-four or sixty-eight bodies moved out of there to Killeen cemetery and Copperas Cove cemetery and Gatesville cemetery, and my dad had to go over there and identify people. His dad and mother was in the bunch, and he had several cousins and such in there. It just amazed me the number of people that was in it. He had an uncle, old Uncle John Gault, buried there. And he said when they dug him up, after all those years, said you could recognize him. Had his bow tie on, leather bow tie on like he always wore. 'Course, after he's exposed to that air, he collapsed pretty quick. Dad said most of them you could put in a kitchen bag.

Supposed to have moved everybody, I don't know what they did. They moved my grandparents and my brother and my brother's boy over to Killeen. I've got brothers, one on the east side of the cemetery and one buried clear on the west side now. We don't know whether the right people got in the right place or not. Dad said they're awful careless with the tagging. You know, contract deal, that's part of what the government did. I'd have hated to have gone up there and identified them, but Dad said, well, somebody had to do it, and he knew more about it than anybody else did, because he'd been there all the time.

Dad was just like a fish out of water the rest of his life. He never did settle down after that. He bought a little place up there at Turnersville, north of Gatesville twenty miles, and he was restless. He'd go to see one of the kids one day and the next day somewhere else. He died in '47.

### NORMAN RICKETTS HALL

I was teaching at Spanish Oak when they decided to build Fort Hood. That was quite a shock to the people, they couldn't believe it at first. They didn't have any concept of what this was gonna mean.

When the camp came, a lot of people said, "This is gonna be great. We're gonna get to sell this land at a high price." But when the army came in, they had pretty much of a thumbnail sketch. They paid twenty-seven dollars an acre for cultivated land [and] eleven dollars an acre for pastureland. But of course the problem was that there were so many people who were dispossessed of their place, they went looking for places and it drove the price up. That put a bad taste in a lot of people's mouths. Because, in other words, when they take my land, I can't replace it.

When they first came, they sent in about a hundred surveyors just to start surveying. They couldn't even accommodate a hundred people in Killeen. I think there was probably one hotel, and they'd never heard of a tourist court. Couldn't even spell it! Most of [the surveyors] were living in Temple or Gatesville, or had their own camping facilities. And then, gosh, it wasn't a year until there you had 80,000 troops out there under the cedar brakes in tents. We'd never heard of a taxi either, but that got to be a pretty growing business when taxis would go out and pick up the troops when they wanted to go to town. And to come to Killeen was a real letdown, 'cause only 1,263 people lived in Killeen when the camp came. It was just a little farming and ranching community.

They did not take our ranch in the first Fort Hood expansion. It was on two sides of us, and quite often some of the fellows driving tanks didn't know where the boundary was, because they would cut across our land. My dad had goats, and one time about 275 goats got out. So he went to Fort Hood to place a claim, and they said, "Well, Mr. Hall, it's just one of those things, we'll look for them." [They] never found them, but they did send troops out to fix the fence. One day Dad went to see the fence, and they'd stuck the little part of the pole in the ground because you didn't have to dig as big a hole. They must've had a hundred yards of fence like that.

When the Korean War came along, by then they had built Belton Lake, and so they wanted to have amphibious training. So they took several thousand more acres so they could go to the shores of Lake Belton, and it became necessary for them to take our land. They paid us a certain amount, and then we moved the house. Had to move it four miles [into Killeen], and my folks had bought a lot in town to move it on.

It was quite a project to jack it up and all that business, and [get it] ready to move. They couldn't move it down the roads for some reason, but they could move it through some of the pastures, and they made arrangement to start moving. They couldn't move it in one day, so they were going to come to spend the night with us after they got squared away and started the move. They didn't come in at four o'clock, they didn't come in at five. It got dark, and they hadn't come, and we thought something was the matter. I drove out to the homeplace. The house was gone, I looked all around. I started back to town, and as I did, I looked down in a pasture where there was a branch, and I saw a light down there, and there's not supposed to be a light down there.

I parked the car as close as I could, and I walked, and there was the house. It was propped up on rollers, and I found the steps and got in the house. There was kerosene lanterns in use. My mother was in the kitchen, I guess preparing a meal, and Dad was sitting in his chair by the radio reading a book. I asked, "What is the matter with you people? I thought you all were going to come to our house?" [Dad said,] "Well, we just decided we would just stay here." Couldn't leave that house, you know.

They actually lived in that in Killeen until they both passed away. Dad must have been in his late seventies when [the house had to be moved], and he never gave up. He lived to be ninety. He could sit on that front porch and I guess dream of the days that had gone by. Mother adjusted real well, because she'd always worked in town, went back and forth, and town was part of her life. But Dad didn't, he never adjusted to going to town. He could sit on the front porch and dream or visualize the past. And here's a funny thing. He had always tilled the soil. He would voluntarily go to a neighbor's yard, and if it had Johnson grass or weeds, he would get it out. He was supervising a new kind of farm, it was a block in town.

But there was a dream. Everybody that moved off that Fort Hood reservation dreamed of the day that, when the war was over and the army left, they could come back. My mother had said, "When we come back, we're gonna put the house here, and we'll turn it like this, and then we'll move this over here." She lived for ten years hoping that would happen, and so many of them were like that.

As I recall, there were two or three suicides where people didn't want to leave their ranch. When they saw them coming and they had to leave, well, they took it real serious. They wanted to hold on to that way of life. 'Course, they had no idea what other kind of life there'd be, but they were satisfied with the one they had.

### CLEMENTS W. "SPEEDY" DUNCAN

In 1937 we came back over here to Okay. That's where we stayed until the army took Pa's rock pile over there one day and took me the next. He was real lucky, he got shut of [his land] one day and me the next.

The army [had] sent me a letter. Allen Hanes owned many acres of land between here and Florence. I was walking. He had a car, and he picked me up. They was drafting people for the army in World War II, and he wanted me to come work on his ranch because it was getting hard to get help. He was going to pay me a dollar a day. I was already making a dollar an hour, but he was going to give me a dollar a day and feed me and keep me out of the army. I said, "Well, Mr. Hanes, I ain't going to volunteer, but when they call me, I'm ready to go," and I got out. About two days later I got an invitation to go to the army. [Later] I found out that Allan Hanes was on the draft board down at Belton! He had drove straight on to Belton and [said], "Get him!"

The army took the farm, and I got back in time to help them move. I worked day and night, three days and three nights, that was my seven-day leave. A fine barbed-wire fence, brand new, joined my daddy's, and it was a full moon that night. I could go a long stretch, like from here to my mail-box up yonder, and take down two wires at a time, pull the staples, and pile them over to the side and tie them to a tree. When I got enough slack and I got to the other end, I could pull on them and get the two together and make a large loop, five or six foot high, and pull back on it and roll it. I rolled up a thousand pounds of new barbed wire in three days and three nights.

This was in February of 1943. It was getting along toward daylight, and the wind come out of the north. And I said, "I better get my shirt on." I was unusually cold, so I headed for the house, and when they tore that house down, they'd tore that Wall-Rite wallpaper off of the old walls, and it was blowing around out there and hanging up on whatever. I went and gathered me up a whole big armload of that Wall-Rite paper and threw it down in this old cellar hole and jumped down in there, crawled in under that paper, and I went to sleep.

My daddy came from over east of Killeen, where they moved to, in a wagon and team, and he went over there and loaded all that wire up by hisself, bless his heart. He didn't know what had happened to me. He come by the old homeplace, and he told me. "Son, I hollered as loud as I could holler and I couldn't get you up." He said, "I don't know why I walked up to that old cellar, but I did." He said, "I looked down in there and said, 'He ain't in there,' and I started to walk off, and then I said, 'That's his boot heel!'"

I'll tell you, a wagon won't knock off much wind, it sure don't. And them old mules was pulling a pretty big load of wire, and I can remember them shaking and quivering they was so cold, pulling that wagon. I had to be in Killeen at the bus station at five o'clock the next morning, so I couldn't go to sleep. I went in there and kissed my mama good-bye, and I said, "I'm going out of town." I went to the bus station, and cold, my God, it was cold! So we told the old boy that was running the bus station that we were going down to the railroad depot, the railroad depot had a coal stove. Need-less to say, that was the first eating-out I got when the sergeant came by to pick us up, and they never did quit.

**JOHN DANIEL WOLF**

Pearl Harbor was December 7, 1941, and in early 1942 there were rumors going around. There was a kind of army vehicle that come up the road in our community. Survey teams of different kinds, people strange in the community, were coming everywhere. People said, "What in the world are they gonna do? What are they here for?"—and nobody could seem to find the answer. Then the rumor got to spreading that they were going to take over the whole thing and make a training camp out of it for Army, and everybody was gonna have to move out. Well, that was so farfetched that most of us didn't believe it for three or four months. Actually, we didn't believe it until we got a Department of Army notice that it is happening. Boy-hidey, you're going to move!

Everybody had to be out by April '42, I believe. The thing was, these people just didn't have any money, we were just coming out of the Depression. Maybe they had a little savings, but they didn't have very much. My parents didn't have anything to amount to anything, just a derned old pickup that ran half the time. They took my dad's land, and he protested the value they put on it, and therefore they didn't pay him anything! So we moved out of here without one dime. We moved to Evant, he bought that place up there without a dime. He had a good connection with the banks and with the people he'd been dealing with, and they trusted him. They stood by him until they got it all worked out. How in the world he managed it, I don't know.

Well, I was at the age that I should have gone in the army in 1943, but I didn't get my draft notice. I was classified I-A, but I didn't get a notice to report for almost a year. I was working twelve hours a day digging post holes at that new place up there [at Evant]. The banker at Evant was on the draft board here in Gatesville and had helped Dad get a deferment for me, and I didn't know it. My dad, I heard this later, had gone down there and told the banker, said, "Aw, dammit, they took my farm and everything else, and now they gonna take the only helper I've got. I've got to have that boy to help me up there."

I found out about it when I came up for renewal of [the deferment], and I told my dad, "Daddy, I don't want you to do that anymore. People in the community and everybody is asking me why I haven't gone in the service!" He said, "Well, if you feel that way." We had most of the fence holes [dug] anyway. I was reclassified, and in three months they had me.

## Epilogue: Sixty Years Afterward

*Looking back from the perspective of 2001, people interviewed by the Fort Hood Oral History Project often commented that their lives had passed very quickly, but that the circumstances and society in which they had grown up seemed very distant from the present. "That was like another world," Andy Wolf recounted, shrugging his shoulders at the inadequacy of those few words and the complexities left unsaid. Nineteenth-century lifestyles lasted through the first third of the twentieth century in places like rural Coryell and Bell counties, then World War II—and the government takeover—arrived to transform all. The rural present is very different. Historian Pete Daniel wrote in his history of Southern agriculture, Breaking the Land, "The rural traveler sees constant reminders of the agricultural system that once characterized the South." These stand beside a New South of brick houses, mobile homes, tractors, and cattle pastures. "In the eleven southern states, farms declined from 2.4 million in 1940 to 723,000 in 1974, while the average size grew from 86 to 235 acres. Farming as a culture was superseded by large-scale farming as a commercial enterprise." Twenty-first-century survivors of the old farming culture at the Fort Hood settlements recalled their lost world with juxtaposed memories of light and dark, but all knew that they could never return.*

### JAMES W. CALHOUN

Dad was just a renter [at Maple]. I remember one time after Daddy paid the rent on a bale of cotton, ginned out right here at Killeen, and he bought whatever Mama told him to get at the grocery store, he had five dollars left and [was] very discouraged.

I've seen Mama cry silently lots of times when things would get so rough. Daddy, if he ever let his feelings be known, he got away from the house. People don't think anything about crying anymore. If their feelings are hurt or something, they don't mind crying. Back in them days, crying was a sign of weakness. That went back to the pioneers.

Bless his heart. I've seen Daddy so beat following plow or teams or something he'd come in and his feet just almost be scalded from walking in the hot dirt. It was a hard, hard life. I sit up there now in a John Deere tractor with cold air blowing on me. Sometimes I have to turn the air conditioner off, it gets so cold. I get to thinking about them days.

### CLEMENTS W. "SPEEDY" DUNCAN

I can find the right spot, right where I was born, but the cedars has literally took it. I'd been gone fifty years and laying in there and ain't thought of the government, the reservation, when I dreamed a soldier fell in a well my daddy dug, a hand-dug well, and it bugged me ever since.

I went out there with them people, but it had been raining and it was awful foggy and wet. I had to walk for a quarter of a mile or so to find it. Where we used to raise what we eat or eat what we raised, it's grown up in cedars. I found it, I definitely know where the house was. Mother had an old tree, we called them pepper trees or sage trees, right at the edge of the yard. We grabbed a handful of these little balls and put them in sausage when we killed a hog and made sausage with a hand grinder.

The well I was worried about was off down in the field. It was hand-dug, and it was fairly deep and awful wide. There's a possibility the army filled it up, but it was a weird dream. I dreamed a soldier fell off in there, and they couldn't find him, and when they found him he was dead. I woke up, and I thought, "I've got to go check on that old well!"

### JOE D. INSALL

We had a lot of good times. I don't know much about playing football, but I can trail an ant across a rock pile if he's bleeding. I learned how to hunt and fish pretty good, and grow things. And I still kind of like to live the way we did back then. It sort of warps the mind.

### T. A. WILHITE

I always said if I had five hundred dollars in the bank and a good set of mules, I had nothing to worry about. Well, I ain't much different now. I don't get no good out of worrying, that's the bad end of living.

# The Fort Hood Oral History Project

The Fort Hood Oral History Project was conceived and implemented by the U.S. Army Fort Hood and its cultural resources contractor, Prewitt and Associates, Inc., of Austin, Texas. Extensive archival research and some oral history work pertaining to the Fort Hood lands had been done by Prewitt and Associates between 1995 and 1999, but it was not until September 2000 that the oral history project officially came into being (Delivery Order No. 7 of Contract DAKF48-99-D-009). The project's purpose was to gather and preserve historical recollections of life in the rural settlements that preceded Fort Hood. Researchers accomplished this primarily by means of audiotaped interviews, but they also conducted videotaped interviews and copied historic photographs in private hands. The project accumulated eighty-one hours of audiotaped interviews, thirty hours of videotaped interviews, and more than 900 historic photographs. Copies of some of the historical records generated by the project are housed on Fort Hood at the Cultural Resource Management Program office (Environmental Division, Directorate of Public Works), but the original records (including the audiotapes and videotapes, photographic negatives, and additional ephemera) are permanently held in trust for the federal government at the Texas Collection of the Baylor University Library System in Waco, Texas, where they are easily accessible to historical researchers.

The oral history project also created a portable exhibit of historical photographs entitled "Lost Worlds: Historic Images from Fort Hood Lands." Many of the photographs used in this book became part of that traveling exhibit, which is maintained by the Cultural Resource Management Program at Fort Hood.

The project published all audiotape interviews compiled during the research phase verbatim and in their entirety in a large anthology entitled *"Just Like Yesterday": Recollections of Life on the Fort Hood Lands*, by

Amy E. Dase, Martha Doty Freeman, William S. Pugsley III, Marie E. Blake, and Thad Sitton. The personal accounts edited for *Harder Than Hardscrabble* derive from that anthology.

Historians made initial contact with most of the interviewees at school, community, or family reunions held in the vicinity of Fort Hood. They tried to locate articulate individuals associated with different communities and socioeconomic groups. Despite this quest for diversity, informants and their forebears tended to be landowners, resulting in an underrepresentation of testimonies from tenants and sharecroppers. Gender was well balanced in the selection of interviewees, but they were almost all Anglo Americans of Southern cultural heritage. This was inevitable, since few if any African Americans or Hispanics had lived in the Fort Hood settlements before 1942. A few informants identified strongly with German or Czechoslovakian cultural traditions.

The oral history project built upon historic research that had been ongoing for many years at Fort Hood. In its efforts to comply with certain federal laws pertaining to cultural resources, the U.S. Army had identified over 1,100 historical sites on Fort Hood lands. Historians and historical archaeologists conducted research to understand the significance of these sites, and the army is trying to protect the ones that are most important. The army has also compiled and published much historical data and interpretation, both in technical and popular formats. Two previous publications by the Cultural Resource Management Program relate directly to historical topics: a technical research report entitled "Agriculture and Rural Development on Fort Hood Lands, 1849–1942: National Register Assessments of 710 Historic Archeological Properties," by Martha Doty Freeman, Amy E. Dase, and Marie E. Blake (2001), and a popular history entitled *Imprint on the Land: Life before Camp Hood, 1820–1942*, by William S. Pugsley III (2001).

From all perspectives, the Fort Hood Oral History Project attained its objectives. Besides amassing a great deal of historical information and making it easily accessible in published form, the project was well received by local persons, many of whom have an intense interest in the history of the region. The U.S. Army Fort Hood and Prewitt and Associates, Inc., are pleased to have been a part of the effort.

## Topical Interview Guide of the Fort Hood Oral History Project

When the Fort Hood Oral History Project began, the five participating historians collaborated to develop a general list of research topics to guide their interviews. The topics listed below represent their responses to the overriding issue: What questions will elicit from memoirists a full and complete account of the life they lived at these rural settlements—to record a "folk" ethnography of the farmers' world?

Except for the interview topic relating to forced land sales during World War II, we believe this interview guide is of relevance to any oral history study of Southern farming settlements before the war.

### FAMILY FARM LIFE, SUBSISTENCE ACTIVITIES

Home gardens and subsistence field crops (melons, field peas, sorghum cane, etc.)

Domestic livestock (milk cows, hogs, chickens, turkeys, geese, etc.)

Corn crop (multiple-resource crop)

Wild animal and plant foods (deer, turkeys, small game, wild hogs, fish, wild greens, fruits)

Household economies (cooking, food preservation, weekly clothes washings, home crafts, recycling, etc.)

Family division of labor regarding subsistence crops and domesticated livestock

Physical circumstances of farmstead (house layout; lighting, heating, and cooking technologies; outbuildings; fencing)

Water sources (wells, cisterns, springs, etc.)

Family-based recreation (games, readings, hunting and fishing, etc.)

Home remedies for illness

Reciprocities with neighbors outside of cash economy (food exchanges, swap work, free-range cooperations, communal work events, etc.)

### FAMILY FARM LIFE, CASH CROP ACTIVITIES

Major field crops sold for cash (cotton, corn, grains, etc.)

Domestic animals or animal products marketed for cash (cattle, sheep, goats, chickens, etc.)

Family division of labor regarding cash crops and domestic animals marketed for cash

Other family-produced products for cash sale (charcoal, cedar posts, firewood, eggs, milk products, etc.)
Day work for neighbors (chopping and picking cotton, fence building, land clearing, etc.)
Landlord-renter relationships
Work stock

### FAMILY FARM AND MARKET TOWN INTERACTIONS
Ginning cotton and sale of cotton (also corn, etc.)
Marketing of livestock or livestock products
Credit relationships with town landlords, banks, mercantile stores, etc.
Recreational/business trips to town
Town doctors, hospitals, and formal medical care
Relations with county officials (commissioners, tax assessors, sheriffs, etc.)
Automobiles and roads
Early telephone systems
Early radios
Visitors from town (mailmen, relatives, law officers, etc.)
Peddling (farm produce peddled in town; peddlers from town at the farm)
Effects of New Deal programs during the Great Depression
Forced land sales of 1942 and 1943: reactions to the coming of Camp Hood

### SETTLEMENT LIFE
Infrastructure (schools, churches, post offices, gins, syrup mills, gristmills, sawmills, etc.)
Different settlements characterized (when persons have lived in more than one)
Relations of home settlement with nearby settlements
Settlements' development and decline, reasons for
Communication within the settlement (trails, roads, blowing horns, telephones, etc.)
Neighborly help in emergencies
Communal work events (grain thrashings, sheep/goat shearings, goose pluckings, quiltings, log rollings, fence buildings, funerals, hayings, house [or barn] raisings, beef clubs, hog killings, etc.)
Local "free range" customs (stock raising, trespass, hunting and fishing, firewood gathering, etc.)

Persons living in settlement who worked as part-time specialists to perform special services (preachers, teachers, well diggers, midwives,
chimney builders, water witchers, blacksmiths, liquor makers, etc.)

Bartering, food swaps, work swaps, and other in-community reciprocities

Cash day labor for neighbors

Landlord-renter relationships within communities

Community-wide social events (house parties, school celebrations,
church-related social occasions, and various males-only "sporting life"
socializings)

Conflict incidents and conflict resolution within the settlement (in-fam-
ily quarrels, feuds between families, outlaws and deviants and informal social controls of these)

### Interviewees

The oral history project recorded forty-two audiotaped interviews with
fifty-two people. Researchers interviewed a few people several times, while
in other instances a single interview involved several people. In all cases,
participants shared freely their recollections of life on farms and ranches
before Camp Hood arrived. Although not interviewed for this project, Jerome
Keener Blackwell gave us permission to use his unpublished autobiography, "Vapors of Life," which we quoted in this book in the same manner as
the oral histories.

The following individuals contributed audio interviews:

John Darel Bay

Melba Goodwin Bennett

Frank Aubrey Black

Margaret Bert Wilhite Bounds

Mrs. F. A. Barrington Bowen

John D. Bowen

H. P. Brookshire Jr.

James W. Calhoun

J. M. Carroll

Margaret Hunt Carroll

Lois Pearl Shults Cathey

Gladys Merle Keener Chastain

Ernest Allen Cole Jr.

Zell Kinsey Copeland

Clements W. "Speedy" Duncan

Juanita Griffin Duncan
John Easley
John Gail Edwards
Wilma Earl Colvin Edwards
Christine Fleming Esparza
Edith York Faris
Juanita Manning Fleming
Wayne E. Fleming
Robert E. Gault
Norris Sidney Graves Jr.
Mary Edwards Groves
Florence Joyce Haedge
John A. Haedge
Tommie L. Shults Haferkamp
Norman Ricketts Hall
Weldon Hicks
Kyle Hilliard
Joe D. Insall
Myrna R. Insall
Cecil L. Newton
Estelle L. Newton
Mary Alice Dorsey Powell
Mary Lou "Honey" Hudson Powell
William Ake Powell
Joyce Calhoun Ritchie
J. W. Shults
Doris Lee White Thomas
Murrel L. Thompson
Louis J. Tomastik
Frankie Juanita Wright Trantham
Hope Edwards Turner
T. A. Wilhite
Hazel Graham Wilkinson
Andy Gordon Wolf
John Daniel Wolf Jr.
Archie Spivy Wright
James W. Yancy

# Selected Bibliography

*Further Reading about the Farming Life, with Emphasis on Texas*

Excellent scholarly overviews of the Southern farmer's world in all its complexity include Gilbert Fite, *Cotton Fields No More: Cotton Agriculture, 1864–1980* (Lexington: University of Kentucky Press, 1984); Pete Daniel, *Breaking the Land: The Transformation of Cotton, Tobacco, and Rice Cultures Since 1880* (Urbana: University of Illinois Press, 1986); and Jack Temple Kirby, *Rural Worlds Lost: The American South, 1920–1960* (Baton Rouge: Louisiana State University Press, 1990).

No comparable book confines itself to Texas, but see Thad Sitton and Dan K. Utley's study of the farming life in Washington, Fayette, and adjacent counties, *From Can See To Can't: Texas Cotton Farmers on the Southern Prairies* (Austin: University of Texas Press, 1997). See also the recent important works by Neil Foley, *The White Scourge: Mexicans, Blacks, and Poor Whites in Texas Cotton Culture* (Berkeley: University of California Press, 1997), and by Mary Rebecca Sharpless, *Fertile Ground, Narrow Choices: Women on Texas Cotton Farms, 1900–1940* (Chapel Hill: University of North Carolina Press, 1999).

Written memoirs and oral autobiographies of the Southern farming life are rich in the elements that most scholarly histories neglect, the daily details of farm families' existence, and we learn much by reading them. Significant personal accounts from outside Texas are those of Cecil Brown, *Coming Up Down Home: A Memoir of a Southern Childhood* (Hopewell, New Jersey.: Ecco Press, 1993); Ed Brown, *On Shares: Ed Brown's Story* (New York: Norton, 1975); Harry Crews, *A Childhood: The Biography of a Place* (New York: Harper and Row, 1978); and Ned Cobb and Theodore Rosengarten's prize-winning oral autobiography, *All God's Dangers: The Life of Nate Shaw* (New York: Alfred A. Knopf, 1974), perhaps the best personal account of the Southern farming life.

Important Texas farming memoirs include Troy Crenshaw, *Texas Black-*

*land Heritage* (Waco: Texian Press, 1983); Dorothy Howard, *Dorothy's World: Childhood in Sabine Bottom, 1902–1910* (New York: Prentice-Hall, 1977); Mance Lipscomb and Glen Alyn, *I Say Me for a Parable* (New York: Norton, 1993); William A. Owens, *This Stubborn Soil: A Frontier Boyhood* (New York: Charles Scribner's Sons, 1973); Robert Skrabanek, *We're Czechs* (College Station: Texas A&M University Press, 1988); Eddie Stimpson Jr., *My Remembers: A Black Sharecropper's Recollections of the Depression* (Denton: University of North Texas Press, 1995); George Lester Vaughn, *The Cotton Renter's Son* (Wolf City, Texas: Hennington Publishing Company, 1967); and C. C. White and Ada M. Holland, *No Quittin' Sense* (Austin: University of Texas Press, 1969).

# Index

**A**

Adams, S. B., 7
airplanes, 261–262
Antelope, 5, 6, 11 fig., 17, 22, 25, 118,
    164, 167–169, 198, 209–210, 212–
    213, 230, 235, 241, 243, 247
Armen, Hugh, 268
automobiles, 64, 87, 118–119, 123,
    176, 184, 254, 257–261
Autrey, Charlie, 156

**B**

Bay, Ike, 98
Bay, John Darel, 229–230, 236
Bear Creek, 105
Beck, Frances, 120
Becker, Carl, 13
"beef clubs," 49
Bee House Creek, 85, 247
Bell, Morgan, 119
Belton, 3, 68, 117, 120, 126, 193, 278
Bennett, Melba Goodwin, 34–35, 66,
    77, 81, 242–243
Beverly, 11 fig.
Birdsong, John, 232
Black, Frank "Noog," 129, 224
Black, Frank "Noog" and Ara Mae,
    155

blacksmithing, 26, 107–109, 120
Blackwell, Amos, 127
Blackwell, Jerome Keener, 87, 100,
    113, 222, 227, 241–242, 266–267
Blackwell, Joel and Sara, 130
Blackwell Mountain, 130
Blanchard, Wayne, 181
Bland, 11 fig.
Blankenship, Gladys, 158
Boaz, 11 fig., 186, 253
Boren, Johnny, 41
Bounds, Margaret Bert Wilhite, 38–
    39, 61, 78–79, 109–110, 112, 193–
    194, 200, 204–205, 208–209, 220,
    230–231, 232–233, 236–237, 247–
    248
Bowen, Mrs. F. A. Barrington, 229
Bowles, Tom, 124
Brashear, Christy, 174
Brashear, Christy and Katherine, 136
Brashear, John, 154, 166
Brashear, John and Carrie, 131, 137
"breaking," of horse and mules. *See*
    work stock
Brookhaven, 11 fig., 22, 196, 203, 208,
    244, 248
Brookshire, H. P., 45–46, 54, 254
broomcorn, 8, 71, 87–90

Brown, Carl and W. L., 153
Brown, Velma, 166
Brown's Creek, 6, 11 fig., 87, 195, 210, 222, 224–225, 227–228, 241–242, 248, 251, 266–267
Bundon, Ralph, 205

**C**

Calhoun, James W., 59, 66, 206, 265–266, 280
canning and other food preservations, 18, 23–24, 35–44, 46–49, 236
Carroll, J. M., 258–259
Carroll, Margaret Hunt, 74–77, 100–101, 229
Carter, William and Lydia Norman, 138
cattle, 6, 45, 49, 90–91
"cedar chopping." See cedar posts
cedar posts, 98, 100–102, 117, 119–120, 196, 202–203
Chaffin, Lou, 124
Chastain, Gladys Merle Keener, 19–20, 33–34, 65, 66–67, 78, 194–195, 215–216, 228–229
chickens, 2, 24, 29, 30, 31, 44–46, 115, 145–146, 246
chores, household, 19–20, 29–44
Christmas, 220–222
churches, 170–177, 195, 241–249
Civilian Conservation Corps, 10
Clear Creek, 11 fig., 17, 51, 121
clothing, washing of, 19–20, 33–34
Cold Springs, 11 fig.
Cole, Ernest Allen, 27–28, 33, 39–40, 47–48, 51, 54–55, 59–60, 81–82, 92–93, 99–100, 107–108, 115, 119–120, 123–124, 197, 199, 204, 220–221
Cole, Walter, 3

Colvin, Barney, 140
Colvin, Bill, 108
Colvin, John Fletcher, 186
Colvin, Nella Mae, 150
Colvin, William Franklin, 142
communities. See settlements, characteristics of
cooking, 22, 27
Copeland, Zell Kinsey, 79–80, 272
Copperas Cove, 3, 44, 72, 91, 120–121, 134, 209, 240, 267, 269, 275
corn, 6–7, 32–33, 36–37, 38, 42–43, 82, 117
cotton agriculture, 1–2, 8–9, 27, 71, 75–84, 113–114, 121–124, 148–150, 212. See also cotton gins
cotton gins, 2, 9, 72, 74, 85–87, 121–124
Cottonwood Creek, 34, 51
"courting," 178–179, 228, 231
Cousins, Joy, 213
Cowhouse Creek, 6, 22, 51, 56–57, 59, 68, 90, 99, 173–174, 178–180, 196, 198, 222–223, 242, 244, 247, 249, 252, 258
Cox, Elder, 269
Cox, Melvin, 207, 268, 273–274
Crossville, 11 fig.
Cummings, R. M., 159, 188
Czechs, 22

**D**

dances, 106, 181, 222, 226–235
Daniel, Pete, 280
DeWare, John, 252
diversification, of agriculture, 98
doctors, medical. See health care
dogs, 14, 18, 67–68, 72, 92, 96–97, 224–226, 240
Dorsey, Bob, 217

Dorsey, Cecil, 233
Doss, Web, 105
Drake, Joe, 104
Drake, Marlis, 104
drouths, 6–8
ducks, 45
Duncan, Clements W. "Speedy," 40, 48–49, 67, 73–74, 82, 90–97, 102–104, 106–107, 123, 222–223, 240, 257–258, 277–278, 281
Duncan, Juanita Griffin, 22–23, 31, 45, 67–68, 238–240, 244–245

**E**

Easley, John, 269–270
Edwards, John Gail, 194, 237, 269
Edwards, Silvia, 11
Edwards, Wilma Earl Colvin, 18–19, 37–38, 68–69, 252
electricity, 9, 120, 123, 253, 255, 264
Eliga, 11 fig., 127, 144, 145, 171, 173, 187, 198, 223, 244, 249
eminent domain. *See* Fort Hood (Camp Hood), land seizures for
entertainments. *See* churches; "courting"; dances; family visits; fishing; hunting; schools, community entertainments at
Esparza, Christine Fleming, 195–196
Evant, 279
Everett, Burl, 218–219
Ewing, 11 fig., 110, 157–159, 197, 210, 213, 268–269

**F**

family visits, 213–222
farmsteads, physical circumstances of, 17–29, 130–132, 136, 166
Federal Emergency Relief Act, 9–10
fiddle players, 230–235

firewood, 102–104
fishing, 51–54
Flat, 11 fig., 121, 211–212
Fleming, Juanita Manning, 24
Fleming, R. E., 113
food preservation. *See* canning and food preservation
football, six man, 211–212
Fort Gates, 6
Fort Hood (Camp Hood), 1–2, 4 fig., 9, 11 fig.; land seizures for, 10–12, 186–188, 190, 263, 267–279
Fort Hood Oral History Project, *ix-x,* 12–13, 283–288
Fort Meade, 274
fox hounds, 224–226
Freeman, Martha Doty, 7
Friendship, 11 fig., 25–27, 78–79, 109, 117, 156, 162–163, 176, 188, 190, 215, 255
funerals, 236, 238–240

**G**

gambling, 222–223
Gannaway Hill, 273
gardens, 2, 13–14, 19, 27–28, 31, 35–44
Gatesville, 3, 6, 7, 36, 44, 62, 65, 66, 109, 118, 120, 189, 193, 198–199, 205–206, 211, 227, 240, 251, 259, 264–265, 273, 275–276, 279
gathering (of useful wild plants), 58–60
Gault, John, 275
Gault, Robert E., 22, 27, 42, 46–47, 52–54, 56–59, 63, 75, 77–78, 87–88, 90–92, 99, 104–105, 113–114, 121, 198–199, 206, 209–210, 216–217, 223, 238, 243–244, 255–256, 263, 273–275

geese, 29, 45, 224
goats. *See* sheep and goats
Golden, Coleman, 147
Goodwin, Carl and Alta Faye, 191
Graham, Milton and Clara, 132, 144
Graham, Ruth, 228
Graham, Vernon, 228
Graves, Norris Sidney, 17, 92, 118–119, 196–197, 220, 239, 245–246, 255, 257, 259–260, 261–262
Gray, Marvin and Della, 187
Gray, Thomas Adolph, 145
Great Depression, 9–10, 36, 51, 55, 58, 71, 83–84, 102, 219, 263–267
Greenway, Luther, 224
Groves, Mary Edwards, 59, 203–204
guineas, 45

**H**

Haedge, Florence Joyce, 47, 116, 272
Haferkamp, Tommie L. Shults, 241, 267–268
Hall, Norman Ricketts, 29, 36–37, 49–50, 58, 62–63, 83, 120–121, 125, 196, 201–203, 214, 238, 253, 256, 259, 261, 264, 275–277
Hall, Weldon, 219
Hallmark, Les, 120
Hanes, Allen, 277
Harmony, 11 fig.
Harris, Oscar, 219
hay baling, 26, 107, 112–113, 147
health care, 18, 60–69, 115, 236–237
Henderson, Finis, 28
Henson's Creek, 11 fig., 110, 121
Hicks, W. T., 235
"high gear." *See* sorghum
Hilliard, Joe and Edith, 218
Hilliard, Kyle, 58, 63–64, 83–84, 114, 116–117, 121–122, 193, 200, 208, 218–220, 221–222, 244, 255, 260–261
Hilliard, Ray and Donna, 222
Hilliard, R. M. and Clara, 218
hogs, 2, 22, 39, 44–49
horses. *See* work stock
Hotel Simpson, 134
House Creek, 53, 121, 144
House Creek School, 198, 274
houses. *See* farmsteads, physical circumstances of
Howell, Sydney, 197
Hubbard, 11 fig.
Humphrey, Frank, 106
hunting, 7–8, 20, 51, 54, 57–58, 155, 222, 224–226

**I**

ice delivery, 252–253
Indians, 6
Insall, Howard, 209
Insall, Joe D., 17–18, 25, 30–31, 34, 41, 49, 51, 55–56, 61–62, 92, 118, 121, 209, 221, 230, 247, 252, 260, 265, 267, 281

**K**

Keener, W. B., 242
Killeen, 50, 53, 62–63, 65, 67, 73, 91, 117, 120–124, 138, 200, 256, 259, 264, 269, 275–278
Kindler, Mrs. Albert, 217
Kinsey, Tinie Taylor, 133

**L**

Lampasas, 93, 269
Lathan Prairie, 198, 275
Leon Junction, 235
Leon River, 6, 222
Levita, 213

Lewis, Oscar, 6
Louer, Leila "Dutch," 139

**M**

Magen, Bill, 125
mail delivery, 251–253
Manning, Doyle and Stela May, 177
Manning Mountain, 11 fig., 24, 195, 214
Maple, 119, 161, 166, 205–206, 210, 215, 251, 265, 280
McGlothlin, Jim and Dewie, 189
McHenry, Tom, 219
medical doctors. *See* health care
milk cows, 2, 30, 31, 32, 44–45, 49–50
Moffett, 125
Montgomery, Mollie, 206
Mound, 266
movies, 119, 125
mules. *See* work stock
mutual aid. *See* neighborliness, practices of

**N**

neighborliness, practices of, 6, 49, 66–67, 107, 193, 235–240
New Deal programs, 9–10, 108, 261, 263–267
New Hope, 11 fig.
New Liberty Hill (Okay), 29
New Sugar Loaf, 11 fig.
Newton, Cecil, L., 85–87
Nolanville, 11 fig.
Northcutt, G. G., 207

**O**

Oakalla, 48, 66, 104
Oenaville, 77
Okay, 11 fig., 27–28, 39–40, 51, 99, 197, 199, 204, 240, 257, 277

Old Sugar Loaf, 6, 11 fig.
outbuildings. *See* farmsteads, physical circumstances of
Overton, Dick, 114, 219
Owens, Ben, 106
Owl Creek, 11 fig., 26, 40, 51, 156, 162–163, 197, 216, 246

**P**

Palo Alto, 7, 11 fig., 83, 116, 193, 200, 208, 244, 255
Paul, Arlee and Randall, 227
Peabody, 76
pecans, 98, 104–105, 119
peddlers, 18, 45–46, 93, 115–118, 252–253, 260
Pidcoke, 5, 11 fig., 17, 85–87, 149, 178, 196, 213, 239, 245, 247, 257, 259, 261
Pilot Knob, 11 fig.
Pleasant Grove, 11 fig.
population, 8, 9
Porter, Robert, 149
Post Oak Mountain, 218
Potter's Crossing, 179
Powell, Jimmie and Jane, 128
Powell, William Ake, 25–27, 32–33, 40–41, 49, 51–52, 80–81, 90, 98, 101–102, 107, 109, 110–112, 116–118, 121, 159, 197–198, 203, 211–212, 214–215, 225, 233–235, 237, 252, 255–256, 267
Powell String Band, 234

**Q**

quiltings, 235

**R**

Radar Hill, 106
radio, 253–255

railroads, 6
recyclings, 13, 30–31, 33, 34, 51
Reese Creek, 11 fig.
Refuge, 11 fig., 242
religious life. *See* churches
rent farmers, 8–9, 12, 18, 82–84, 132,
    195–196, 280
reunions, 14, 190
roads. *See* travel and transportation
Roberts, Ross and Thelma, 241
Ross School, 198
Ruth, 6, 11 fig., 117

## S

Salem, 175, 206, 275
Schley, 11 fig.
schools, 5–6, 9, 28, 44, 50, 120, 142,
    156–169, 193, 251; travel to and
    from, 193–199; instruction at,
    199–203; discipline problems of,
    203–207; community entertain-
    ments at, 208–213
Seattle, 11 fig.
Second War Powers Act, 10
self sufficiency, practices of, 13–14.
    *See* neighborliness, practices of
settlements, characteristics of, 5–6,
    11 fig., 13. *See* neighborliness,
    practices of
sharecroppers. *See* rent farmers
sheep and goats, 6, 8, 28–29, 90–97,
    152–153
Shults, J. W., 30, 71–72, 200–201, 246,
    271
Shults, Thomas and Virgie, 185
Siler, George, 242
Silver City, 102, 112, 227–228
slavery, 7
Smith, Bob, 219
Smith, Frank, 141

snakes, 14, 21, 26, 44, 67–68, 72–73,
    77–78, 82, 98–100, 106–107, 238
social life. *See* churches; "courting";
    dances; family visits; fishing; hunt-
    ing; schools, entertainments at
Soil Conservation Service, 10
Sonnichsen, C. L., 3
sorghum, 43–44
South Nolan, 11 fig.
Spanish Oak, 201, 275
Sparta, 5, 11 fig., 79, 90, 106, 120, 200,
    203–204, 230, 232, 237, 247–248,
    269
Spring Hill, 6, 11 fig., 37, 75–76, 211,
    214, 243
Stampede, 11 fig., 66, 165, 191, 194,
    204, 237
Stevenson, Jim, 271
stores, rural, 9, 115, 117–120, 154–155
Straw's Mill, 118, 181, 221
Stray, Charles Lee, 181
Strickland, George Augustus, 259–260
Styles, W. F., 165
Sugar Loaf, 244
suicides, 12, 271, 277
syrup cane, 71, 87, 107, 111–112
syrup milling. *See* syrup cane

## T

Table Rock School, 198
Tama, 11 fig., 68, 117, 131, 154
telephones, 23, 118, 255–258
Temple, 21, 117, 201, 235, 276
tenants. *See* rent farmers
Tennessee Valley, 208, 230–231, 233
Thomas, Doris Lee White, 60–61, 75–
    76, 109, 211, 214, 216, 221, 243
Thomas, Genieva White, 211
Thompson, Burton, 233
Thompson, Leslie, 210

Thompson, Murrel L., 63, 72, 227, 235, 241, 270–271

Thornton, J. E., 117

threshing, 26, 110–111, 151, 260

Tomastik, Louis J., 21–22, 60, 207–208, 209

towns. *See* settlements

toys and play, 31, 34, 182, 220–221

tractors, 72, 113, 262

Trantham, Frankie Jaunita, 30, 212–213, 272–273

trapping, 54–57, 194

travel and transportation, 6, 32, 64, 115, 123, 137, 160, 171, 176–177, 183–184, 209, 216, 251–252, 257–262

turkeys, 2, 29, 45, 98–100

Turner, Hope Edwards, 194

Turnersville, 274

Turnover, 11 fig., 181

Union Hill, 11 fig., 208, 237

violence, 13, 105, 205–206, 227–229, 232, 234–235, 240

well digging, 107

whisky making, 98, 227

Whitehead, Sonny, 240

Whitney, Eli, 1

Wilhite, Ira, 106

Wilhite, T. A., 35, 41–42, 57, 81, 90, 102, 105–106, 120, 124–125, 226, 232, 237, 248, 268–269, 281

Williams, Frank, 147

Willow Springs, 11 fig., 229

Wilson, Will, 223–224

Wiseman, John, 226

Wittie, Ruby, 221

Wolf, Andy Gordon, 20, 52, 64–65, 84–85, 88, 93, 98–99, 106, 108, 112, 115, 119, 205–206, 214, 217, 223–224, 227–228

Wolf, Francis, 160, 234–235

Wolf, John Daniel, 21, 35–36, 65, 88–90, 102, 117, 205–206, 210, 224–225, 248–249, 251–252, 262, 279

Wolf, William Doyle, 206

Wolf Valley, 20, 64–65, 225

wood cutting. *See* firewood

Woods, Dr. D. L., 63–64, 67

work stock, 41–43, 72–75, 107, 109–110, 116, 123–125, 137, 271

Wright, Archie Spivy, 32, 206–207

Yancy, James. W., 91, 263–264

Yancy, J. R., 91